Founding a Company

Michael J. Munkert · Stephan Stubner ·
Torsten Wulf

Editors

Founding a Company

Handbook of Legal Forms in Europe

 Springer

Editors
Dr. Michael J. Munkert
MUNKERT · KUGLER + PARTNER GbR
Äußere Sulzbacher Straße 29
90491 Nürnberg
Germany
m.munkert@munkert-kugler.de

Dr. Stephan Stubner
Prof. Dr. Torsten Wulf
HHL – Leipzig Graduate School of
Management
Chair of Strategic Management and
Organization
Jahnallee 59
04109 Leipzig
Germany
stephan.stubner@hhl.de
torsten.wulf@hhl.de

MUNKERT · KUGLER + PARTNER
Steuerberater · Wirtschaftsprüfer · Rechtsanwälte GbR

ISBN 978-3-642-11258-4   e-ISBN 978-3-642-11259-1
DOI 10.1007/978-3-642-11259-1
Springer Heidelberg Dordrecht London New York

Library of Congress Control Number: 2010923235

Cover design: WMXDesign GmbH, Heidelberg

Printed on acid-free paper

Springer is part of Springer Science+Business Media (www.springer.com)

Preface

From our daily practice as scholars, consultants and entrepreneurs we know how critical it is to make the right decisions that can shape the future of a company. One of the earliest of such decisions is surely the selection of the appropriate legal form as it is hardly reversible and has major implications on the running business.

Accordingly, we can find a wealth of information about the pros and cons of specific legal forms. However, so far there is only scarce information available once you decide to enter a foreign market. There are offerings, e.g. from the Chambers of Commerce and you can search the Internet. When information is provided in the local language, comprehension becomes difficult. Furthermore, the material that is available today only seldom allows for a structured analysis and comparison of legal forms in different countries.

From discussions with entrepreneurs we know that this situation has not only been cumbersome for us, but actually everybody who is thinking about starting up a business or widening the operations across country borders is faced with the complex task of deciding on a legal form.

With this handbook on legal forms in Europe we strive to provide a starting point for practitioners and students who need to better understand the implications of different legal forms in different countries. We have involved experts from ten countries that are associated with the Geneva Group International, multidisciplinary network of lawyers, consultants, auditors and tax consultants with 412 offices in 72 countries. Each expert has provided a thorough introduction into important aspects of their national legal forms. To facilitate comprehension and comparison we equipped them with a standard framework to prepare these analyses and to summarize the findings in a country-specific recommendation.

Many people helped us to compile this work. We especially want to emphasize the contribution of the participants of the course "Legal aspects in entrepreneurship" at HHL – Leipzig Graduate School of Management in the spring term of 2008 who were instrumental in discussing our ideas and in compiling the first summaries for each country: Dominique Ehler, Hans-Christian Erdmann, Emelie Eriksson, Alexander Hiller, Lucas Kohlmann, Lutz Kregel, Johannes Kreibohm, Kevin Lair, Edmée Lamarre, Nikolaj de Lousanoff, Henrik Medla, Philip Meißner, Janis Münch, Verena Nedorn, Max Radtke, Alexander Schlagenhaufer, Frederic von Dallwitz and

Justus von Grone. In addition, our special thanks go to Katharina Zmich and Kati Roleder who provided vital support in administering all contributions and compiling the final manuscript.

Nuremberg, Germany   Michael J. Munkert
Leipzig, Germany   Stephan Stubner
Leipzig, Germany   Torsten Wulf

Disclaimer

The information available in this handbook is based on the legal regulations of the year 2009. Each contribution focuses on providing an introduction into the norms and requirements of a particular country and should be appropriate to make most decisions on a suitable legal form. However, we strongly advise to assess each decision process individually, because a variety of other factors like the strategy of the company or the financial background of the stakeholders can influence the optimal solution.

Especially when talking about the legal form of a company, there is no one-size-fits-all approach that we can present. In addition, although we put a lot of effort into the preparation of each article, we might have deviated from the original meanings during the translation process, or regulations could have changed over time.Thus, we cannot take any legal responsibility for decisions made on the basis of this handbook but ask the reader to use it as an introduction for his information needs on legal forms.

When reading the handbook you will see that we generally use the term "he" as a neutral denomination for a male or female founder, respectively a founding company. This is done to facilitate easy reading and comprehension.

Contents

About Editors and Authors

Anton W. Blatter † was attorney-at-law and partner of Bratschi Wiederkehr & Buob in Zurich, Switzerland. He worked in the fields of corporate law, banking law, mergers and acquisitions, tax planning, arrangement of corporate successions, corporate restructuring and financial reorganization, international arbitration, trusts and foundations, financial services for private clients. Besides this, he was active in multiple family office companies. Dr. Blatter did his doctorate at University of Bern where he also studied law. Besides this he received his D.E.S. from University of Geneva and studied at the Academy of American and International Law in Dallas, Texas, USA.

Astrid Dorfmeister is a lawyer and partner at Dr. Frühbeck, Abogados & Economistas y Cía. S.C. with offices in Madrid, Barcelona, Marbella, Palma de Mallorca, Las Palmas de Gran Canaria, Gerona and La Habana (Cuba). She is the general manager for the Barcelona, Cuba and Canary Island branches. Before this, she worked as general director of the Spanish Chamber of Commerce in Germany. Her competencies include M&A, companies formation, product liability and consumer law, arbitration and international mediation, family and inheritance law, international investment in Spain and Cuba as well as debt collection. Dr. Dorfmeister received her doctorate and her LLM in international law from University of Hanover, Germany. She speaks Spanish, German, English and French.

Astrid Dorfmeister Dr. Frühbeck, Abogados & Economistas y Cía. S.C., C/Balmes, 368, pr. 2ª, 08006 Barcelona, Spain, barcelona@fruhbeck.com

Sergio Finulli is a certified public accountant and a registered auditor based in Milan, where he is a partner of Studio Bianchi Finulli and appointed by the Court of Milan as a trustee in bankruptcies. Specialized in corporate law, tax law and insolvency law, Mr. Finulli has gained fully qualified experience in EU law and has been appointed as assistant professor of business administration. He is also a member of the International Taxation Practice Group for Geneva Group International.

Sergio Finulli Studio Bianchi Finulli, Via Morozzo della Rocca, 3, 20123 Milan, Italy, sergio.finulli@bianchifinulli.it

Attila Kovács is a partner at Kovács Réti Szegheő, Attorneys-at-law in Budapest. Before this, he gained further professional experiences at several Hungarian and German law offices. His primary areas of practice are corporate law, M&A, bankruptcy, liquidation and execution law, real estate law and international taxation, and he is also an arbitrator at the Arbitration Court attached to the Hungarian Chamber of Agriculture. Dr. Kovács studied at the Faculty of Law of Eötvös Loránd University. He speaks Hungarian, English and German.

Attila Kovacs Kovács Réti Szegheő Attorneys-at-Law, Bimbó út 143, 1024 Budapest, Hungary, kovacs.attila@krs.hu

Klaus Küspert is managing partner and head of the legal division of MUNKERT · KUGLER + PARTNER. He is specialized in international tax planning, restructuring, mergers & acquisitions, company succession and contract negotiations. Before joining MUNKERT · KUGLER + PARTNER in 1988, he studied law and economics at the University of Würzburg and worked for multinational audit firms as well as for one of the major private foundations in Germany. Klaus Küspert is lawyer, certified tax consultant, certified public auditor and specialist advisor in international taxation. He has written several publications and held many lectures in his areas of specialization. He is a member of different professional organizations and examination committees.

Klaus Küspert MUNKERT · KUGLER + PARTNER GbR, Äußere Sulzbacher Straße 29, 90491 Nürnberg, Germany, k.kuespert@munkert-kugler.de

Pieta C. Laarhoven van der Mark is attorney-at-law at the corporate law department of TeekensKarstens, Attorneys-at-Law & Civil Law Notaries. She is specialized in M&A (cross-border), transactions & restructuring and commercial contracting as well as transport law and insurance law. She advises a broad spectrum of clients, ranging from entrepreneurs to multinational companies. Before joining TeekensKarstens, she worked at a civil law notary office and PriceWaterhouseCoopers Legal Services (today Van Doorne, Corporate Finance Group). She is admitted to the The Hague Bar Association and has written several articles in various entrepreneurs' magazines and has made presentations on her areas of specialization. Pieta Laarhoven studied civil and notarial law in Leiden (The Netherlands) and post graduated in comparative commercial and international property law at the University of Copenhagen (Denmark).

Pietia C. Laarhoven van der Mark TeekensKarstens Attorneys-at-Law & Civil Law Notaries, Vondellaan, 51, 2332 AA Leiden, The Netherlands, laarhoven@tklaw.nl

John F. Langelaar is attorney-at-law at the corporate law department of TeekensKarstens, Attorneys-at-Law & Civil Law Notaries. He is specialized in M&A (cross-border), transactions & restructuring and commercial contracting as well as transport law and insurance law. He advises a broad spectrum of clients, ranging from entrepreneurs to multinational companies. Before joining TeekensKarstens, he was a lawyer at Loeff & Van der Ploeg (the predecessor of Loyens & Loeff) in Rotterdam. He is admitted to the The Hague Bar

Association, an arbitrator for the Chamber of Commerce and member of the Executive Committee of Geneva Group International. John F. Langelaar studied law in Germany and graduated in civil and environmental law from Leiden (The Netherlands). TeekensKarstens has offices in Alphen aan de Rijn, Leiden and Lisse, where 160 employees provide services for national and multinational clients. In 2009, TeekensCarstens received the prestigious "Golden Hourglass" award as fastest growing Dutch law firm.

Johan F. Langelaar TeekensKarstens Attorneys-at-Law & Civil Law Notaries, Vondellaan, 51, 2332 AA Leiden , The Netherlands, langelaar@tklaw.nl

Andrew Lindsay is a company and commercial lawyer based in York, in the North of England where he is a partner in Denison Till, a specialist in M&A activities both within the United Kingdom and overseas. He is also a director of the Leeds, York & North Yorkshire Chamber of Commerce and Chair of the Audit & Risk Management Board of the Central Science Laboratory, a government agency dealing with plant health and protection within the United Kingdom. Within the context of M&A activity, Andrew Lindsay handles a large number of acquisitions and sales of companies and businesses and works closely in collaboration with a number of major accountancy firms. He also undertakes banking and securities work and handles management buyouts and succession planning issues. Furthermore, he is chair of the M&A Practice Group for Geneva Group International.

Andrew Lindsay Denison Till, Stamford House, Piccadilly, York YO1 9PP, United Kingdom, cal@denisontill.com

Emanuelle Lutfalla is a partner in the French law firm Soulie & Coste-Floret in Paris. Her trial practice involves all areas of insurance law, with special emphasis on cases involving product liability. In 1998, Emanuelle Lutfalla has given conferences to the Eastern Europe candidates to the European Union, under the auspices of the EEC Commission in Brussels (Belgium). She is a frequent speaker for EFE (Edition Formation Entreprise) in product liability law and presently chairing as a vice-president of the Web page for the IADC. Emanuelle Lutfalla received both her undergraduate and graduate degrees from PARIS II ASSAS University (Université Panthéon – ASSAS (Paris V)) in Paris, earning a Master's degree (DESS) in business law in 1989. She also graduated from Kent University in England, earning a master's degree in international commercial law in 1990. She graduated as a lawyer and was enrolled to the Paris Bar in 1992.

Emmanuèle Lutfalla Avocat à la Cour, SCP Soulie & Coste-Floret, 20 Boulevard Massena, 75013 Paris, France, e.lutfalla@coste-floret.com

Michael J. Munkert is managing partner and head of the corporate finance division of MUNKERT · KUGLER + PARTNER. He is specialized in M&A, company valuation, company succession and strategic tax planning and advices a broad spectrum of clients, ranging from entrepreneurs to multinational companies. Before joining MUNKERT · KUGLER + PARTNER in 2003, Dr. Munkert studied international business administration at the University of Erlangen-Nuremberg. He is a certified tax consultant and holds a Master of Science in accounting and finance from the London School of Economics and Political Science (LSE) and a Master of Laws (M & A) from the University of Münster. Dr. Munkert has written several publications and held many lectures in his areas of specialization. MUNKERT · KUGLER + PARTNER gives its clients comprehensive advice and support ranging from tax and legal advice to accounting, commercial and investment advice. In Germany, 350 employees at 34 locations provide clients with personalized full service. As a member of Geneva Group International (GGI) MUNKERT · KUGLER + PARTNER actively supports its clients in more than 70 countries with 11,400 employees.

Michael J. Munkert MUNKERT · KUGLER + PARTNER GbR, Äußere Sulzbacher Straße 29,90491, Nürnberg, Germany, m.munkert@munkert-kugler.de

Christian Seidl is a partner at Tramposch & Partner since 2005 and works in the Eisenstadt office in Austria. He is an experienced litigator and advises clients on issues in all fields of business law as well as commercial and liability law. He is a member of the Vienna Bar Association and the Lawyers Association. Christian Seidl studied law at the universities of Graz, Austria and Wolverhampton, England. He holds a Magister of Laws degree from the University of Graz. In 2005, he was admitted to the Austrian Bar.

Christian Seidl Tramposch & Partner, Thomas A. Edison Straße 1, 7000 Eisenstadt, Austria, office-eisenstadt@tramposch-partner.com

Roxana Smeu is an associate attorney-at-law and a member of Dragomir & Associates Law Offices. Her practice areas are litigation, arbitration and mediation, real estate, public procurements and public–private partnership, corporate and commercial. Roxana Smeu graduated from the Law School of the University of Bucharest (Romania) and studied post-graduate with specialization in private law. She is a definitive attorney-at-law and member of the Bucharest Bar since 2004.

Roxana Smeu Dragomir & Associates, Constantin Noica nr. 159, sector 6, 060052, Bucuresti, Romania, office@dragomirlaw.ro

Stephan Stubner is assistant professor for strategy and entrepreneurship at HHL – Leipzig Graduate School of Management. As academic director for the International Entrepreneurship Program at HHL he teaches and coaches start-up teams through all stages of their life cycle. He also co-founded two own businesses and is on the advisory boards of a number of growth companies. Stephan Stubner received his doctorate from University of Erlangen-Nuremberg in Germany with a thesis on *Venture Capital Management Support for Start-Ups* and focuses his current research on growth issues in entrepreneurial family businesses and large organizations.

Stephan Stubner HHL – Leipzig Graduate School of Management, Jahnallee 59, 04109 Leipzig, Germany, stephan.stubner@hhl.de

Adriana Turta is an associate attorney-at-law and a member of Dragomir & Associates Law Offices. Her practice areas are litigation, corporate and commercial arbitration and mediation, real estate, public procurements and public–private partnership. Adriana Turta graduated from the Law School of the University of Bucharest (Romania) with a Master's degree in private law. She is a definitive attorney-at-law and member of the Bucharest Bar since 2006.

Adriana Turta Dragomir & Associates, Constantin Noica nr. 159, sector 6, 060052, Bucuresti, Romania, office@dragomirlaw

Torsten Wulf is chaired professor of strategic management and organization at HHL – Leipzig Graduate School of Management. He also is the academic director of the MBA programs and heads the International Entrepreneurship Program at HHL. In addition, Torsten Wulf trains and consults a variety of corporate clients of all sizes on strategic topics. Before coming to HHL, he was professor of strategy and international management at the ENPC School of International Management at Paris, the business school of one of France's Technical Grande Ecoles. His current research focuses on executive succession, scenario planning and growth issues in corporations. HHL – Leipzig Graduate School of Management was founded in 1898 as the first business school in the German-speaking countries. Today it is widely acknowledged as one of the leading business schools in Germany and one of the few universities that has received the highly respected accreditation by AACSB International. All of the programs at HHL (full-time and part-time M.Sc. and MBA) are offered in English.

Torsten Wulf HHL – Leipzig Graduate School of Management, Jahnallee 59, 04109 Leipzig, Germany, torsten.wulf@hhl.de

Part I
The Need for a Better Understanding
of Legal Forms in Europe

Chapter 1
Cross-Border Operations and Enlargement of European Union as Driving Forces for Pan-European Expansion Strategies

Torsten Wulf and Stephan Stubner

Abstract The Handbook on Legal Forms in Europe starts, in this chapter, with an introduction into the strategic need of looking at the subject. The authors Torsten Wulf and Stephan Stubner begin with an outline on the importance for each founder and founding company to critically evaluate the question about which legal form to use. As the evaluation of this question becomes especially complex when looking at foreign markets, they then first take a look at the reasons for setting up businesses abroad. They show the underlying strategic drivers for pan-European expansion strategies and discuss the possible benefits for companies. The authors complement this internal perspective with an overview on external factors that foster cross-border operations and conclude with the discussion of several case examples and an outlook.

Contents

1.1 Introduction

Whenever a firm starts its activities, the decision for a legal form has usually already been made. The founders have done so explicitly by crafting a company constitution, getting advice by lawyers and tax accountants and filing for a legal form with

T. Wulf (✉)
HHL – Leipzig Graduate School of Management, Jahnallee 59, 04109 Leipzig, Germany
e-mail: torsten.wulf@hhl.de

M.J. Munkert et al. (eds.), *Founding a Company*, DOI 10.1007/978-3-642-11259-1_1,
© Springer-Verlag Berlin Heidelberg 2010

the respective legislative authorities, or they have done so implicitly by just shaking hands with their partners and starting their operations. Both approaches can be suitable and are legally binding.

In any case, it is advisable that the process leading to the decision of which approach to take has been structured and analytical because few decisions shape the future of a company so dramatically and are as difficult to reverse as the constitution of a legal form. The selection of the legal form affects a company in many ways. Among other things, it sets the standard for transparency (and accordingly bureaucratic) requirements, impacts the size of tax duties, induces administrative costs for recurring expenses. It also impacts personal liability of managers and shareholders and, last but not the least, transmits a certain image to outside stakeholders about the quality, size and professionalism of the firm. Thus, when starting up a business, the selection of the legal form is one of the earliest and most important administrative decision any founder has to make for the new firm (Weber, 1998; Schick, 2008).

In every European country, numerous support initiatives exist which provide detailed information about different domestic legal forms and their implications for the business and the owners. In Germany, for example, you can obtain information from the Chamber of Commerce, academic and political institutions and, of course, from facilitators like tax accountants, lawyers or consultants. Naturally, these resources are often focused on setting up a local business and accordingly little support is available that helps to understand the requirements, processes, advantages and disadvantages of the legal forms in other countries. But in fact, an increasing number of companies and founders face the need to open up pan-European operations in one or more countries, in order to, e.g., serve certain customer segments or to get access to important resources. This trend is further fuelled by the overall economic, political and technological developments that induce a raise in international business activities on a global scale (Rugman and Hodgetts, 1995).

Founders and companies are, thus, increasingly challenged with the complex task of evaluating legal forms for countries outside their original markets. Today, there is still a lack of multilingual information material for foreign investors even in European countries and, thus, the language barrier poses one major obstacle. More importantly, the range of available legal forms to choose from is not uniform across countries, and even in cases where similarities exist at first sight, a deeper understanding of the exact regulations is needed for a thorough evaluation process. Finally, also the peculiarities of legislatory regulations, cultural norms and economic conditions in different European countries may lead to totally different conclusions as to which legal form to choose in a respective country. And while this challenge to choose a suitable legal form is apparent for start-up companies, it actually affects organizations of any size and maturity, from the born-global start-up considering the ideal place for company headquarters to the established multinational enterprises (MNEs) that are looking into expanding their manufacturing footprint.

With this introductory chapter, we aim to lay the foundation for an expanded overview of legal forms in Europe. Especially, we focus on providing a better understanding of the drivers that lead companies to enlarge their operations and to evaluate legal forms in foreign countries. For this, we discuss both the internal strategic drivers for growth and the external factors which are particularly relevant within the European Union. We close this chapter with an overview of several case examples of pan-European expansion strategies and a conclusion for companies that consider going into new markets.

1.2 Strategic Drivers for Pan-European Expansion

When businesses consider starting operations in a foreign market, they usually do so for an economic reason. Either they want to grow sales or decrease cost by embarking into new regions (Berlemann and Tilgner, 2006). In many companies, growth remains one of the ultimate goals of top management. But growth most often is not seen as a reason in itself; rather it is perceived as a lever that has an impact on a variety of other factors that increase the success of the firm. It is seen to lead to superior competitiveness and has positive impacts on both short-term profitability and long-term prospects of the firm (Schwenker and Bötzel, 2007).

When a company is able to increase its sales and at least keep its current relative cost-position, it will also increase its nominal profitability, i.e. the amount of profits it can generate. If additionally it is able to use its increased sales to leverage on learning-curve effects or economies of scale, it can even improve its relative profitability and make more profit on every unit it sells. Furthermore, a larger size usually leads to a better market position that is beneficial in dealing with suppliers and creditors, thus decreasing overall transaction costs and further improving profitability. Besides sales growth and its accompanying effects, operating in foreign markets can also have a direct impact on the cost-position of a company, when it allows for optimized access to resources (e.g. via offshoring). Companies then benefit from the integration of multinational sourcing activities to lower the cost of talent acquisition, material, components, etc. (Di Gregorio et al., 2008).

Building up good prospects, i.e. a positive expectation of future developments for the company, is especially important for the perception of the firm with external and internal stakeholders. Outside stakeholders value a growth-oriented outlook for a company as it gives them an indication of the viability of the firms' business model. For example, investors and creditors often link prospects to failure risk and companies with better prospects find it easier to get access to capital. With a lower risk perception due to good prospects, the additional cost of capital decreases, again leading to a higher profitability. Also, growth prospects have a large impact on the valuation of a company on the capital markets. Better prospects lead to a higher expected growth rate and thus increase company valuation according to DCF-related valuation methods which are used predominantly. These methods determine the value of a company by discounting cash-flows for a certain number of years in the future (e.g. the following 5 years) plus one "terminal value" that is largely determined by the company's growth rate in the future. Finally, another group of stakeholders who are influenced by the prospects of a company are current and future employees. Good prospects show employees that working for a company can be beneficial and that enough growth possibilities for further personal advancement are available. The most talented people, thus, feel drawn to work for this company and become instrumental to further develop the business in the future, laying ground for a reinforcing circle of growth and success (Schwenker and Bötzel, 2007).

As shown above, going abroad to generate direct cost reductions through looking for cheaper input factors is obvious. Besides this, also a number of growth-related aspects are drivers for internationalization that lead companies to consider foreign markets to grow sales. One aspect can be the limited size of the home market. A company might, e.g., operate in a small regional market or in a very specific niche, where sales potential is not high enough to allow for continued investments and domestic growth. Relatively small countries like Austria and the Netherlands are examples for these conditions as they belong to the top four economically most globalized countries in the world (Dreher et al., 2008). Another driver for internationalization can be the maturity of a market. Especially in saturated markets, competition tends to intensify leading to eroding margins. In such situations companies are tempted to search for easier growth opportunities in other regions, where markets are not as far developed and growth can be achieved easier. And in business-to-business markets, customers might just be located in other regions and business dynamics demand for setting up operations close to the customers.

When companies go abroad to benefit from the results of cross-border operations, they also have to consider how they want to internationalize their organization. Several approaches exist (Kutschker and Schmid, 2006) and the alternative a company chooses has implications on the most appropriate legal form. Thus it should be considered as one decision criterion.

The basic way to embark into cross-border operations is to perform all activities out of the home market. This typically requires no additional subsidiaries and leads to pure export, international sourcing strategies respectively. Alliances and joint ventures are more advanced forms of cross-border operations, where two companies typically team up and create a new entity for a certain period of time. Normally, the partners would set up a new legal entity in one of the operating countries which allows for the most suitable form of cooperation. Finally, companies can also decide to directly form an own sales or production subsidiary to reap the full benefits of cross-border operations. In this most elaborate form of internationalization, a deep understanding of the implications of the different legal forms have is obviously most crucial.

1.3 External Drivers for Pan-European Expansion

International business in general is no new phenomenon, as is the outreach into markets on the European continent. For many decades, technological, sociological and regulatory advances have continued to ease the flow of transport, information and goods/services across national borders and facilitated the globalization of businesses, especially across the European markets (Oviatt and McDougall, 1997; Fletscher, 2004). As a result, transportation and communication have become commodity resources and the associated costs have decreased to an extent where it starts to get interesting even for small businesses to engage into cross-border operations. For example, new forms of telecommunication today allow companies to easily market their products across national borders and even product development and manufacturing can be distributed across several countries and the internet still allows for real-time communication with business units, suppliers and customers (Chetty and Campbell-Hunt, 2004). Increased availability of information and the awareness of different cultures through media, more tourism and global business have also lead to a significant standardization of customer tastes and products/services that are successful in one country often have a high potential to be successful in other markets as well (Oviatt and McDougall, 1997). And with the European Union, an open market has developed where national tariffs and trade barriers do not hinder the exchange of goods and services anymore.

The regulations in the European Union to facilitate cross-border operations are known as the "Four Freedoms". They set a number of rules that aim to enable and protect the possibility to move goods, capital, people and labour freely within the member countries (European Commission, 2009; Barnard, 2007). With the creation of a customs union, a single economic market and an economic and (partial) monetary union, the European Union works on enacting these freedoms for the benefit of the different national economies (European Commission, 2003).

For individual companies these measures are drivers for their expansion strategies. Within the single European market, companies have easier access to necessary information which they need for their location decisions. The European Union also guarantees the free choice of location for individuals and businesses, e.g. a French company can decide freely if it wants to set up operations in Poland. Together, the unified market thus leads to a large decrease in transaction costs, as trade barriers have been abolished and access to the cheapest and best resources within the member countries is facilitated.

1.4 Expansion Examples and Outlook

In the last section of this chapter, we discuss several short examples for different expansion strategies. Furthermore, we provide an outlook for companies that consider pan-European expansion. Although such activities are relevant for large and small firms alike (Bassen et al., 2001; Koller et al., 1998; Henzler, 1992), we have – with reference to the aim of the overall handbook on legal forms in Europe – chosen three examples of companies that followed a rapid cross-border expansion approach, also called "born globals": ciao, Logitech and trivago.

Born globals are young, entrepreneurial companies that expand across national boundaries soon after their foundation. They create subsidiaries abroad to, e.g. enable fast market access, provide the potential for exponential growth and be first movers in their industries (Moen and Servais, 2002; Lehmann and Schlange, 2001; Rennie, 1993; Oviatt and McDougall, 1994; Bloodgood et al., 1996; Rialp et al.,

2005). The three companies we look at here have all chosen a distinct approach to cross-border expansion, as all of them faced specific needs. Thus they serve as suitable examples to highlight the different situations in which a better understanding of legal forms across regions is gained.

The born-global company ciao.com, a consumer community for product reviews was challenged with the need for fast internationalization to be ahead of its market and to create important barriers to entry for companies in other countries. For this purpose it opened up own offices in the most important European markets France, Italy, Spain and the United Kingdom only months after the company was founded in Germany in 1999. Later, subsidiaries in Romania and the United States followed to enlarge the footprint and to get access to important human resources. "With this approach we wanted to bring our innovative business model to all important markets before somebody else did", explains Cyril Jaugey, at that time managing director for the internationalization, "and it allowed us to show investors the potential for the scalability of ciao.com" (Jaugey, 2009). Ciao decided to create an own legal entity in all of the regions it was active in and left operations to local managers. Being 100% subsidiaries of the German headquarters, strategic directions where set centrally, while operational decisions and in-country strategies were devised by local management. With this approach ciao was successful in creating a first-mover advantage and secured a dominant market position. Today, ciao is a subsidiary of Microsoft and an integral part of its internet strategy.

Logitech, the producer of computer periphery, is also a born-global company. Established in Switzerland in 1981, the challenge for the company was very early on to be closer to important markets for suppliers and customers, most remarkably also for human and creative talent. As Switzerland is a rather small market with limited access to necessary resources, the company made a dramatic decision. It moved its headquarters to the United States only one year after its foundation. In the following years, it opened up production facilities in Taiwan and Ireland and chose to institutionalize them as full subsidiaries. Since then, Logitech has followed a step-by-step approach to be closer to customer markets and formed new legal entities in each of the respective countries (Holtbrügge and Enßlinger, 2005).

An example of a company with a totally different approach on cross-border operations is the travel start-up trivago.com. The company was founded in 2005 with the mission to provide a web-service where consumers can inform themselves about the quality and prices of hotels worldwide. Already in the first year of operation, trivago started with its own services in France and the United Kingdom. In contrast to ciao or Logitech, however, the management decided to centralize decision-making and operations and provided all services from their headquarters in Germany without opening any offices abroad. Still, trivago also needed to form several legal entities. In France for example, .fr-internet domain names could only be held by French companies. Thus, trivago needed to set up a subsidiary in France to facilitate the business in this country. "Going abroad was a no-brainer for us; as our service appeals to international consumers, it was just logical to expand our offer to other countries. This also helped us to achieve tremendous growth rates", says Rolf Schrömgens, one of the founders of trivago (Schrömgens, 2009). Today, the service is available in 17 countries and provides the world's largest value and price comparison for hotels.

These examples show that a multitude of different approaches to pan-European expansion exist. For each approach the actual recommendation concerning the most appropriate legal form will be different, as each company has to decide for itself which goals it has and which factors are important in the decision process. Possessing know-how on legal forms, however, is important not only for born globals but also for other types of firms. This includes, e.g. medium-sized "hidden champions", which often are very globalized, and even more for large, multinational enterprises (Zucchella and Scabini, 2007) and so-called born-again global companies that rapidly expand internationally after a rather long period of domestic stabilization (Balldegger and Wyss, 2007; Glowik and Göttert, 2009). Typically, such firms follow a staged process of internationalization and thus have more time to evaluate the suitable legal form (Johansen and Vahlne, 1977). Furthermore, larger firms tend to have the resources to involve specialized lawyers and can already draw on own experiences from prior internationalization effects. Accordingly, especially younger and smaller firms will gain the most benefits from this handbook of legal firms in Europe.

The described strategic drivers for pan-European expansion will continue to put pressure on companies to quickly internationalize. With ongoing discussions within the European Union to include new member states, there will also be a steady basis for further growth into new markets and revived sourcing opportunities abroad. In this environment, companies will need to better understand the impact that different legal forms will have on their business in the respective countries. Thus, the need for a handbook on legal forms in Europe will also continuously increase.

Bibliography

Balldeger RJ, Wyss P (2007) Profiling the hybrid: Born-again global firms. Growth Publisher, Fribourg/Bern/New York

Barnard C (2007) The substantive law of the EU: The four freedoms, 2nd ed. Oxford University Press, Oxford, New York

Bassen A, Behnam M et al (2001) Internationalisierung des Mittelstands. Ergebnisse einer empirischen Studie zum Internationalisierungsverhalten deutscher mittelständischer Unternehmen. Zeitschrift für Betriebswirtschaft 71(4):413–432

Berlemann M, Tilgner J (2006) Determinanten der Standortwahl von Unternehmen – ein Literaturüberblick. ifo Dresden berichtet 14–24

Bloodgood J, Sapienza HJ et al (1996) The internationalization of new high-potential U.S. ventures: Antecedents and outcomes. Entrepreneurship Theo Pract 20(4):61–76

Chetty S, Campbell-Hunt C (2004) A strategic approach to internationalization: A traditional versus a "born global" approach. J Int Market 12(1):57–81

Di Gregorio D, Musteen M et al (2008) International new ventures: The cross-border nexus of individuals and opportunities. J World Bus 43:186–196

Dreher A, Gaston N et al (2008) Measuring globalisation: Gauging its consequences. Springer, Heidelberg

Fletcher D (2004) International entrepreneurship and the small business. Entrepreneurship Reg Devel 16:289–305

Glowik M, Göttert M (2009) Attempt to structure entrepreneurial-based internationalization concepts J Econ Manag 27–46

European Commission (2003) Going for growth manuscript catalogue number: NA-47-02-357-EN-C

European Commission (2009) http://ec.europa.eu/enterprise/regulation/index_en.htm 20 July 2009

Henzler H (1992) Die Globalisierung von Unternehmen im internationalen Vergleich. Zeitschrift für Betriebswirtschaft 62:83–98, Ergänzungsheft 2:92

Holtbrügge D, Enßlinger B (2005) Initialkräfte und Erfolgsfaktoren von Born Global Firms. Working Paper 2/2005, University of Erlangen-Nuremberg, Chair of International Management

Johansen J, Vahlne JE (1977) The internationalization process of the firm: A model of knowledge development and increasing foreign market commitments. J Inter Bus Stud 8(1):23–32

Koller H, Raithel U et al (1998) Internationalisierungsstrategien mittlerer Industrieunternehmen am Standort Deutschland – Ergebnisse einer empirischen Untersuchung. Zeitschrift für Betriebswirtschaft 68(2):175–203

Kutschker M, Schmid S (2006) Internationales management. Oldenbourg, München/Wien

Lehmann R, Schlange LE (2004) Born global – Die Herausforderungen einer internationalen Unternehmensgründung. ZfKE 3:206–224

Moen Ö, Servais P (2002) Born global or gradual global? Examining the export behavior of small- and medium-sized enterprises. J Int Market 10(3):49–72

Oviatt BM, McDougall PP (1994) Toward a theory of international new ventures. J Int Bus Stud 25(1):45–64

Oviatt BM, McDougall PP (1997) Challenges for internationalization process theory: The case of international new ventures. Manag Int Rev 37(2):85–99

Rennie MW (1993) Born Global. The McKinsey Quarterly 4(4):45–52

Rialp A, Rialp J et al (2005) The born-global phenomenon: A comparative case-study research. J Int Entrepreneurship 3:133–171

Schick M (2008) Rechtsformwahl für die Gründungs- und Wachstumsphase. Grin Verlag, Munich

Schwenker B, Bötzel S (2007) Making growth work: How companies can expand and become more efficient. Springer, Heidelberg

Weber A (1998) Standortwahl und Unternehmensbesteuerung in der Europäischen Union. Schriftenreihe des Zentrums für europäische Studien, Universität Trier

Rugman AM, Hodgetts RM (1995) International business: A strategic management approach. McGraw-Hill, Maidenhead, Berks

Zucchella A, Scabini P (2007) International entrepreneurship – Theoretical foundations and paradoxes. Palgrave and Macmillan, New York

Chapter 2
Legislatory Need for a Handbook on Legal Forms in Europe and Selection of Countries

Michael J. Munkert

Abstract In this chapter the author Michael J. Munkert discusses the differences in firm legislation across countries as another important aspect that makes a handbook on legal forms in Europe necessary. He highlights the tension between the European open market and the country-specific rules and regulations for setting up and running businesses and explains the accompanying challenges companies face. Furthermore, he delivers an argumentation for the selection of the ten countries that are included in this handbook and introduces the structure that is used for analysis of each country.

Contents

2.1 Differences in Firm Legislation and Need for a Handbook on Legal Forms in Larger Europe

Through the process of the European integration and due to the age of globalization, the false impression that diverse legal systems in different countries have been simplified and adjusted can easily arise. However, there are still various striking dissimilarities between [the] countries, which often cause legal conflicts. Of course, it is obvious and indisputable that the Hague Convention (see Hague Convention

M.J. Munkert (✉)

MUNKERT • KUGLER + PARTNER GbR, Äußere Sulzbacher Straße 29, 90491 Nürnberg, Germany

e-mail: m.munkert@munkert-kugler.de

M.J. Munkert et al. (eds.), *Founding a Company*, DOI 10.1007/978-3-642-11259-1_2,   11
© Springer-Verlag Berlin Heidelberg 2010

1961, Art.12) enabled debureaucratization and eased legal relations between countries. Thereby, near worldwide legal relations could be established without needing diplomatic services.

The other side of the coin is that all countries still have different regulatory frameworks regarding economic and cultural aspects. The prevailing difficulties lie in language barriers, lettering and firm legislation. The phrase "different strokes for different folks" hits the nail on the head and demonstrates that there is still diversity between the European countries. Many companies and founders are not aware of this fact and thus, are often surprised when unexpected problems concerning firm legislation arise and are confronted with the harsh reality. Hence, a need for a handbook on legal forms in larger Europe that provides a clear, structured overview over ten different European countries is apparent. In addition, this handbook can be very helpful in order to prevent unpleasant side effects of incorporation.

On the one hand, the handbook on legal forms addresses people who dream of starting their own business and being their own boss. Unfortunately, these people often show a lack of the required detailed know-how and for many, it is a mystery as to which legal and fiscal premises are necessary. Especially, when you want to start a business in a country that is not your native land, you have to be informed sufficiently and must acquire accurate knowledge about the legal system in the foreign country. There are many aspects one has to consider when incorporating. This handbook details the most important facts and alleviates the introduction into this complex field of legal forms in a comprehensible way.

On the other hand, established companies seek to expand their scope and seek subsidiaries in different countries. Through the globalization of markets, the incorporation process has become easier, but it is more important to expand one's horizon and to cooperate beyond boarders. The possibility to break into new markets provides growth opportunities for enterprises. However, this involves several risks and influencing factors that are often not kept in mind and are generally underestimated. Therefore, current information is constantly essential. To conclude, the language, different legal forms and missing information propose an enormous challenge.

Figure 2.1 shows that 38 percent of service-industry companies have subsidiaries abroad. Consequently, a certain trend and popularity for this form of internationalization can be assumed. But the cooperation is still the favoured form with 49 percent. This can be attributed to the fact that there is still a high inhibition threshold to incorporation because of the higher risks and challenges involved.

Table 2.1 shows that the number of investment plans in German industrial enterprises abroad has steadily increased and the amount of non-planned investments has declined over the past several years. Therefore, it becomes clear that the German industry still has its focus on internationalization. The share of investing enterprises abroad is 41 percent. This number is well above the results from the previous 10 years (about 30 percent). From these enterprises, 40 percent seek to increase their engagements in foreign countries and only 11 percent are planning a reduction.

Figure 2.1 and Table 2.1, accompanied by the previously mentioned assertion, illustrate that there is a high demand for incorporation and internationalization in other countries. For this reason, this handbook on legal forms in greater Europe

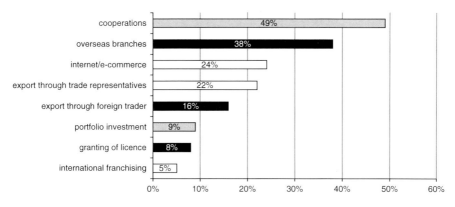

Fig. 2.1 Forms of internationalization of service-industry companies

Table 2.1 Investment plans of German industrial enterprises abroad as percentage[a]

Industrial enterprises for the year	2000	2001	2002	2003	2004	2005	2006	2007
Investments abroad	36	34	38	43	40	41	43	41
No investments abroad	64	66	62	57	60	59	57	59

Industrial enterprises which seek to invest in countries abroad in comparison to the previous year	2000	2001	2003	2004	2005	2006	2007	2008
Higher investments abroad	33	34	35	31	42	43	40	40
Same amount of investments abroad	52	54	44	50	46	47	52	49
Less investments abroad	15	12	21	19	12	10	8	11
Balance	18	22	14	12	30	33	32	29

[a]Until 2000 only industrial enterprises from western Germany; since 2001 industrial enterprises from Western and Eastern Germany; no survey in 2002 regarding investments abroad

has been published in order to meet this demand. It serves as a guideline for the selection of the best legal form in each individual case. It names the pros and cons and explains the steps that have to be taken to found a company in a given country.

2.2 Approach and Selection of Countries

The handbook on legal forms in Europe deals with ten different countries and analyses their most relevant legal forms. For this reason, 12 criteria with an important influence on the legal form selection have been identified, as tabulated in Table 2.2. First, it is vital to know whether the chosen legal form has legal capacity and power of agency. Second, the whole process and the requirements of incorporation are

Table 2.2 Overview on analysis criteria for each legal form

Legal capacity and power of disposition	Regulations concerning corporate name
Process and requirements of incorporation	Transfer of shares/regulations in the case of death of a shareholder
Requirements for associates/shareholders and regulations concerning shareholders' meetings	Liability of shareholders and directors
Articles of Association	Applicable accounting standards
Minimum contribution/initial capital	Disclosure requirements
Commercial register	Employee participation

explained in detail. Another crucial aspect is whether there are requirements for partners and regulations concerning shareholder's meetings. The articles/memorandum of association are then described. Furthermore, it is important to know if a minimum contribution or initial capital is required. Another section broaches the issue of the commercial register. It is also significant to know if there are any regulations concerning the corporate name of this legal form. Moreover, it is relevant to know what will occur in the case of shareholder death. Additionally, questions regarding the liability of shareholders and directors will be discussed. Applicable accounting standards is another topic. In addition, it is necessary to know if any disclosure requirements exist. Finally, it is also important to clarify if employees can or have to participate in this legal form. All in all, these different aspects cover the most crucial facts about one legal form – tax issues aside.

It is clear that one can only decide between these various legal forms if the advantages are contrasted with the disadvantages. Therefore, this handbook outlines the pros and cons of different legal forms. By the same token, an objective recommendation including tendency statements is given depending on the individual case for each country.

But why exactly did we choose the ten countries discussed in this handbook? First of all, these countries have economic and fiscal advantages, which make them very interesting for German enterprises to invest in. The countries with high economic interest and power are France, Germany, the United Kingdom, Spain and Italy. Additionally, the neighbouring countries Austria, Swiss and the Netherlands, are attractive for German companies. Moreover, the Netherlands and Switzerland have mainly fiscal advantages.

In 2007, German enterprises invested more than EUR 122.5 billion in their subsidiaries abroad. That is about EUR 47 billion more than 2006. The money was invested mainly in the Netherlands (EUR 25.5 billion), the United Kingdom (EUR 14 billion) and Switzerland (EUR 13 billion). Furthermore, the profits of EUR 30 billion were invested again. This can be ascribed to the profitability of the subsidiaries.[1] Figure 2.2 shows the "big foreign trade partners" for Germany.

---

[1] http://www.spiegel.de/wirtschaft/0,1518,541947,00.html, version. Accessed 4 Mar 2009
Deutscher Industrie und Handelskammertag (2008) Ergebnisse einer DIHK-Umfrage bei den Industrie und Handelskammern Frühjahr 2008, www.dihk.de. Accessed 4 Mar 2009

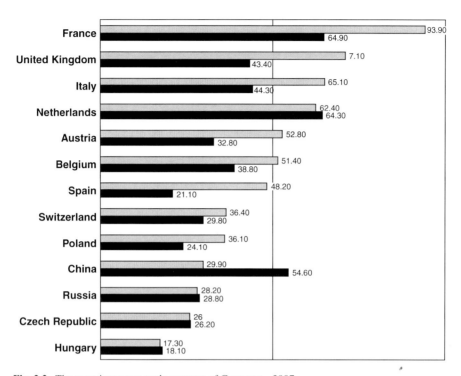

Fig. 2.2 The most important trade partners of Germany – 2007

The coalescence of the European domestic market attracts many enterprises. About 43 percent of companies name the EU-15 as their main goal (see Fig. 2.3). The reasons for this are mainly the positive economic activity, the advantages of a nearly unitary currency area, and the secure legal framework of the domestic market. The proximity of the home country is also a vital influencing factor.

Figure 2.3 illustrates that new EU member-states, mainly from Central and Eastern Europe are getting more and more attractive for German enterprises (37 percent). Therefore, Romania and Hungary can be seen as representatives of these new EU member-states. One motivation for investors to start business in one of these countries is the low costs of production. Thus, the new EU member-states are gaining importance.

Moreover, these countries are now close to the category "countries of the old EU-15" which is, however, still the most relevant destination for investments abroad (43 percent).

Figure 2.4 illustrates the reinvestments made by German enterprises in the year 2007 abroad and emphasizes the importance of the EU-countries (27) to German investors. From a total of EUR 162,577 million, EUR 108,968 million of the reinvestments were made in EU-countries.

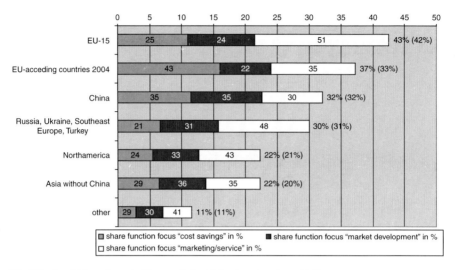

Fig. 2.3 In which regions do German industrial enterprises invest in?

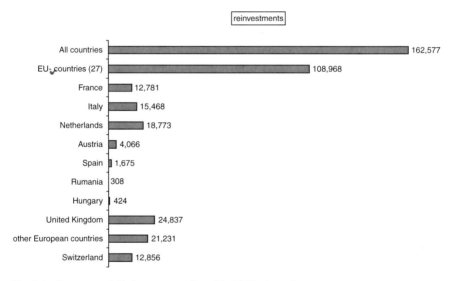

Fig. 2.4 German portfolio investments abroad in 2007 – in m €

To sum up, these countries have been selected due to their economic or fiscal benefits, their location and their recent EU membership. All these named criteria make them attractive for foreign investment and incorporation.

Part II
Legal Forms of Company Foundation

Chapter 3
Austria

Michael J. Munkert and Christian Seidl

Abstract In the chapter on Austria, the authors Michael J. Munkert and Christian Seidl start with an overview of the laws that are relevant for setting up and running a business in Austria. They use the general analysis framework for the handbook on legal forms in Europe to discuss eight relevant legal forms that are possible in Austria: the sole proprietorship (Einzelunternehmen), the general business partnership (Offene Gesellschaft), the limited commercial partnership (Kommanditgesellschaft), the silent partnership (Stille Partnerschaft), the company constituted under civil law (Gesellschaft Bürgerlichen Rechts), the limited partnership with a limited company as general partner (GmbH & Co. KG), the limited company (GmbH) and the public limited company (AG).

They conclude their discussions with an evaluation of the advantages and disadvantages of the different legal forms and provide exemplary recommendations depending on individual cases of the founders.

Contents

C. Seidl (✉)
Tramposch & Partner, Thomas A. Edison Straße 1, 7000 Eisenstadt, Austria
e-mail: office-eisenstadt@tramposch-partner.com

M.J. Munkert et al. (eds.), *Founding a Company*, DOI 10.1007/978-3-642-11259-1_3,
© Springer-Verlag Berlin Heidelberg 2010

3.1 Introduction

As an entrepreneur in Austria, one can choose between different legal forms, which are more or less similar to German legal entities. In the year 2007, the company law regulations for new business establishments changed partially due to a reformation of the Austrian legal system. The Austrian commercial code (Handelsgesetzbuch/HGB), in particular the former legal basis, was replaced by a new commercial code – the so-called "Unternehmensgesetzbuch" (UGB).

Thus, existing law regulations, which often create complicated difficulties in the formation of subsidiaries and particularly in the selection of the appropriate company name, should be reversed by a new and modern company law. One of the central reconfigurations was the combination or consolidation of both, the business law and the corporate law, in the new "Unternehmensgesetzbuch".

Overall, the Austrian commercial law can be described as special private law. The former business law was already described as a special private law, but was especially used for businessmen and -women. As already mentioned, the Austrian legal forms are quite similar to the German legal forms; though with minor differences. The most common and important legal forms, which will be further described in this chapter, are the following:

1. The sole proprietorship (der Einzelunternehmer/EU)
2. General partnerships, including the general business partnership (Offene Gesellschaft/OG), the limited commercial partnership (Kommanditgesellschaft/KG), the silent partnership (Stille Gesellschaft/StG), the company constituted under civil law (Gesellschaft bürgerlichen Rechts/GesBR) and a special form of a limited company, limited partnership with a limited liability company as general partner (GmbH und Co. KG)
3. Stock corporations, including the limited liability company (Gesellschaft mit beschränkter Haftung/GmbH) and the corporation (Aktiengesellschaft/AG).

Any other special forms, e.g. the commercial partnership limited by shares (KGaA) or the corporation and Co. limited partnership (AG & Co. KG), are not discussed in this chapter because they are less common and not as important as the others, previously mentioned.

3.2 Description of Relevant Legal Forms

For a founder of any business, these questions arise: Which entrepreneurial form is the best one for starting the business? Should it be a sole proprietorship, or is a registered company more advantageous? If so, what type of company? And what will it be called then?

Complex and important decisions need to take into account the factors of trade and tenant law, liability, social security and tax law. One has to determine how decision making is to be structured and establish whether the legal form being considered seems advantageous in terms of founding costs, ongoing expenses and business management. For these reasons, it makes sense to include experts in decision making who can estimate the advantages and drawbacks with regards to individual plans and circumstances. The information below is intended to give introduction into the options available when determining a legal form in Austria. Four key questions should guide anybody who is faced with making this decision:

1. How strong is the commitment you want to have to your potential business partner(s)?
2. Do you wish to assume personal liability – perhaps even for your business partner's errors?
3. Does the legal form also make sense in terms of business management?
4. In comparison, what are the main advantages and drawbacks of each legal form?

3.2.1 The Sole Proprietorship (Einzelunternehmen)

The fact that one is a sole proprietor (Einzelunternehmer/EU) does not mean that one is entirely dependent upon himself alone. He can hire employees, conclude work contracts and avail himself of the support and cooperation of the family. For this specific kind of business, no particular regulations exist. Registration takes place only in special cases (when it is beyond the size of a small firm) and only if the firm is registered does the sole proprietorship have a company name.

The following points describe the most important issues that should be kept in mind when considering a sole proprietorship.

3.2.1.1 Legal Capacity and Power of Disposition

The legal capacity of a sole proprietorship is identical with the individual person leading this one-man business.

3.2.1.2 Process and Requirements for Incorporation

Initially, a specific foundation is not needed, but the registration of the sole proprietorship is necessary. As a rule, a sole proprietorship commences upon registering the business and/or receiving authorization.

Additionally, corporate law registration is possible. However, it is important to keep in mind that a single person (one-man businesses) with a reporting liability need to be listed in the commercial register (see section on Commercial Register).

3.2.1.3 Requirements for Associates/Shareholders and Regulations Concerning Shareholders' Meetings

A sole proprietor is a business that is owned and controlled by one person. The business is known as a "one-man business". The business is either owned by private individuals, for example, friends and family – this is called the private sector – or by the public, for example, the government – this is called the public sector.

The owner of a sole proprietorship is

- The sole owner of the business
- The person who makes all the decisions
- The person who is responsible should anything go wrong.

3.2.1.4 Articles of Association

For a sole proprietorship, no corporation agreement is necessary because the business will not be listed as a corporation.

3.2.1.5 Minimum Contribution/Initial Capital

For a sole proprietorship, no own capital is required because the sole proprietor holds absolute liability.

3.2.1.6 Commercial Register

As a sole proprietor, one must be entered in the commercial register once you have reached the level of accountability. The limit for this obligation lies generally at EUR 400,000.00 in annual sales. If this threshold is not reached, one may register voluntarily, but without accounting obligation. This could be an interesting option due to the opportunities it offers under corporate law.

3.2.1.7 Regulations Concerning Corporate Name

If not entered in the commercial register, one must use his surname and at least one written-out given name to externally designate the workplace and business documents. Registered sole proprietors may use the names of people, things or imaginary names, but an appendix indicating the legal form must be appended, such as registered proprietor ("eingetragener Unternehmer") or a generally comprehensible abbreviation of that designation, e.g. "e.U". Sole proprietors must also give their names if they are different from the company name, for example personnel company: Schmidt e.U., commodities company: XY Lumber Trading e.U., imaginative name: Complex e.U. An additional designation indicating the type of business can also be used (§ 17 UGB). If the owner operates more than one business, a registration for every single business is possible.

3.2.1.8 Transfer of Shares/Regulations in the Case of Death of a Shareholder

The transfer of the business is possible. It must be pointed out that the continuation of the sole proprietorship is mandatory, if business does not stop. After the acquisition of a business/firm, the continuation with or without an additional name (e.g. Müller's successor) is possible if the former owner or his heirs agree to the given name.

Furthermore, the sole proprietorship cannot be sold without the business itself as the proprietorship and the liability for it is assumed to be known. (This holds true for business partnerships and public limited companies as well.)

3.2.1.9 Liability of Shareholders and Directors

As a sole proprietor, one is unrestrictedly liable – with all personal assets at risk – for the business's debts. The sole proprietor bears all the risks – but because he does so, he also reaps all the benefits.

3.2.1.10 Applicable Accounting Standards

Simple cash basis accounting is possible as long as the accounting limit is not exceeded. Double entry bookkeeping and drawing up an official balance sheet are necessary if the business exceeds five million Euros in revenues.

3.2.1.11 Disclosure Requirements

For a sole proprietorship, disclosure requirements do not exist.

3.2.1.12 Employee Participation

A supervisory board with employee's representatives is not necessary.

3.2.2 The General Business Partnership (Offene Gesellschaft)

A general business partnership ("Offene Gesellschaft/OG") is composed of at least two shareholders, who are directly liable and whose personal assets are at risk. In questionable cases, the shareholders must provide equal contributions; however, the contributions in the form of services may also be accepted. The following points describe the most important issues to keep in mind when dealing with a general partnership.

3.2.2.1 Legal Capacity and Power of Disposition

The general business partnership is capable of holding rights. This kind of partnership can have every permitted function, including freelancing and agriculture and forestry activities.

3.2.2.2 Process and Requirements for Incorporation

The foundation of a general business partnership starts with a business or partnership agreement. At least two partners are required (§ 105 UGB). The public perception generally starts with the beginning of the business, but in any case with the registration in the commercial register.

The agreement regulates all rights and liabilities for the shareholders (Among each other and to the company). For example: profit and loss statement or liquidation.

3.2.2.3 Requirements for Associates/Shareholders and Regulations Concerning Shareholders' Meetings

The assets of the business are owned on behalf of the other partners, and they are each personally liable – jointly and severally – for business debts, taxes or tortuous liability. For example if a partnership defaults on a payment to a creditor, the partners' personal assets are subject to confiscation and liquidation to pay the creditor.

Each general partner is deemed the agent of the partnership. Therefore, if that partner is carrying on partnership business, all general partners can be held liable for his dealings with third persons.

3.2.2.4 Articles of Association

Articles of association between at least two shareholders are a prerequisite for founding a general business partnership. The articles are not bound to any legal forms. They can even be made orally. However, we do recommend that they be made in writing. Notaries public or attorneys need not be involved. All the partners' rights and obligations towards each other and to the company should be set out in the articles, including company management and representation, profit and loss sharing, voting rights for important decisions, provisions for death, resignations and dismissals, liquidating the company, etc.

After you have drawn up the articles of association, you must apply to have the partnership entered in the commercial register, in which all facts important to people having business contacts with the partnership are available (e.g. shareholder liability, authority of representation, company name, etc.). Only an entry in the commercial register gives the general business partnership its legal status.

3.2.2.5 Minimum Contribution/Initial Capital

For a general business partnership, no capital or minimum deposit is required.

3.2.2.6 Commercial Register

The registration in the commercial register is obligatory. Furthermore, the registration has to cover the following clauses: § 3 Z 2–4, 5, 7, 8 and 16, if necessary in § 3

Z 6, 9, 11 and 15 and § 4 Z 2, 3, 5 and 7 FBG as well (§ 106 UGB). The shareholder, who represents the corporation, has to lodge a deed with his signature.

3.2.2.7 Regulations Concerning Corporate Name

The company must provide proper identification of itself to differentiate itself from others. The company name of a general business partnership can be derived from a surname, the object of the company or an imaginative name, whereby the designation "offene Gesellschaft" or a generally comprehensible abbreviation of that term (e.g. "OG") must be used, for example:

- Name derived from the surname: Schmidt OG;
- Named derived from the object of the company: XY Lumber Trading OG
- Imaginative name: Complex OG.

An additional designation indicating the type of business can also be used.

3.2.2.8 Transfer of Shares/Regulations in the Case of Death of a Shareholder

The transfer of shares is possible, but every existing, every new and every dropped shareholder (and all limited and general partners) have to verify the transfer. Transfer of general partnership shares can only occur if all shareholders agree, but deviant arrangements within the partnership agreement are possible.

3.2.2.9 Liability of Shareholders and Directors

The distinguishing feature of a general business partnership is the partners' unlimited liability. Each partner is personally liable for all of the partnership's debts. That includes any debts incurred by any of the other partners on behalf of the partnership. Any partner is able to bind the partnership by entering into a contract on behalf of the partnership. If Müller and Meyer are partners, and Meyer signs a contract on behalf of the partnership, Müller will be personally liable for the full amount. This is true regardless of whether Müller authorized the contract or whether he even knew of its existence. This feature of unlimited liability contrasts with the limited liability of a corporation's owners. As discussed later on, when a contract is entered into on behalf of a corporation, the owners are not personally liable for its performance.

Due to the fact that each of the partners has unlimited personal liability, a general partnership is the single most dangerous form for conducting one's business. Not only is a partner liable for contracts entered into by other partners, each partner is also liable for the other partner's negligence. When two or more physicians or other professionals practice together in a partnership, each partner is liable for the negligence or malpractice of any other partner.

In addition, each partner is personally liable for the entire amount of any of the partnership's debts. For example, Dr. Wolter may be one of ten partners in a medical partnership, but he is not responsible for only 10 percent of partnership obligations. He is responsible for 100 percent – even though he owns only a 10 percent interest. If Dr. Wolter's other partners are unable to pay their respective shares, he must pay the entire amount.

According to law, every unrestrictedly liable shareholder has the right and the obligation to represent his company. Should one or more of such shareholders be precluded from company management, this circumstance must be set out in the articles of association and entered in the commercial register. Restriction of representation authority and/or company management does not constitute a limitation of liability towards creditors.

3.2.2.10 Applicable Accounting Standards

Simple cash basis accounting is possible as long as the accounting limit is not exceeded. Double entry bookkeeping and drawing up an official balance sheet are necessary if the business exceeds five million Euros in revenues.

3.2.2.11 Disclosure Requirements

No obligations for publication exist. The regulations for sole proprietorship can be applied.

3.2.2.12 Employee Participation

No supervisory board with employee's representatives is obligatory.

3.2.3 The Limited Commercial Partnership (Kommanditgesellschaft)

A limited commercial partnership ("Kommanditgesellschaft/KG") is a form of partnership similar to a general partnership, except that in addition to one or more general partners (GPs), there are one or more limited partners (LPs). The following points describe the most important issues that should be kept in mind when dealing with a limited partnership.

3.2.3.1 Legal Capacity and Power of Disposition

The limited commercial partnership is capable of holding rights. According to Austrian legal regulations, everybody is able to acquire rights as per the conditions stipulated.

3.2.3.2 Process and Requirements for Incorporation

Incorporation occurs with the partnership agreement, which has a common intention and delivery responsibility of at least one person (Komplementär: partner with unlimited liability) and at least one limited partner (Kommanditist).

3.2.3.3 Requirements for Associates/Shareholders and Regulations Concerning Shareholders' Meetings

At least two shareholders are needed to found the partnership, usually natural or legal persons. OG and KG can be shareholders by themselves. If this would be the case, there is a need for at least one general partner and one limited partner. The limited partners are not permitted to manage the company. They have to accept the acts of the general partners, unless the act is beyond the general business and Para. § 16, 3 UGB is not valid.

In all major respects, the GPs are in the same legal position as partners in a conventional firm, i.e. they have management control, share the right to use partnership property, share the profits of the firm in predefined proportions, and have joint and several liabilities for the partnership debts.

As in a general partnership, the GPs have actual authority as agents of the firm to bind all the other partners in contracts with third parties when this is in the ordinary course of the partnership's business. As with a general partnership, an act of a general partner that is not apparently in line with carrying on the ordinary course of the limited partnership's activities or activities binds the limited partnership only if the act was actually authorized by all the other partners.

3.2.3.4 Articles of Association

Articles of association between at least one general partner and one limited partner are a prerequisite for founding a KG. The articles are not bound to any legal form. They can even be concluded orally. However, it is recommended to make them in written form. Public notaries or attorneys need not be involved. All the partners' rights and obligations towards each other and to the company should be set out in the articles, including company management and representation, profit and loss sharing, voting ratios for important decisions, provisions for death, resignations and dismissals, liquidation of the business, etc.

Changes to corporation agreement require the agreements of all shareholders.

3.2.3.5 Minimum Contribution/Initial Capital

In a limited commercial partnership, fixed capital and a minimum deposit are not mandatory for general partners, but fixed deposits for limited partners are necessary. The amount varies depending on the case.

3.2.3.6 Commercial Register

Once the articles of association have been drawn up, the commercial register has to be notified of the partnership for entry. All facts concerning the public aspect of the business, which are of importance to anyone having commercial contacts with it (e.g. shareholder liability, authority of representation, official company name, etc.) must be entered in the commercial register. The entry in the commercial register gives a KG its legal status.

Additionally, the registration has to cover the facts mentioned in the following paragraphs: § 3 Z 2–4, 5, 7, 8 and 16 as well as in § 4 Z 6, if necessary in § 3 Z 6, 9, 11 and 15 and in § 4 Z 2, 3, 5 and 7 FBG (Firmengesetzbuch – commercial code).

3.2.3.7 Regulations Concerning Corporate Name

The name of a limited commercial partnership consists of at least one of the general partner's names and the specification "KG" (or limited partnership). The name must be derived from a surname, the objective of the company or an imaginative name. It must be followed by "Kommanditgesellschaft" or a generally comprehensible abbreviation (e.g. "KG"). The partner's name may not be included in the wording:

- Name derived from a surname: Schmidt KG
- Name derived from the purpose of the company: XY Lumber Trading KG
- Imaginative name: Complex KG.

In addition, a designation of the type of business can be used.

Property, individual or fantasy names are also permissible. The name of the limited partners should not be used. Additionally, it is possible to use extras such as "and", "/", "and partner".

3.2.3.8 Transfer of Shares/Regulations in the Case of Death of a Shareholder

The transfer of shares requires the agreement of all shareholders if it is not differently stated in the articles of association. In the case of the general partner's death, his shares are not automatically inheritable. The continuation of the company with the heirs is only possible if all other shareholders agree to that. It is common to solve this by a succession or accession clause. In the case of a limited partner's death, the continuation of the company with the heirs results as long as it is not differently stated in the articles of association.

3.2.3.9 Liability of Shareholders and Directors

The unlimited partners have unlimited liability. The limited partners are only liable up to the amount of capital they have invested (according to the register).

When the partnership is being constituted or the composition of the firm is changing, LPs are generally required to file documents with the relevant state registration office. LPs must also explicitly disclose their LP status when dealing with other parties, so that such parties are on notice that the individual negotiating with them carries limited liability. It is customary that the letter paper, other documentation and electronic materials issued to the public by the firm will carry a clear statement identifying the legal nature of the firm and listing the partners separately as general and limited. Hence, unlike the GPs, the LPs do not have inherent agency authority to bind the firm unless they are subsequently preserved as agents and thus, create agency by estoppels; or acts of ratification by the firm create ostensible authority.

According to law, every unrestrictedly liable shareholder has the right and the obligation to represent his company. Should one or more of such shareholders be excluded from company management, this circumstance must be set out in the articles of association and entered in the commercial register. Restriction of representation authority and/or company management does not effectuate a limitation of liability towards creditors. Limited partners are not entitled to represent the company externally. They merely have certain control rights, which can be amended through the articles of association.

Limited partnerships are distinct from limited liability partnerships, in which all partners have limited liability.

3.2.3.10 Applicable Accounting Standards

Simple cash basis accounting is possible as long as the accounting limit is not exceeded. Double entry bookkeeping and drawing up an official balance sheet are necessary if the business exceeds five million Euros in revenues.

3.2.3.11 Disclosure Requirements

There are no obligations for publication as long as there is nothing that is especially relevant.

3.2.3.12 Employee Participation

No supervisory board with employee's representatives is obligatory.

3.2.4 The Silent Partnership (Stille Partnerschaft)

This type of partnership is neither registered nor publicly declared. In Austria as well as in Germany, the silent partnership is the classic form of mezzanine financing. There are two main types: the typical silent partnership and the atypical silent partnership. The silent partner contributes a share of the capital and obtains a share of the profit in return. The participation in losses is typically limited to the capital contribution, but can be higher in atypical partnerships.

The typical silent partner does not influence the management of the company and expects a minimum rate of return on a regular basis (usually yearly). By comparison, participation in management and risk is an inherent part of the atypical silent partnership, and for this reason, the atypical silent partner demands an extraordinary return. The typical silent partnership is widely used in public funding. Public venture capital companies or public–private equity enterprises take minority shares in technological ventures or growing small and medium-sized enterprises (SME).

The following points describe the most important issues that should be kept in mind when considering a silent partnership.

3.2.4.1 Legal Capacity and Power of Disposition

As mentioned before, one can differentiate between a typical and an atypical silent partnership. Typical silent partners participate only in partnership profits and losses. Atypical silent partners are part of the management and have a holding in the company's assets if this is agreed upon by contract.

The silent partnership is an undisclosed partnership without legal capacity as well as without title register capacity, the capacity to conduct proceedings in its own name or delict capability. Undisclosed partnerships can belong to a partnership or public–private partnership (with legal or partial legal capacity).

3.2.4.2 Process and Requirements for Incorporation

The silent partnership, as all other legal forms mentioned before, starts with the partnership agreement. As an undisclosed partnership, the silent partnership does not have a face to the public.

3.2.4.3 Requirements for Associates/Shareholders and Regulations Concerning Shareholders' Meetings

The owner as well as the silent partners can be legal or natural persons, as well as OG, KG or GbR. If there is more than one silent partner, a partnership exists with every single partner. If a silent partner holds several shares of different corporations, every relation is characterized by different partnerships.

3.2.4.4 Articles of Association

A silent partnership has no formal regulations and verbal contracts and no implied actions are permissible.

3.2.4.5 Minimum Contribution/Initial Capital

Fixed capital and minimum deposit are not mandatory, but nominal specification of deposit of the silent partner is obligatory. The silent partner is not committed to raise the agreed deposit or to add to the deposit after losing money.

3.2.4.6 Commercial Register

No registration in the commercial agreement is needed for a silent partnership.

3.2.4.7 Regulations Concerning Corporate Name

The silent partnership has no name because it does not make an appearance in public.

3.2.4.8 Transfer of Shares/Regulations in the Case of Death of a Shareholder

The transfer and bequeath of the silent partner's shares is generally possible, but restrictions can be made in the articles of association. Furthermore, the transfer requires the agreement of the company's owner.

3.2.4.9 Liability of Shareholders and Directors

The owner of the corporation bears the liability of a silent partnership only up to the amount of invested capital.

3.2.4.10 Applicable Accounting Standards

According to the UGB, there is no obligation for accounting regarding the silent partnership. In case of an atypical silent partnership, the balance sheet is prepared for tax purposes. The obligation for accounting only concerns the proprietor of the business in which the silent partner is involved.

3.2.4.11 Disclosure Requirements

There are no obligations for publication that are directly related to the silent partnership. The legal form of the proprietor of a business is a significant factor affected by the disclosure requirements.

3.2.4.12 Employee Participation

No supervisory board with employee's representatives is obligatory.

3.2.5 The Company Constituted Under Civil Law (GesbR)

A company constituted under civil law ("Gesellschaft bürgerlichen Rechts"/GesbR) consists of at least two companies that can be thought of as being under one roof. The idea is to unite money and/or monetary-value services or workers for purposes of joint benefit. As a rule, founding a GesbR is only possible up to annual sales of

EUR 400,000.00. A GesbR differs from other partnerships and corporations in the way that it has no legal personality. Consequently, a GesbR

1. Has no qualification under trade law,
2. Has no capacity to be a party in a lawsuit (i.e. it may not litigated or be sued as a company),
3. Has no title register capacity (i.e. it cannot be a landowner. The shareholders – not the company – are entered in the land, trademark and patent registers),
4. Has no official company name. There is, however, an exception under sales tax law; a GesbR also has a type of legal personality within this framework.

The company acts like as a sole trader towards non-partners. This legal form can only be used for enterprises not surpassing the size of an SME. The following points describe the most important issues that should be kept in mind when considering a private partnership.

3.2.5.1 Legal Capacity and Power of Disposition

The civil law association does not hold legal entities of its own. The subjects of rights and duties are always single shareholders, due to the company agreement. Civil law associations cannot be listed in the commercial register.

3.2.5.2 Process and Requirements for Incorporation

Foundation starts with a partnership agreement of two or more persons, for a collaborative acquisition (§ 1175 ff. ABGB). The maximum annual sales for a civil law association is EUR 400,000.

3.2.5.3 Requirements for Associates/Shareholders and Regulations Concerning Shareholders' Meetings

For a civil law association, at least two shareholders are necessary. The shareholders can be any single, natural person or every kind of corporation.

3.2.5.4 Articles of Association

The required articles of association are concluded between at least two shareholders if you want to found a GesbR. In terms of the law, such articles of association are not bound to any form. That is why one may also conduct them orally. However, it is recommended that they be put down in writing. You do not need to involve a notary public or an attorney. The articles of association should regulate all the shareholders' rights and obligations among each other and towards the company, including company management and representation, profit and loss sharing, voting conditions for important decisions, provisions for death, resignations and dismissals, liquidation of the business, etc.

3.2.5.5 Minimum Contribution/Initial Capital

For a civil law association, no capital or minimum deposit is required.

3.2.5.6 Commercial Register

Due to the lack of entity status, the enterprise cannot be entered in the commercial register. If more than one person operates the association (§§ 1175 ff. ABGB – Allgemeines bürgerliches Gesetzbuch, the Civil Code of Austria) and the marginal value for a financial statement will be achieved (more than EUR 600,000 in sales revenue for two consecutive years or more than EUR 600,000 sales revenue in 1 year), the company constituted under civil law has to be registered as an OG or KG.

3.2.5.7 Regulations Concerning Corporate Name

There are no regulations concerning the company's name. The own corporation is not managed by the company. The public appearance occurs with the name of the shareholders. Additionally, property, individual or made-up names are possible.

Since a GesbR itself is not a corporation, it is imperative that all the shareholders publicly represent the firm with their company designation. In addition, a joint designation of the type of business can be used.

3.2.5.8 Transfer of Shares/Regulations in the Case of Death of a Shareholder

The transfer of shares is only possible if all shareholders agree upon it. In the case of death, the company is generally liquidated. However, it is possible to add different regulations in the articles of association.

3.2.5.9 Liability of Shareholders and Directors

In a company constituted under civil law, unlimited liabilities of all members exist (including private properties). As a rule, the provisions on representation may be freely negotiated; otherwise, the capital majority is entitled to representation. In general, with the exception of labour shareholders, all shareholders are entitled to authorization to manage the company. Restriction of authority of representation and/or company management does not effectuate a limitation of liability towards creditors.

3.2.5.10 Applicable Accounting Standards

According to the UGB, there is no obligation for accounting.

3.2.5.11 Disclosure Requirements

There are no obligations for publication as long as there is nothing that is especially relevant.

3.2.5.12 Employee Participation

No supervisory board with employee's representatives is necessary.

3.2.6 The Limited Partnership with a Limited Liability Company as General Partner (GmbH & Co. KG)

For a limited partnership with a limited liability company as general partner, a registration of both "Ges.m.b.H." and "KG" is necessary. The following points describe the most important issues that should be kept in mind when considering a limited company and Co. limited partnership.

3.2.6.1 Legal Capacity and Power of Disposition

As a hybrid between GmbH and KG, the GmbH & Co. KG is a private company that has legal capacity. The legal capacity starts with the registration of the GmbH & Co. KG with the commercial register.

3.2.6.2 Process and Requirements for Incorporation

A limited partnership with a limited liability company as general partner occurs with a partnership agreement of at least one person (Komplementär: partner with unlimited liability) and at least one limited partner (Kommanditist). Assets in kind or monetary contributions are possible (assets in kind with special statutory report). The foundation starts with the registration in the commercial register. To build a GmbH & Co. KG, first a GmbH is necessary. However, the registration of both "Ges.m.b.H." and "KG" is necessary to set up a GmbH & Co. KG.

3.2.6.3 Requirements for Associates/Shareholders and Regulations Concerning Shareholders' Meetings

For a GmbH & Co. KG, at least two shareholders are necessary (natural or legal persons). An OG, KG or GesbR could be shareholders by themselves. If this would be the case, there is a need for at least one general partner and one limited partner. Shareholders of the general-partner-GmbH can be the same person as the limited partner. The GmbH & Co. KG could be shareholder of the general-partner-GmbH as well.

3.2.6.4 Articles of Association

For a GmbH & Co. KG, no formal regulations are possible. Moreover, a verbal conclusion of the contract is permissible. A change in the partnership agreement requires the acceptance of every shareholder.

3.2.6.5 Minimum Contribution/Initial Capital

No minimal contribution is needed from the general partner, but limited partnership interest from the limited partner is required. However, the amount of the limited partnership interest is not prescribed.

3.2.6.6 Commercial Register

The business of the GmbH & Co. KG starts with the registration in the commercial register. For a partnership agreement, notarization is needed. Registration has declarative effect. The limitation of liabilities of the limited partners starts with the day of registration.

3.2.6.7 Regulations Concerning Corporate Name

The name of a GmbH & Co. KG has to be used for identification of the company, to differentiate against others. Therefore, the name should include the name of the unlimited partner. However, property or made-up names are also possible as long as it is not misleading. Another requirement is that the company's name must include the additional term "limited company & Co. KG" (with a limited liability company as general partner – Gesellschaft mit beschränkter Haftung or "GmbH & Co. KG" or "GesellschaftmbH & Co. KG" or "GesmbH & Co. KG"). The name of any other individual person cannot be included in the company's name.

3.2.6.8 Transfer of Shares/Regulations in the Case of Death of a Shareholder

The transfer of shares requires the agreement of all shareholders if it is not differently stated in the articles of association. If the general partner dies, his shares are not automatically inheritable. The continuation of the company with the heirs is only possible if all other shareholders agree upon that. It is common to solve this by a succession or accession clause. In the case of a limited partner's death, the continuation of the company with the heirs results if it is not differently stated in the articles of association.

3.2.6.9 Liability of Shareholders and Directors

The GmbH & Co. KG is liable as an unlimited partner with its total assets. The limited partner is only liable with his capital investment.

3.2.6.10 Applicable Accounting Standards

The regulations that are valid for capital companies also have to be applied for the GmbH & Co. KG. Within the first 5 months of a year, the GmbH has to prepare an annual statement of the last fiscal year, which includes the balance sheet, profit and loss account as well as explanatory notes. Furthermore, a status report has to be prepared. Small and mid-sized GmbHs can benefit from some relaxations of the accounting standards. They only have to prepare a reduced version of an annual statement, which includes the shortened balance sheet, profit and loss account as well as explanatory notes. Additionally, small and mid-size GmbHs do not need to prepare a status report.

3.2.6.11 Disclosure Requirements

The regulations that are valid for capital companies also have to be applied for GmbH & Co. KG. Right after preparation, both the annual report and status report have to be sent to the shareholders. Moreover, in order to enable the shareholders to check these reports before the general meeting, which has to take place within the first 8 months of the new fiscal year, the company has to allow the shareholders to have a look at the books of the company. Furthermore, the company with limited liability has to submit the annual report and status report to the commercial register within 9 months after the past fiscal year.

3.2.6.12 Employee Participation

A supervisory board with employee's representatives is not obligatory.

3.2.7 The Limited Company (GmbH)

Literally translated as company with limited liability, the concept mit beschränk-ter Haftung inspired the creation of the limited liability company form in other countries. The name of the GmbH form emphasizes the fact that the owners (Gesellschafter, also known as members) of the entity are not personally liable for the company's debts. Other variations include mbH (used when the term Gesellschaft is part of the company name itself), and gGmbH (gemeinnützige GmbH) for non-profit companies. The following points describe the most important issues to keep in mind about a limited company.

3.2.7.1 Legal Capacity and Power of Disposition

According to § 61 GmbHG (Gesetz betreffend die Gesellschaften mit Beschränkter Haftung – Limited Liability Corporation Act), a company with limited liability can have its individual and independent rights and obligations, i.e. legal capacity as cor-porate body. Registration with the commercial register needs to be done before the company can even begin to exist, according to § 2 GmbHG.

3.2.7.2 Process and Requirements for Incorporation

The initial contribution and the conclusion of the articles of association can be done by one or several persons. The incorporation itself requires a notarization and the signature of all directors [§ 4 (3) and § 9 GmbHG]. The legal capacity starts with the registration of the company (with limited liability) in the commercial register [§ 2 (1) GmbHG]. Contribution in kind and deposits are possible, whereas in-kind contributions require a special statutory report.

It is widely accepted that a GmbH is formed in three stages: the founding association, which is regarded as a private partnership with full liability of the founding partners/members; the founded company (often qualified with "i.G.", meaning "in Gründung"); and the fully registered GmbH. Only the registration of the company in the commercial register (Firmenbuch) provides the GmbH with its full legal status.

3.2.7.3 Requirements for Associates/Shareholders and Regulations Concerning Shareholders' Meetings

Shareholders can be any natural person or any kind of corporation (private company or Capital Company). According to § 3 (2) GmbHG, the foundation of a single-member company is also possible.

3.2.7.4 Articles of Association

According to §9 (2) GmbHG, the articles of association need to be notarized. Regarding amendments of the articles of association, §§ 49–60 and especially §§ 49–51 GmbHG have to be considered. An amendment to the articles of association can only be effected by a resolution of the shareholders. More precisely, it shall be resolved with a majority of three-quarters of the votes cast. Furthermore, the resolution needs to be recorded by a notary and only has legal effect if it is registered with the commercial register [§49 GmbHG].

3.2.7.5 Minimum Contribution/Initial Capital

The nominal capital has to amount to at least EUR 35,000 and consists of the initial contributions of the individual shareholders, each of which must amount to at least EUR 70. The amount of initial contribution may be determined differently for the individual shareholders because every shareholder can only hold one share, but shares can have different par values [§ 6 GmbHG]. At least half of the nominal capital must be fully raised by the initial contribution in cash, i.e. cash contribution has to be at least EUR 17,500 [§ 6a GmbHG and § 10 GmbHG]. However, exceptions apply for the continuation of an enterprise and for contributions in kind. At least one quarter of every initial contribution (but an amount of EUR 70 in any case) has to be paid in cash [§ 10 GmbHG]. According to § 63 (1) GmbHG, each shareholder is obligated to pay the full amount of the initial contribution he subscribed, as provided in the articles of association and the validly adopted resolutions of the shareholders. The discharge of this payment obligation can neither be waived nor deferred using individual shareholders. It cannot be discharged by initiating a claim against the company.

3.2.7.6 Commercial Register

The formation of a GmbH starts with the registration in the commercial register [§ 2 (1) GmbHG]. The partnership agreement requires a notarization. According to § 3 (1) GmbHG, the registration of a company with liability in the commercial register requires the conclusion of the articles of association and the appointment of directors (the management board).

3.2.7.7 Regulations Concerning Corporate Name

According to § 5 GmbHG, the name of the company is used to identify the company in order to differentiate itself from others. Therefore, the name should be taken from the objective of the business or needs to include the names of the shareholders or at least of one of them. The names of persons other than the shareholders cannot be included in the company's name. Notwithstanding the above, the continuation of the name of an organization that has been transferred to the company need not be barred. Another requirement is that the company's name has to include the additional term "Gesellschaft mit beschränkter Haftung" ("company with limited liability"). The term may also be abbreviated accordingly (e.g. "GmbH" or "GesellschaftmbH" or "GesmbH").

3.2.7.8 Transfer of Shares/Regulations in the Case of Death of a Shareholder

According to § 76 (1) GmbHG, the shares are transferable and inheritable. A notary deed is required to transfer shares by an inter-vivo legal transaction. Agreements relating to a shareholder's obligation to transfer a share in the future require the same form. The articles of association may subject the transfer to further conditions, in particular to the approval of the company [§ 76 (2) GmbHG]. The permission to transfer also has to include the permission to pledge it by contract. For the latter, a notary deed is not required [§ 76 (3) GmbHG]. According to § 77 GmbHG, if the articles of association require an approval of the company for the transfer of a share, a shareholder who has fully deposited the initial contribution may, if such approval is refused, be allowed by the commercial court for the company's head-quarters to transfer the shares if sufficient reasons for the refusal of the approval do not exist and if the transfer can be conducted without damaging the company, the other shareholders and the creditors.

3.2.7.9 Liability of Shareholders and Directors

According to § 61 GmbHG, the company with limited liability has its independent rights and obligations. Only the company's assets are liable to its creditors for the debts of the company. Basically, the company is liable for all responsibilities itself. The shareholders are only liable for the capital invested. The manager is personally liable in case of negligence and is usually also responsible for the observation of trade laws.

3.2.7.10 Applicable Accounting Standards

Within the first 5 months of a year, the GmbH has to prepare an annual statement of the last fiscal year, which includes the balance sheet, profit and loss account as well as explanatory notes. Furthermore, a status report has to be prepared. Small and mid-size GmbHs can benefit from some relaxations of the accounting standards. They only have to prepare a reduced version of an annual statement, which includes the shortened balance sheet, profit and loss account as well as explanatory notes. Furthermore, small and mid-sized GmbHs do not need to prepare a status report.

3.2.7.11 Disclosure Requirements

The regulations that are valid for capital companies are also to be applied for a GmbH & Co. KG. Right after preparation, both the annual report and status report have to be sent to the shareholders. Moreover, in order to allow the shareholders to check these reports before the general meeting, which has to take place within the first 8 months of the new fiscal year, the shareholders must be able to have a look at the books of the company. Furthermore, the company with limited liability has to submit the annual report and status report to the commercial register within 9 months after the past fiscal year.

3.2.7.12 Employee Participation

A supervisory board (Aufsichtsrat) has to be formed if the nominal capital exceeds the amount of EUR 70,000 and more than 50 shareholders are involved or the number of employees exceeds 300 or the articles of association stipulate it. One employee representative for every two shareholders' representative shall be appointed to the supervisory board. The supervisory board has to have a minimum of three members. If the number of shareholders' representatives is odd, one additional employee representative must be appointed.

A supervisory board is required if the company has more than 500 employees; otherwise the company is run only by the managing directors (Geschäftsführer), who have unrestricted authority. The members acting collectively may restrict the powers of the managing directors by giving them binding orders. In most cases, the articles of association list the business activities for which the directors must obtain prior consent from the members. Under Austrian as well as German law, a violation of these duties by a managing director will not affect the validity of a contract with a third party, but the GmbH may hold the managing director in question liable for damages.

3.2.8 The Public Limited Company (AG)

The public limited company is a capital company, where the nominal capital is divided into shares. The following points describe the most important issues that should be kept in mind when considering a public limited company.

3.2.8.1 Legal Capacity and Power of Disposition

According to § 1 Aktiengesetz (AktG – law on stock corporations), the stock corporation is a company with separate legal personality, i.e. legal capacity as a corporate body whose shareholders participate through contributions in the share capital, which is divided into shares. The legal capacity starts with the registration of the stock corporation with the commercial register, and all founders and members of the management board and of the supervisory board have to apply for the registration [§ 28 AktG].

3.2.8.2 Process and Requirements for Incorporation

The contribution in the share capital divided into shares can be done by one or more persons [§ 2 AktG]. The regulations regarding company formation and formation audit in §§ 16–47 AktG have to be considered. For agreements about special benefits or contributions in kind and acquisitions of assets, special regulations [§§19 and 20 AktG] have to be applied. These formations require an audit from special persons (auditors of the formation e.g. sworn accountants etc.) [§25 (2) AktG]. The legal capacity starts with the registration of the stock corporation with the commercial register, where all founders and members of the management board and of the supervisory board have to apply for registration [§28 AktG].

3.2.8.3 Requirements for Associates/Shareholders and Regulations Concerning Shareholders' Meetings

Shareholder can be any natural person or any kind of corporation (private company or Capital Company). According to §35 AktG, the foundation of a single-member company is possible.

3.2.8.4 Articles of Association

According to §16 (1) AktG, the articles of incorporation have to be notarized. Furthermore, §17 AktG gives an overview about the minimal standards of the articles of incorporation regarding the content. For amendments to the articles of incorporation, §§ 145–148 AktG have to be considered. An amendment to the articles of association requires a resolution of the shareholders' meeting [§145 (1) AktG]. The resolution of the shareholders' meeting requires a majority of at least three-quarters of the share capital represented at the adoption of the resolution [§146 (1) AktG]. Furthermore, the resolution has to be recorded by a notary and only has legal effect if it is registered with the commercial register [§148 AktG].

3.2.8.5 Minimum Contribution/Initial Capital

The share capital should be at least EUR 70,000 [§7 AktG]. At least 25 percent of the share capital has to be paid in cash. Shares may be issued as par value shares or as no-par value shares [§8 AktG]. They are denominated in a value of at least EUR 1 or multiples thereof or, in case of no-par value shares, the pro rata amount of the share capital allocated to each share is to be at least EUR 1 [§8 AktG]. Shares may not be issued at a price lower than the nominal amount or the pro rata amount of the share capital allocated to each share. Furthermore, shares have to be made out to the name of the holder if they are issued before the full payment of the issue price [§10 (2) AktG]. The required amount (for the shares) must be at least one-fourth of the lowest issue price and, in the event of the issue of shares for an amount higher than that, it must also include the additional amount [§28a AktG].

3.2.8.6 Commercial Register

After registration in the commercial register, the public limited company becomes incorporated [§28 AktG].

3.2.8.7 Regulations Concerning Corporate Name

According to §4 AktG, the company name of a stock corporation allows for the identification of the company and the differentiation from others. Therefore, the company's name is derived from the objective of the company's business. One can only deviate from this provision if important circumstances arise. Names derived from the object or fantasy names are also possible as long as the name is not misleading. Another requirement is that the company's name contains the additional term "Aktiengesellschaft" ("stock corporation"); the term can be abbreviated as "AG". If the stock corporation continues to use the company name of the business that it has acquired, then according to the general provisions of commercial law, the company name needs also to include the term "Aktiengesellschaft" ("stock corporation").

3.2.8.8 Transfer of Shares/Regulations in the Case of Death of a Shareholder

The transfer and passing down of shares is generally possible and quite easy as no notary deed is required. According to § 61 (2) AktG, name shares may be transferred by endorsement. With regard to the form of the endorsement, the legitimacy of the holder and his obligation to surrender, Articles 12, 13 and 16 of the Bills of Exchange Act ("Wechselgesetz") 1955, Federal Law Gazette No. 49 apply accordingly. The transfer of the name share is to be reported to the company and the shares are to be presented and the transfer proofed. The company must register the transfer in the share register [§61 (3) AktG]. These provisions accordingly apply to interim share certificates. According to § 62 (1) AktG, the articles of incorporation may require the consensus of the company for the transfer of shares. The consensus is granted by the management board, unless the articles of incorporation state differently. The consensus may only be refused for an important reason.

3.2.8.9 Liability of Shareholders and Directors

According to § 48 AktG, only the stock corporation's assets are liable for the debts of the company to its creditors. According to § 1 AktG, shareholders only participate through contributions in the share capital, which is divided into shares; however, shareholders are personally not liable for the liabilities and debts of the company. The obligation of the shareholders to make a contribution is limited by the issue price of the shares [§ 49 (1) AktG]. Unless in-kind contributions are determined in the articles of incorporation, the shareholders shall be required to pay the issue price of the share [§ 49 (2) AktG].

3.2.8.10 Applicable Accounting Standards

The regulations that are valid for the GmbH are also to be applied for AG.

3.2.8.11 Disclosure Requirements

According to § 24 AktG, the founders must issue a written report on the course of the formation (formation report). According to § 127 AktG, within the first 5 months of the business year, the management board shall prepare a report on the state of the company for the previous business year and present it together with the annual financial statements and the proposal for the distribution of profits to the supervisory board. The publication of the annual financial statements has to be made in accordance with § 277 Commercial Code (HGB). Besides, the regulations of the GmbH shall be applied.

3.2.8.12 Employee Participation

The supervisory board consists of at least three and at most, 20 members. The exact number depends on the capital stock [§ 86 AktG]:

- up to EUR 350,000 – seven members
- more than EUR 350,000 – twelve members
- more than EUR 3,500,000 – 20 members.

Employee representatives (group employees' representatives) are entitled, but not obligated to appoint one employee representative for every two shareholder representatives to the supervisory board. Resolutions of the supervisor board generally require a simple majority of the votes. The employee representatives have no special status.

3.3 Summary

There is no such thing as an "ideal" legal form, as every choice depends on the function the business is supposed to have and the requirements set on the legal form.

Therefore, considering the pros and cons of each legal form in advance is the best way to evaluate the different ways of starting a business. Keeping in mind that none of the legal forms will be permanently advantageous, no matter how many reasons there are for making a selection at the outset, any one of them can change with time.

Before giving any recommendations, a summary of the pros and cons of all the legal forms described above will help to draw useful conclusions.

3.3.1 Advantages and Disadvantages of the Different Legal Forms

3.3.1.1 The Sole Proprietor

The first advantage of a sole proprietorship is the fast, easy and relatively cheap start of the business. Furthermore, only few formalities have to be considered, no additional contracts have to be made and no partners are required.

The disadvantage, however, of this legal form is the unlimited, personal liability of the founder. The founder is liable to the full extent of his private fortune. In addition, all trade regulations have to be fulfilled by the entrepreneur and the whole foundation costs are to be met by the entrepreneur. Another problem arises because the sole proprietor has (from the point of view of financing institutions) a reduced credit rating, since the fate of the enterprise depends only on the entrepreneur. Moreover, the entrepreneur needs to have and contribute business acumen, as he does not have a partner who would take care of those issues. If the entrepreneur does not have these capabilities, he needs to employ a business manager. In addition to that, the founder gets no help from a partner in entrepreneurial decisions. Another disadvantage is that the founder does not have the possibility to work as employee and thus, has no tax privileges.

3.3.1.2 The General Partnership

The advantage of a general partnership is the fast and relatively cheap start of business. Furthermore, the general partnership has legal capacity, which means that it has its individual and independent rights and is able to take out loans. Additionally, the second partner increases the creditability of the company. Therefore, the opportunities for financing are extended. Another advantage of this legal form is the possibility to divide the work between the partners. This implies that it is enough if at least one of the partners has the necessary business acumen. Finally, the entrepreneurs have the advantage that the simple income and expenditure accounting is possible as long as the accounting limit is not exceeded.

The most significant disadvantage is quite possibly the unlimited fixed liability of the shareholders. This is even true 5 years after a shareholder leaves the partnership. For instance, if the company is in debt at the time of the shareholder drop out and the remaining time to maturity is 5 years at most, the retired shareholder stays liable for the debts. Due to these circumstances, the shareholders are tied very strongly to the company. Another disadvantage is the strong focus on persons in this legal form, which can lead to major difficulties if it comes to internal disputes.

3.3.1.3 The Limited Company

The advantages and disadvantages of the limited company are similar to the pros and cons of the general partnership. The main difference, however, is the existence of the limited partner and the related advantages and disadvantages.

One advantage is that the limited partner only has a limited liability. Furthermore, the role of the limited partner is quite flexible in its design. The limited partner can choose to only have a share in the company, to have a real employment status, or to work independently. Another advantage is the increased creditability. The higher the deposits of the limited partners are, the higher the creditability is.

The disadvantage is that only the limited partner has limited liability, but the general partner still has individual and unlimited liability.

3.3.1.4 The Silent Company

In general, an advantage of the silent company is the good opportunity to invest in a business of an entrepreneur/corporation without being registered in the commercial register. Furthermore, the untypical silent partnership offers tax benefits with regard to the optimal utilization of tax losses.

3.3.1.5 The Civil Law Association/Private Partnership

The positive aspect of a private partnership is the very easy and relatively cheap start of business.

The negative aspect, however, is the unlimited liability of the shareholders. Another disadvantage is that this legal form is strongly individual oriented, which can lead to great difficulties if it comes to internal disputes. Furthermore, the discussion can be very difficult in the case of voluntary or involuntary retirement. Another problem is the reduced creditability of the sole proprietor (from the point of view of financing institutions) because the fate of the enterprise depends only on the entrepreneur.

3.3.1.6 The Limited Company and Co. Limited Partnership

The main purpose of setting up a GmbH & Co. KG is to combine fiscal advantages of partnerships (i.e. netting the company's profits and losses against the shareholders' other income) with limited liability. The general partner is the GmbH, which is characterized by limited liability. Thus, it is possible to manage the enterprise as a general partner and still appear as partnership. The management can be done by the limited partner or another person. Another advantage is the possibility of a flexible equity financing.

The biggest issue is that two companies have to be founded, which leads to higher founding costs and ongoing expenses. For example, the foundation of the GmbH requires a minimum contribution of EUR 35,000. A further weakness of this legal form is its difficult legal construction, which makes it to be quite non-transparent.

Furthermore, the GmbH & Co. KG only has low creditworthiness due to the general partner's limitation of liability.

3.3.1.7 The Limited Company

The main advantage of the limited company is that the shareholders are not personally liable; their liability is limited to the extent of their share of capital. Basically, the amount of equity capital is the upper liability limit. The preconditions for trade regulations can also be made by persons other than the entrepreneur. Another advantage is flexible fiscal design, i.e. entrepreneur can have employee status.

The disadvantage is the cost of founding of a GmbH. The nominal capital has to amount to at least EUR 35,000 and has to consist of the initial contributions of the individual shareholders, each of which must amount to at least EUR 70). Furthermore, the foundation procedure, contract modifications as well as administration of the limited company are comparably complex due to the need for notary attestation. Furthermore, under trade law, the managing director may also be liable. The creditability of the limited company strongly depends on the amount of equity capital.

3.3.1.8 The Public Limited Company

The benefit of the public limited company is its liability, which is limited to the company's own assets. Furthermore, it is easily possible to transfer the shares. Not even a notary attestation is needed to transfer these. This contributes to the continuation of the company, since it assures the continuation in case of changing shareholders or shareholders' death. Another important advantage is the possibility to go public. This implies that financing through equity capital is possible on a quite broad basis, which decreases the dependency on debts. Furthermore, the separation of power between the board of directors and the supervisory board is an effective management tool.

A crucial aspect of the AG is the high effort and the costs that are required for the foundation. The capital stock has to amount to at least EUR 70,000. Moreover, the foundation procedure of the limited company is comparably complex due to the need for notary attestation. In addition, there is an increased effort for organization, as three boards (board of managers, supervisory board and general meeting) work in parallel.

3.3.2 Recommendations Depending on the Individual Case

A company's legal form defines both the legal relations within the enterprise and its surroundings. The aspects of personal, tax, administrative and commercial law criteria must be carefully considered when choosing a legal form for a business. In many cases and for many entrepreneurs, the question arises as to whether or not a business should be found alone (sole proprietorship), or maybe with acquaintances or partners (partnership). Due to this question, this recommendation reflects this topic because it deals with one of the most important decisions that has to be made.

It is also contingent upon the business concept and the framework conditions surrounding the planned business start-up. However, the drawbacks are that individual decision making is restricted, every partner is liable for the others' errors, and it often takes longer to reach firm decisions. As an alternative, it is worth looking into whether, as an individual, it is possible to agree on cooperation with others. The activities can cover all business functions, from acquiring raw and auxiliary materials and fuel, to manufacturing, all the way to distribution and service provision or sharing equipment. The regularity of the cooperation can be freely organized.

Depending on the objective, both a loose cooperation with independent enterprises and founding a joint company are conceivable. In a nutshell, the advantages for a start up together with partners are

- Complementary experience, knowledge and skills
- Better work distribution and time savings
- Easier capital accumulation
- Less founding risk
- More dynamic business growth
- Greater chances of success.

In the end, it is always an individual decision as to whether a business will be started together with a partner or not. When founding a partnership, there is a risk in choosing a partner, i.e. the choice might be made on an emotional basis rather than a purely professional one. However, this does not mean that feelings and intuition should be ignored. One of the most important prerequisite for success in business is being able to trust the partner.

Bibliography

Birnbacher D (ed) (2007) Das neue Unternehmensgesetzbuch (UGB), Kanzlei Dr. Dietrich Birnbacher Villach

Brugger W (2000) Offenlegung der Jahresabschlüsse. DBJ. http://www.dbj.at/phps/start.php?noie=1&lang=de&content=publikationen_show.php&navi=publikationen&publikation_nr=7. Accessed 7 June 2008

Miller F. (ed) (2007) Das neue Unternehmensgesetzbuch – aus HGB wird UGB. Schruns

OV (ed) (2004) Die Limited Company – Das Handbuch. Wien 2007.

Pössinger A (2005) Die Wahl der "geeignetsten" Rechtsform nach der Steuerreform 2004/2005. Wesonig. http://www.wesonig.at/download/wahl_02.pdf. Accessed 7 June 2008

Preslmayer R (2005) Investing in Austria. Deloitte. http://www.deloitte.com/dtt/cda/doc/content/Investing%20in%20Austria%2061).pdf. Accessed 7 June 2008

Roth GH, Fitz H (2006) Unternehmensrecht, Handels-und Gesellschaftsrecht, 2. Aufl, Wien

Schneider C, Temmel C (2004a) Das österreichische Aktiengesetz: deutsch/englisch = The Austrian Stock Corporation Act. Letis Netis ARD ORAC Wien

Schneider C, Temmel C (2004b) Das österreichische GmbH-Gesetz : deutsch/englisch = The Austrian Companies with Limited Liability Act. Wien

Schönherr R (2004) Unternehmensgründung in Österreich. Salzburgagentur. http://www.
    salzburgagentur.at/C1256D7B005829AE/o/E09805B0BFA9B437C1256ED60053B9E8/$file/
    Unternehmensgruendung.pdf. Accessed 7 June 2008
Wirtschaftskammer Ö (ed) (2005) Gründung einer Niederlassung eines ausländischen
    Unternehmens, 5th edn. Wirtschaftskammer Wien
Wirtschaftskammer Ö (ed) (2008a) Gesellschaft mit beschränkter Haftung – Rechtsinfo, 2nd edn.
    Wien
Wirtschaftskammer Ö (ed) (2008b) Guide for Business Start-Ups, 7th edn. Wien

Chapter 4
France

Emmanuèle Lutfalla and Michael J. Munkert

Abstract In the chapter on France, the authors Emmanuèle Lutfalla and Michael J. Munkert start with an overview of the multitude of organizational forms that can be used in France and provide the rationale for the selection of six legal forms that are discussed in this chapter. They use the general analysis framework for the handbook on legal forms in Europe to analyse the sole proprietorship (L'Entreprise Individuelle – EI), the corporation (Société Anonyme – SA), the limited liability company (Société par Actions Simplifiée – SAS), the private limited liability company (Société à Responsabilité Limitée – SARL), the special private limited liability company (Entreprise Unipersonnelle à Responsabilité Limitée – EURL) and the general partnership (Société en Nom Collectif – SNC).

The authors conclude their discussions with an evaluation of the advantages and disadvantages of the different legal forms and provide exemplary recommendations depending on the individual case of the founders.

Contents

E. Lutfalla (✉)
SCP Soulie & Coste-Floret, 20 Boulevard MASSENA, 75013, Paris, France
e-mail: e.lutfalla@coste-floret.com

M.J. Munkert et al. (eds.), *Founding a Company*, DOI 10.1007/978-3-642-11259-1_4,   49
© Springer-Verlag Berlin Heidelberg 2010

4.1 Introduction

The types of legal forms in France are split into two main categories, the "Sociétés" – the corporate entity – and the individual firms, called "Entreprise Individuelle" in French, which is less risky and easier to create.

There are 17 different types of organizations in France; SCS, SARL, SCA, SCOP, SCIC, Société civile, SCM, GIE, SCI et enterprise, EURL, SARL de famille, SNC, SA, SAS/SASU, SEP, SCP and SEL. The majority of these forms are not commonly used and are essentially highly specific or subcategories of major legal forms.

For the purpose of providing a general insight into the French business system, seven types of legal forms have been chosen for an assessment. This choice is based on the relevance of each legal form for an entrepreneur or group of entrepreneurs, and it outlines the most common legal forms in France. Consequently, some diversified legal forms such as non-profit organizations and cooperatives have been excluded from this summary. We estimate that these firms only play a secondary role in the choice of a legal entity for an entrepreneur.

The main characteristics of the six chosen forms are summed up below.

4.1.1 Entreprise Individuelle (EI)

The individual enterprise or sole proprietorship is one of the most frequently used legal forms in France and many start-ups begin as EIs. The "Entreprise Individuelle" is the easiest form to manage and also the easiest to create. It also is the most common type of legal form for organizations in France, with 53% of all companies in being EIs. Mostly used for craftsmen, liberal professions, etc. the EI differs fundamentally from the other types of organizations mentioned in this chapter, as the owner is solely responsible for the firm and personally liable in case of financial hardships.

4.1.2 Société Anonyme (SA)

Besides the EI, the "Société Anonyme" is one of the most common legal entities in France. It requires a total of seven shareholders and a starting capital of EUR 37,000, thus making it expensive and complex to start, with many bureaucratic requirements.

4.1.3 Société par Actions Simplifiée (SAS)

The SAS is a simplified form of the SA with fewer legal requirements in terms of organizational structure, making it fairly flexible (limited liability company). There must be at least two shareholders (with a maximum of 50), and the starting capital requirement is lower than that of the SA.

4.1.4 Société à Responsabilité Limitée (SARL)

The SARL is a private limited liability company with at least two shareholders. It is the most widely used limited legal form in France, mainly because of the reduced complexity of this entity compared to the SA. The SARL, like the SAS, is suitable for SMEs (small- and mid-sized enterprises). An additional benefit, from a small enterprise perspective, is that there are no requirements regarding starting capital. The EURL is a subcategory of the SARL with only one shareholder.

4.1.5 Société en Nom Collectif (SNC)

This company's form is similar to a general partnership in the United Kingdom. It is not costly to create and the partners take on personal responsibility. Nevertheless, it is not as common as SARL or SA because the responsibility is not shared between the partners, but all members share equal responsibility if the company goes bankrupt.

A separate section discusses employee participation in France, as this topic does not differ, irrespective of which private legal entity the company chooses.

4.2 Description of Relevant Legal Forms

4.2.1 The Sole Proprietorship (L'Entreprise Individuelle – EI)

4.2.1.1 Legal Capacity and Power of Disposition

The legal capacity of the EI is identical to that of the natural person running it. Under French law, the manager of an EI has to be over 18 years of age to create it, and must be able to lead the business, i.e. the person must be able to spend money for the firm without the authorization of a third party. The EI is normally composed of only one person, the manager. The manager is free to lead the company and make all decisions unanimously and with full sovereignty, meaning there are no partners or shareholders. Since the owner represents the company in all legal matters, he is personally responsible, with his own personal property, for all company debt.

4.2.1.2 Process and Requirements for Incorporation

It is necessary to differentiate between three types of business activities since the costs and the modus operandi of formation will differ. These types are "professions", "small-scale enterprises", and "trading companies".

For professional activities, there are no costs of formation. The owner must register with the URSSAF, the social security authorities. For a trading company, the cost of registering with the trade registry, the RCS (Registre du Commerce et des Sociétés), is approximately EUR 56. Finally, the formation of a small-scale enterprise requires registration with the guild chamber directory, and the cost of this ranges from EUR 91–168, depending on the circumstances. The registration of the firm with its various authorities must occur 1 month before formation, or 15 days after it at the latest. The process of legally forming the EI lasts at least 12 days. Subsequent to forming the EI, a notice must be published in a legal notice journal.

In regard to the location of operations, the EI may operate in any type of location, even the manager's home. If the location is the manager's home, there are some additional requirements that need to be met. This arrangement can only last for 5 years and no longer than the specified duration of his private housing contract.

The last step of the registration process is to go to the Centre de Formalité des Entreprises, CFE, where final documents are drafted for the company's operations.

4.2.1.3 Requirements for Associates/Shareholders and Regulations Concerning Shareholders' Meeting

As the manager alone is the head of the company and has no partners, there are no requirements for shareholder meetings.

4.2.1.4 Articles of Association

Contrary to other types of organizations, it is not compulsory to write a document about the statutes in the company. Nevertheless, some other documents have to be written, such as the lease for the store or office, or if it is purchased, the document that states the actual purchase.

4.2.1.5 Minimum Contribution/Initial Capital

For the creation of an EI, there is no minimum capital required. This is due to the small size of the firm, which rarely employs more than five employees. The initial capital is in the amount of the manager's contribution.

4.2.1.6 Commercial Register

As a sole proprietor, the founder has to have an entry in the RCS, the French commercial trade register. In order to have the organization registered, the manager has to meet some conditions: he has to give identification documents, his marriage status (it has to be published in the RCS), documents about the activity of the company and the location. In addition, a natural person can only be registered as the owner of an EI once.

4.2.1.7 Regulations Concerning Corporate Name

For the corporate name, it is necessary to make a distinction between the different commercial activities that the sole proprietor can perform. The professional enterprise must take the name of the owner. For a trading company, the choice of name is wide open, i.e. the owner may choose a name reflecting the activity of the company, or may choose a completely different name. Nevertheless, prior to starting the business, the owner must ensure that the name is not in use elsewhere. This information can be obtained at the INPI, the national organization for patent rights.

4.2.1.8 Transfer of Shares/Regulations in the Case of Death of a Shareholder

When creating an EI, there is no transfer of shares because there are no shareholders, but there can be transfer of the plant or facilities (for commercial and small-scale activities) or transfer of the business (the clients) for a professional activity. Such transfers occur when the manager wants to retire or wants to stop operating. The manager also has the option of leasing his activity to someone else.

4.2.1.9 Liability of Shareholders and Directors

The director is responsible for everything in the organization, as he is the only decision maker. Thus, there is no difference between his personal capital and the company's capital; meaning that the sole proprietor is legally liable with his entire business and private wealth (i.e. unlimited liability of the owner). This implies that if the company's finances are not strong enough to cover the debts, the director's personal belongings can be taken.

4.2.1.10 Applicable Accounting Standards

The EI is only subject to income tax of the proprietor due to its legal status. For the trading company, the income tax is declared in the industrial and commercial profits category, whereas the professional activities firms declare their profits on a non-commercial profits basis.

4.2.1.11 Disclosure Requirements

The manager does not have to annually publish the balance sheet statements or justify his management decisions. The disclosure requirements are different for each scheme of organization. If the scheme is considered as normal, the books have to be comprehensive. In a case of a very small organization, the manager does not have to disclose any financial statements to the authorities or the IRS.

4.2.2 Corporation (Société Anonyme – SA)

4.2.2.1 Legal Capacity and Power of Disposition

Comparable to the American corporation, the SA is a legal entity and may therefore act legally in its own right.

4.2.2.2 Process and Requirements for Incorporation

Forming the SA involves several steps. First of all, the articles of incorporation must be drafted. The articles of incorporation are important; if they are not present, there will be legal and fiscal consequences. The board of directors is appointed in the memorandum/articles of incorporation. Once the board has been chosen, it will nominate a manager, who is also appointed in the memorandum. The company's articles of association must be registered with the appropriate tax collector's office within 1 month after all board members signed it.

After appointing the manager, a statement of the actions carried out on behalf of the company being formed must be prepared, and registration with the commercial trade register (RCS) must take place for the company to become a legal entity. By filing the registration with the CFE, all registration-related issues are taken care of by a single agency and this takes about 15 days. The company's in-kind contributions must then be deposited in a bank or in the Deposit and Consignment Office, so that they can be used at the company's discretion. Finally, a notice in a legal notice journal should be published. This notice must contain the name of the company and its manager, share capital and the address of the registered office.

The total cost of setting up the SA is about EUR 130 (for registering in the Trade Register) plus EUR 150 (for publication in legal notice journals). The time needed to set up an SA is at least 29 days.

4.2.2.3 Requirements for Associates/Shareholders and Regulations Concerning Shareholders' Meetings

The capital of the corporation is divided into shares. In order to form an SA, at least seven shareholders are required. The shareholders can be natural persons (of French or of foreign descent) as well as legal entities, and there is no maximum number of shareholders. The duration of an SA is limited to 99 years, although this licence can be renewed.

There are two kinds of management structures that can be followed by an SA. The most commonly followed type of structure is the appointment of a general manager and a board of directors. In this management structure, the board, which consists of 3–18 shareholder members, appoints a manager and runs the corporation. The manager can be a natural person or a legal entity. If it is a legal entity, a person who can act on behalf of the legal entity must be appointed. There is also a second option, known as the dual structure, where a directorate and a supervisory council are used – similar to German management structures.

The SA's shareholders must meet within 6 months after the end of a fiscal year to approve the company's annual reports. Revoking or appointing members of the board, approving the company accounts and decisions that modify the articles of incorporation require a majority of the quorum of a quarter of the shareholders.

4.2.2.4 Articles of Association

In the articles of association, the directors are first appointed. Following this, the board of directors appoints the chairman. The articles of incorporation outline the company's structure, including corporate name, purpose, ownership structure, share capital invested, the value of each share, any limitations to the free transferability of shares, a description of operations, the naming and description of legal power of the manager or director and the required appointment of a statutory auditor.

4.2.2.5 Minimum Contribution/Initial Capital

The minimum capital requirement is currently EUR 37,000. At least half of that capital (EUR 18,500) has to be paid upon forming the company and the other half must be paid within 5 years. If the company is listed on the stock exchange, the capital must be at least EUR 225,000. The initial capital can consist of cash or in-kind contributions, for instance, tangible assets or intellectual property. An expert appointed by the commercial court must appraise the book value of the latter.

4.2.2.6 Commercial Register

The SA must be registered with the commercial trade register (Tribunal de Commerce) in order to be regarded as a legal entity. Before registration has occurred, the company is not entitled to make any commitments.

4.2.2.7 Regulations Concerning Corporate Name

The name can reflect the activities of the company, the names of founders, or it can be a completely made-up name, as long as all partners agree on the name. Companies are advised to add "SA" to the company name in order to make it easier for those researching the organization. However, companies that do not comply with this suggestion can no longer be penalized.

4.2.2.8 Transfer of Shares/Regulations in the Case of Death of a Shareholder

The SA uses a simplified system of share transfer. The transfer between existing shareholders is unrestricted, but transfers involving third parties involve more limitations. The taxation of share transfer carries a registration fee of 1.1% (with a EUR 4,000 cap), and profit taxed as income tax.

4.2.2.9 Liability of Shareholders and Directors

The shareholders are only liable to the extent of their contribution, whereas the liability of board members is more extensive. The board members' responsibility can be extended to their personal property in case of poor management. Poor management could involve negligent behaviour as well as cases of fraud.

4.2.2.10 Applicable Accounting Standards

The SA is subject to corporate income tax. For corporations, there is a distinction between company profits and managers' salaries. After managers' salaries have been deducted from the net profit, a flat corporate tax rate is applied to the rest of the profit regardless of the amount. The standard tax rate on profit is currently 33.33%. A corporation also has to pay an "additional contribution" (contribution additionnelle) to the extent of 3% of the total amount of the corporate tax.

   Moreover, the social contribution equals 3.3% of the total corporate income tax in excess of EUR 763,000. For an SME, there is a tax reduction for amounts earned less than EUR 38,120, where a tax rate of 15% applies. Tax payments are paid in four instalments yearly and are based on the company's taxable income of the previous fiscal year. The special form no. P279 is sent along with the payment.

4.2.2.11 Disclosure Requirements

The company must file an annual financial statement along with the management report and the general financial report of the statutory auditor. The documents are filed with the local commercial court 1 month after a general shareholders' meeting (AGM) at the latest. The auditor is appointed for a period of 6 years at the annual shareholders' meeting, and a renewal of the contract is possible upon request and on the approval of the shareholders. The statutory auditor is paid a salary, but must remain impartial as he can be held liable if anomalies are discovered. In addition to the annual report, the statutory auditor issues a report disclosing regulated transactions.

4.2.3 Limited Liability Company (Société par Actions Simplifiée – SAS)

4.2.3.1 Legal Capacity and Power of Disposition

As a corporation, the SAS is a legal entity and may therefore act legally in its own right.

4.2.3.2 Process and Requirements for Incorporation

In order to form an SAS, several steps must be taken. First of all, the articles of incorporation must be drafted. Since the SAS allows founders to exercise more freedom in the design of the organization, the main requirement is then to appoint a president in the articles of incorporation.

Subsequent to appointing the president, a statement of the actions carried out on behalf of the company being formed must be prepared, and registration with the commercial trade register (RCS) must take place in order for the company to become a legal entity. Filing for full registration with the CFE is also recommended. The company's in-kind contributions must then be deposited in a bank or in the Deposit and Consignment Office, so that they can be used at the company's discretion. Finally, a notice in a legal notice journal should be published. This notice must contain the name of the company and its manager, share capital and the address of the registered office.

The total cost of setting up an SAS is about EUR 130 (for registering in the commercial register) plus EUR 50 (for publication in legal notice journals). At least 29 days are needed in order to settle the issues regarding the formation of an SAS.

4.2.3.3 Requirements for Associates/Shareholders and Regulations Concerning Shareholders' Meetings

The capital of the corporation is divided into shares, and there must be at least one shareholder, who can be a natural person or a professional body, upon formation. Unlike the SA, the SAS is prohibited from going public. The duration of an SAS is limited to 99 years, although this licence can be renewed if the company wishes to do so.

Partners are free to choose their organizational rules according to company articles. The only legal requirement is that a president must be nominated. Moreover, partners can freely decide on how collective decisions are taken; although some decisions, such as approval of accounts and changes to the share capital, must always be made collectively.

There are few restrictions on shareholders' meetings. Unlike other forms, where regulations regarding such meetings are firmly stated, the annual general meetings may be held over the telephone or by e-mail, thus making the structure highly flexible.

4.2.3.4 Articles of Association

The articles of association must describe the structure of organization as well as the organizational rules, because this information is not normally contained elsewhere for the SAS. This is because the SAS allows freer structuring of the organization for shareholders. Moreover, the memorandum must contain detailed information as to how collective decisions are made. The articles of incorporation outline the company's structure, including corporate name, the purpose, ownership structure, share capital invested, the value of each share, any limitations to the free transferability of shares, a description of operations, the naming and description of legal power of the manager or director and the appointment of a statutory auditor.

4.2.3.5 Minimum Contribution/Initial Capital

The minimum capital requirement is currently EUR 37,000. At least half of that capital (EUR 18,500) has to be paid upon forming the company and the other half must be paid within 5 years. The initial capital can consist of cash or in-kind contributions, for instance, tangible assets or intellectual property. An expert appointed by the commercial court must appraise the book value of the latter.

4.2.3.6 Commercial Register

The SAS must be registered with the commercial trade register in order to be regarded as a legal entity. Before registration has occurred, the company is not entitled to make any commitments.

4.2.3.7 Regulations Concerning Corporate Name

A name can reflect the activities of the company, the names of founders, or it may be a completely made-up name, as long as all partners agree on the name. Companies are advised to add "SAS" to the company name in order to make it easier for those researching the organization. However, the company will not be penalised for not including it.

4.2.3.8 Transfer of Shares/Regulations in the Case of Death of a Shareholder

Similar to the SA, the SAS has a simplified system of share transfer. The transfer between existing shareholders is unrestricted, although involving third parties creates more limitations. The taxation of share transfer has a registration fee of 1.1% (with a EUR 4,000 cap), and profit is taxed as income tax.

4.2.3.9 Liability of Shareholders and Directors

The shareholders are only liable to the extent of their contribution, whereas the liability of board members is greater, as responsibility may be extended to their personal property if they have managed the company poorly. Poor management could involve negligent behaviour as well as cases of minor and major fraud.

4.2.3.10 Applicable Accounting Standards

The SAS is subject to corporate income tax. For corporations, there is a distinction between company profits and managers' salaries. After managers' salaries have been deducted from the net profit, a flat corporate tax rate is applied to the rest of the profit regardless of the amount. The standard tax rate on profit is currently 33.33%. A corporation also has to pay an "additional contribution" (contribution additionnelle) to the extent of 3% of the total corporate tax amount.

Moreover, the social contribution equals 3.3% of the total corporate income tax in excess of EUR 763,000. For an SME, there is a tax reduction for amounts earned less than EUR 38,120, where a tax rate of 15% applies. Tax payments are paid in four instalments yearly and are based on the company's taxable income of the previous fiscal year. The special form no. P279 is sent along with the payment.

4.2.3.11 Disclosure Requirements

The SAS must prepare annual reports. Moreover, the corporation is required to appoint a statutory auditor (commissaire aux comptes). The company must file an annual financial statement along with the management report and the general financial report of the statutory auditor. The documents are filed with the local commercial court 1 month after a general shareholders' meeting (AGM) at the latest.

4.2.4 Private Limited Liability Company (Société à Responsabilité Limitée – SARL)

4.2.4.1 Legal Capacity and Power of Disposition

The SARL is a legal entity and therefore, can act legally in its own right, and its liability is limited.

4.2.4.2 Process and Requirements for Incorporation

In order to form a SARL, several steps must be taken. First, the articles of incorporation are drafted. After appointing the manager, a statement of the actions carried out on behalf of the company being formed must be prepared, and registration with the commercial trade register (RCS) must take place in order for the company to become a legal entity. By filing the registration with the CFE, all registration-related issues are taken care of by a single agency, and this takes about 15 days. The company's in-kind contributions must then be deposited in a bank or in the Deposit and Consignment Office, so that they can be used at the company's discretion. Finally, a notice in a legal notice journal is to be published. This notice must contain the name of the company and its manager, share capital and the address of the registered office.

The total cost of setting up the SARL is about EUR 130 (for registering in the commercial register) plus EUR 150 (for publication in legal notice journals). The total time required for starting a SARL is 29 days.

The duration of a SARL is 99 years; this period starts when the company's registration is complete.

4.2.4.3 Requirements for Associates/Shareholders and Regulations Concerning Shareholders' Meetings

One or several managers run the SARL. The number of managers must be specified in the articles of incorporation. These managers can be third parties, shareholders or salaried employees; however unlike an SA, they must be natural persons. The minimum requirement of shareholders upon formation is one. A maximum of 100 shareholders is allowed. The maximum duration of the SARL is 99 years; renewal is possible upon expiry.

The SARL does not have a manager; it has a CEO, called the gérant, who legally represents the SARL. The CEO is directly responsible to the shareholders through the annual general meeting. There is no need for an annual meeting of shareholders if the number of shareholders is less than 25.

4.2.4.4 Articles of Association

It is very important to draft the articles of association, as these affect the legal status of the manager, who is appointed in the articles of association, and how the SARL is run. The information contained in the articles of incorporation include

- Company name
- Location of company's operations
- Description of business activity
- Shareholders' names, address, marital status, date of birth
- Ownership structure
- Appointment of the manager
- Amount of starting capital
- Date on which the financial statements will be disclosed

4.2.4.5 Minimum Contribution/Initial Capital

There is no minimum capital requirement to form a SARL; therefore, the capital may be as low as EUR 1. It is, however, advised that the initial capital is at least EUR 8,000 for owners to be able to start the business successfully. Upon formation, 20% of contributions must be paid up front, and the rest must be paid within 5 years. These contributions can be paid in cash or in kind, with in-kind contributions including, for instance, tangible assets and intellectual property. Know-how and similar assets can be added as in-kind contributions; however, special rules apply to such instances. Like the SA and SAS, the SARL requires an expert appraiser to be appointed to determine the book value of the in-kind contributions.

4.2.4.6 Commercial Register

The SARL must be registered with the commercial trade register in order to be regarded as a legal entity.

4.2.4.7 Regulations Concerning Corporate Name

The corporate name can reflect the activities of the company, the names of founders, or it can be a completely made-up name, as long as all partners agree on the name.

4.2.4.8 Transfer of Shares/Regulations in the Case of Death of a Shareholder

The transfer of shares is free between shareholders. In the case of a share transfer to third parties, the approval of the majority of shareholders holding at least half the shares is required. Normally, shares may be transferred freely to family members. In every case, share transfers must be reported. Taxes are 5% of the transfer price and there is no cap.

4.2.4.9 Liability of Shareholders and Directors

The shareholders are liable only to the extent of their contribution. However, managers can be held civilly and criminally liable for breaching the memorandum of association, for breaking civil or corporate law, or for cases of mismanagement. Mismanagement can refer to cases of negligent behaviour or minor or severe cases of fraud.

4.2.4.10 Applicable Accounting Standards

The SARL is normally subject to the same regulations that apply to SAs and SASs; however, under certain circumstances, it is possible for a SARL to opt for a pass-through regime instead. The pass-through regime is normally used for the SNC, the SCS and the EURL. Under the pass-through regime, profits are reportable on the shareholders' tax returns. Thus, in case the shareholder is a natural person, he must include the profits in his income tax return. On the other hand, if the shareholder is a legal entity, the profits will be reported in the legal entity's corporate tax return.

4.2.4.11 Disclosure Requirements

The company must file an annual financial statement along with the management report and the general financial report of the statutory auditor. The documents are filed with the local commercial court 1 month after a general shareholders' meeting (AGM). The SARL is obligated to appoint a statutory auditor if the assets are in excess of EUR 1,550,000, if the profits are more than EUR 3,100,000 or if the company has more than 50 employees.

4.2.5 Special Private Limited Liability Company (Entreprise Unipersonnelle à Responsabilité Limitée – EURL)

4.2.5.1 General Overview

A EURL is a private limited company under sole ownership. Essentially, the EURL is a SARL with only one partner. There being only one partner may be the result of a conscious choice upon formation or from acquiring all the shares from other shareholders. The shareholder can be a legal entity or a natural person; however, it cannot be another EURL.

4.2.5.2 Applicable Accounting Standards

Although the rules regarding the general meetings of shareholders cannot be applied to a EURL (due to number of shareholders), the single shareholder must record decisions taken in the corporate minute book of the company. One difference between the EURL and the SARL is the taxation system. Unlike the SARL, the pass-through regime is normally used for the EURL, which essentially means that the profits are reportable on the shareholders' tax returns. The manager of the EURL may opt to switch to the normal system traditionally used by the SA, the SAS and the SARL.

4.2.6 General Partnership (Société en Nom Collectif – SNC)

4.2.6.1 Legal Capacity and Power of Disposition

All partners are equally liable for the company with their personal wealth. This is called the "solidarity principle". In case the company collapses, all partners are responsible and have to pay with their own capital.

4.2.6.2 Process and Requirements for Incorporation

In order to incorporate an SNC, the organization's leaders have to complete several steps. First, all legal documents concerning the incorporation must be drafted in order to specify the conditions of the company. The articles of association must be notarized and signed by an attorney.

Following the completion of the first step, additional elements need to be approved before the start of the company's activities. Examples of such elements include a clear definition of the legal power and responsibility of each partner, details about the shareholders' meetings and their power, and the conditions regarding the dismissal of the manager.

The last step to complete the legal groundwork of formation is to have the legal documents registered with the fiscal administration. Then, the company has to get published in the legal notice journal (EUR 160). An additional cost is the matriculation in order to be registered in the commercial trade registry, Registre du Commerce et des Sociétés (RCS), which costs EUR 86. The process will last at least 30 days.

4.2.6.3 Requirements for Associates/Shareholders and Regulations Concerning Share-holders' Meetings

In order to create an SNC, a minimum of two partners is required. Conversely, there is no limit regarding the maximum amount of shareholders allowed. The partners can be natural persons, who are of legal age, or legal entities.

Because the SNC is a partnership, there are one or several managers. They can be third parties or partners. If nothing is specified in the statutes during the first steps of the creation, all partners have managerial status according to French law. Although it is possible to assign a corporate body as the head of the company, the responsibilities stay the same. Partners enjoy a lot of freedom in terms of the organization and management structure, and this flexibility calls for a specific articles of association.

The annual meeting of the partners is a requirement for the SNC to discuss and approve the financial report. In addition, partners must meet when specifically requested by one of the partners or the manager. During the course of the meeting, all decisions are taken unanimously; still, the articles of association may contain a clause stating that a certain type of decision can be made in a different manner. However, in some instances, unanimous decision making is a requirement. These cases are the dismissal of the manager, the transmission of shares, change of the type of company to SARL and the proposed practice following a call for bankruptcy.

4.2.6.4 Articles of Association

The statutes have to be written and approved, and some elements are required for the document. It has to be composed of the type of the company (an SNC), the duration of the business, the name of the company, location, description of the business and, finally, the amount of capital for the business.

4.2.6.5 Minimum Contribution/Initial Capital

There is no minimum contribution to the starting capital, though partners may bring capital to the company, be it cash or in-kind payments. The capital will be divided into shares and all partners have to agree on the ownership structure, as there are no regulations concerning this.

4.2.6.6 Commercial Register

The company must register with the RCS.

4.2.6.7 Regulations Concerning Corporate Name

The partners are free to name the company as they wish, be it naming for the shareholders or using a made-up name. However, the binding condition is that the company has to comply with French trade regulations.

4.2.6.8 Transfer of Shares/Regulations in the Case of Death of a Shareholder

When one leads an SNC, there are four different reasons for a transfer of shares. The first case is when the manager does not have the right to lead the company any longer due to the expiration of his right to manage the company as specified in the articles of association. The second case is when the manager is unable to continue leading the company for personal reasons, such as illness. In the third case, the shareholders can decide to unanimously dismiss the manager. Finally, the manager may resign from his position.

According to French law, the death of one of the shareholders leads to the end of the company. However, it is possible for the company to go on with the other shareholders or with heir of the deceased shareholder. A transfer of shares is completed only when it is documented and approved by a bailiff. If the recipient of the share transfer is an external third party, the partners must unanimously agree.

4.2.6.9 Liability of Shareholders and Directors

Every partner is liable should the company go bankrupt. This means that every partner can be sued by a creditor, even if he is not responsible for the mismanagement. Thus, every partner is liable to cover the company's debt, without any restriction as to the extent of his own capital.

4.2.6.10 Applicable Accounting Standards

The profits earned by the SNC are not subject to corporate taxation; however, profits are taxed on the income statement of the shareholders as income tax.

4.2.6.11 Disclosure Requirements

There are few disclosure requirements for the SNC, and the appointment of a statutory auditor is not mandatory. Nevertheless, an auditor is needed in order to certify the validity of the company's balance sheet if the company meets two out of the following three criteria: the assets are worth more than EUR 1.5 million, the net sales are higher than EUR 3 million and if the company has more than 50 employees.

4.2.7 Employee Participation in France

France is the country with the highest number of unions and surprisingly enough, the lowest rate of union membership, with a current rate lower than 10%. Moreover, the ability to strike is an individual right for French citizens, and 35 working days per year are normally lost due to strikes. Usually, disagreements between employers and employees turn into strikes (Altmeyer and Dufour, 2007/01).

The laws regulating the employee participation in a firm are fairly lax in France, which means that there are no financial or legal repercussions of not fulfilling the employee participation requirements. As a result, firms often refrain from organizing a structured workers' council, etc.

For a private company of any sort (including societies, individual enterprises) with more than 11 employees, some kind of committee for co-determination of employees is advisable. The same rules apply for every private company.

Fig. 4.1 Levels of employee integration in French business

Differences in the regulations occur only at a private/public level; no distinctions are made between these legal forms in this chapter.

The French committee of employees (CE) meets with the representative of the employer. Matters discussed include job descriptions and processes and current events. The CE is also responsible for leisure activities within the company, such as the company cafeteria, cultural events and sporting activities. The company committee, committee enterprise, must be present in a firm with more than 50 employees. The members of the committee represent the employees and they have to be in a labour union. CHSCT is the committee for the company's safety representatives. This organization evaluates and improves office and factory conformity and safety for workers. A quarter of firms have not appointed such a group; it is not mandatory to have one. The discussion of employee participation in France is summarized in Fig. 4.1.

4.3 Summary

4.3.1 Advantages and Disadvantages of the Different Legal Forms

4.3.1.1 SA

The main advantage of an SA is that shareholders are only liable to the extent of the amount they have invested in the company. The structure of the firm allows for high flexibility of operations. Moreover, it is possible for the owner of the SA to be a salaried employee of the company. The option of floating the company through an IPO allows the SA to raise additional capital, which may then be used to carry out large investments necessary for sustained future growth.

Finally, the SA is very flexible in terms of the system – regulating transfer of shares and the high level of bureaucracy that the company must adhere to prior to forming the SA. It gives more credibility to the members when they meet bankers, suppliers and clients, as the form of the SA signals a large size and diversity of shareholders.

The sheer number of shareholders required indicates that the company must be of a certain size for the SA form to be implementable. Moreover, the minimum capital requirement of EUR 37,000 excludes most SME start-ups. The CEO of an SA is in an unstable position, since he can be dismissed without any notice and any indemnity; this may result in lack of company loyalty and long-term strategic consistency.

4.3.1.2 SAS

An SAS is a simplified version of the SA. Therefore, the advantages of the SA apply to the SAS. However, due to the fact that the SAS is somewhat simplified, additional benefits of this legal form arise. For one, only one shareholder is needed to form the company. Moreover, it gives the management more power to organize the company's operations due to the flexible organizational requirements as stated in regulations regarding the SAS. Similar to other legal forms, the shareholders of the SAS are only liable to the extent of the amount they have invested, as the company is a legal entity in its own right.

Shareholders of an SAS enjoy a certain degree of flexibility as they may form their own rules of share transfer and organizational structure. As a result, forming an SAS is easier than an SA.

Many of the disadvantages of the SA hold true for the SAS as well; particularly all the legal requirements and the requirements of the articles of incorporation. The flipside of the coin is that the company is prohibited from floating the company, which mainly results in limitations as to how the company can raise new capital.

4.3.1.3 SARL

As the required starting capital is zero, the SARL is suitable for small- and medium-sized businesses. Because liability is limited, shareholders are not responsible for the company's losses except for the amounts they have invested and they do not act in the name of the corporation in legal matters. An additional benefit of the specific form of SARL, the EURL, is that it only takes one partner to form the company. Furthermore, the structure is easy to change into a partnership.

The main disadvantage of the SARL is the time-consuming formation process and the fact that the company's shares cannot be traded on the stock exchange.

4.3.1.4 SNC

The main advantage of the SNC is the lack of minimum starting capital required. For the director(s), managing the SNC is more stable due to the fact that all decisions are taken unanimously, especially in the case of dismissal. Moreover, the manager is not alone at the head of the firm; rather the responsibility is shared among all members. An additional benefit of the SNC is that it can stop operating immediately after unanimously selling all the shares, which increases the flexibility of this legal form. Finally, the regulations concerning corporate taxes for the SNC are highly lenient, allowing the company to waive tax payments if profits are below a certain limit.

The main disadvantage is the equal and unlimited liability of all members involved in the SNC. Subsequently, the process of decision making is very long and not very flexible; the unanimity principle applies for all decisions. This latter disadvantage can lead to the difficulty for a member to leave the company because he needs unanimity in the shareholders' meeting. Finally, the members have to declare all profits of the company on their income statement when paying the income tax.

4.3.1.5 EI

An EI is comparatively easy to create because it does not require any capital upon formation. Furthermore, the manager is the only decision maker and the only person leading the company, which makes the process of forming the EI less complex and bureaucratic. This is mainly due to the fact that the owner of the EI need not submit much documentation to the authorities, thereby reducing the time taken to create the firm by at least two-thirds. Lastly, the costs of forming and running the EI are low, the EI is not subject to corporate tax and, because there are no requirements to have a statutory accountant or extensive annual financial reports, costs can be kept at a minimum.

In spite of the prevalence of the EI as the most popular legal form in France, there are undoubtedly some drawbacks. The private liability of the manager constitutes a problem for the owner of the EI – he is responsible for the financial status of the company and its debt; he risks his personal wealth in case of bankruptcy, which is why it is sometimes less risky to create a EURL as a unique partner or even create a SARL.

4.3.2 Recommendations Depending on the Individual Case

The EI and the SARL are the most commonly used legal forms in France, indicating that there are several benefits to these forms. However, the choice of legal form depends largely on the circumstances surrounding the formation and the purpose of the business. If one does not know which type of organization one should choose as legal form, it is possible to take a test on the website of the French national agency of company creation (www.apce.fr), where businessmen are able to find all relevant information regarding firm creation.

There are three major factors that influence the decision of which legal form to use: the number of partners, the amount of investment required, and whether the entrepreneur wants to have his capital protected. In order to make it clearer, the four major possibilities will be examined.

4.3.2.1 First Scenario

- Number of partners: one
- Investment requirement: High
- Capital protection: Yes

In this situation, the entrepreneur will be advised to build a EURL or a SASU (which is a particular form of the SAS), because it does not require more than one person and the liability is restricted in the case of bankruptcy. Nevertheless, the entrepreneur will have to get used to the constraint that this kind of firm requires and the fact that fees of forming the company are higher than when creating an individual firm (due to the liability). A SASU is also a good solution, especially if the company is likely to expand quickly.

4.3.2.2 Second Scenario

- Number of partners: Multiple
- Investment requirement: High
- Capital protection: Yes

This group of potential entrepreneurs should opt for the SARL, the SA or the SAS, because those forms protect the private capital of all partners. The SARL is a very flexible form that can adapt to every kind of project, and the starting capital is determined by the partners and by the size of the company with no minimum requirement. The SA and SAS are adapted to firms needing a large starting amount of money from external sources, and are suitable if the firm is expected to grow quickly.

4.3.2.3 Third Scenario

- Number of partners: Multiple
- Investment requirement: Low
- Capital protection: Yes

In this case, where the starting capital requirement is low, but the restricted liability of private wealth is essential, the group of people should go for SARL due to the fact that SARL is highly flexible and protects the personal wealth of its partners.

4.3.2.4 Fourth Scenario

- Number of partners: one
- Investment requirement: Low
- Capital protection: No

The optimal solution for the requirements of scenario four is to form a single business firm, the Entreprise Individuelle. The process of creating an EI is the least complex one. However, no distinction is made between the manager's wealth and the firm's capital, which implies the full liability of the manager. Choosing a sole proprietorship typically is a very first step, and mostly suited for small-scale or single-person businesses. If starting small is only the first step of a long-term plan, the founder should instead opt for the EURL form, where the owner is still the sole manager, but with no personal liability. An added benefit is that the EURL now has the option to expand to become a SARL by bringing in additional shareholders.

Last but not least, as the SNC has not been mentioned above, here is a brief description as to when it should be chosen when starting a business. The SNC is well suited for companies with a limited number of partners who want to create a closed organization with people they trust. Indeed, the shares are transmitted only if all the associates decide together. The required unanimous consent of all the shareholders to transfer one's shares is often the key factor for choosing such a type of company and, in addition to that, there are no requirements concerning the starting amount of capital, which makes it easy to start.

Bibliography

Altmeyer W, Dufour C (2007/01) Interessenvertretung in Frankreich – Vive La France. Der Betriebsrat (DBR)
APCE: Agence pour la création d'entreprises. http://www.apce.fr
CCI: de Clermont-Ferrand/Issoire. http://www.clermont-fd.cci.fr
Doing Business (2007) Starting a business. http://www.doingbusiness.org/ExploreTopics/Starting Business/
Euro Info Center, EIC (2007) Att starta företag I Frankrike. www.euroinfo.se
Just Landed (2008) Business entities in France. http://www.justlanded.com/english/France/Tools/Just-Landed-Guide/Business/Business-entities-in-France
SODIP – Audit de France (2004) Doing business in France. www.sodip.com/images/Produits/A91DADB5-8743-4455-B2A3-BA3D9A696D71.PDF
The government of Canada how to set up a company in France. www.international.gc.ca/canada-europa/france/commerce/STATUSofFrenchcompanies.pdf
Thieffry associes French legal structures: Incorporate or not? http://www.thieffry.com/doingbusiness/corporations.htm

Chapter 5
Germany

Michael J. Munkert and Klaus Küspert

Abstract In the chapter on Germany, the authors Michael J. Munkert and Klaus Küspert start with a short introduction into the company forms in Germany and present the legal forms that are discussed. They use the general analysis framework for the handbook on legal forms in Europe to analyse eight legal forms: the sole proprietorship (Einzelunternehmen), the private (non commercial) partnership (BGB-Gesellschaft), the commercial partnership and private partnership company (OHG und Partnerschaftsgesellschaft), the limited partnership (Kommanditgesellschaft), the silent partnership (Stille Gesellschaft), the limited commercial partnership (GmbH & Co. KG), the limited liability corporation (GmbH) and the corporation (Aktiengesellschaft).

The authors conclude their discussions with an evaluation of the advantages and disadvantages of the different legal forms and provide exemplary recommendations depending on the individual case of the founders.

Contents

K. Küspert (✉)
MUNKERT KUGLER + PARTNER GbR, Äußere Sulzbacher Straße 29, 90491 Nürnberg,
Germany
e-mail: k.kuespert@munkert-kugler.de

M.J. Munkert et al. (eds.), *Founding a Company*, DOI 10.1007/978-3-642-11259-1_5,
© Springer-Verlag Berlin Heidelberg 2010

5.1 Introduction

The subsequent description and discussion of various legal forms covers the main relevant business entities used in Germany for legal and/or tax purposes.

In general, the typical German legal forms can be divided into proprietor-based forms and capital-oriented forms. In addition, there are legal entities that include features from both of the above-mentioned forms. Influenced by the liberalization of the legal framework for business entities within the European Economic Community (EEC), foreign entities are also used to manage German enterprises.

In the following paragraphs, we present a short description of the relevant legal forms and then explain the typical features of each form in detail. After explaining all relevant forms, we conclude with a summary, including a comparison of the different legal forms and possible recommendations for using them.

The typical legal forms in Germany comprise the following:

- Sole proprietorship (Einzelunternehmen),
- General commercial partnership and partner company (OHG und Partnerschaftsgesellschaft),
- Limited partnership (Kommanditgesellschaft),
- Silent partnership (stille Gesellschaft),
- Private (non-commerical) partnership (BGB-Gesellschaft),
- Limited commercial partnership (GmbH & Co. KG),
- Limited liability company (GmbH), and
- Corporation (Aktiengesellschaft).

5.2 Description of Relevant Legal Forms

5.2.1 Sole Proprietorship (Einzelunternehmen)

5.2.1.1 Legal Capacity and Power of Disposition

A sole proprietor must be a natural person running the business. The proprietor acts in his own name and on his own account. The owner may give a power of attorney to someone to fully act for his enterprise (Prokura) or partly represent him (Handlungsbevollmächtigte).

5.2.1.2 Process and Requirements for Incorporation

The registration costs involved are relatively low.

5.2.1.3   Requirements for Associates/Shareholders and Regulations Concerning Shareholders' Meetings

No regulations are applicable.

5.2.1.4   Articles of Association

As a single entrepreneurship does not include different persons, no articles of associations or other regulations are applicable to run the business.

5.2.1.5   Minimum Contribution/Initial Capital

There is no requirement of having a minimum capital paid in or registered.

5.2.1.6   Commercial Register

The single proprietor may apply for registration in the local commercial register.

5.2.1.7   Regulations Concerning Corporate Name

If a single proprietor uses a brand or trade name, he is obligated to register this name including a link to his own name as proprietor.

5.2.1.8   Transfer of Shares/Regulations in the Case of Death of a Shareholder

The transfer of shares is not necessary as the business of a single proprietor includes all assets and liabilities in regard to the proprietor's business. A sale of the business is made via an asset sale and has to be performed accordingly. If the single proprietor dies, his business is inherited by the heirs, who are fully liable for debts incurred by the business. The heirs may limit this liability to the net worth belonging to the business itself. This limitation has to be applied for with the local register in order to be valid.

5.2.1.9   Liability of Shareholders and Directors

As the single proprietor is fully liable for any debts or liabilities regarding his business, he is fully liable to any creditors unless he limits his liability by a special arrangement with the single creditor upon fixing a single deal.

5.2.1.10   Applicable Accounting Standards

The single proprietor is subject to all relevant statutes covering financial statements and legal reporting. However, a single proprietor is not subject to audit unless he runs a very large business.

5.2.1.11 Disclosure Requirements

A single proprietor is not subject to disclosure unless he is subject to the regulations of a big business (Publizitätsgesetz).

5.2.1.12 Employee Participation

If the single proprietor has more than three employees, the total group of employees may have participation rights in personal affairs. However, a single proprietor does not have a statutory employee participation requirement concerning business affairs.

5.2.2 Private (Non Commercial) Partnership (BGB-Gesellschaft)

5.2.2.1 Legal Capacity and Power of Disposition

The private partnership is the basic model for partnership interests. This legal form has a partly legal capacity and may act as a partnership itself. Partner may be any person or corporation. Each partner is fully liable. All partners have full rights of disposition, but have to act together unless the articles of association provide for single representation.

5.2.2.2 Process and Requirements for Incorporation

There are no incorporation stipulations in order to form this legal entity and no costs of processing or maintaining the legal form are incurred.

A private partnership needs at least two partners to become effective. As there are relatively detailed statutory laws, articles of association or contractual agreements binding the partners are only necessary to establish rules differing from the statutory laws or in order to supplement them.

5.2.2.3 Requirements for Associates/Shareholders and Regulations Concerning Shareholders' Meetings

Statutory laws have no special rules for shareholder meetings or similar items. For this reason, articles of association or similar agreements are useful in order to regulate the partnership.

5.2.2.4 Articles of Association

Articles of association or similar agreements are useful for establishing rules differing from the statutory laws or in order to supplement them.

5.2.2.5 Minimum Contribution/Initial Capital

No minimum capital is needed unless provided for in the articles of association.

5.2.2.6 Commercial Register

A private partnership is not registered in a legal commercial register.

5.2.2.7 Regulations Concerning Corporate Name

A private partnership has no registered trade name. However, the private partnership may act similar to a business by using a particular name.

5.2.2.8 Transfer of Shares/Regulations in the Case of Death of a Shareholder

Any transfer of a partner's interest is subject to approval by all other partners. If a partner dies, this constitutes an event to dissolve the partnership. Under most articles of association concepts, the remaining partners, however, may continue the partnership with the heirs or may continue the partnership after paying severance to the heirs.

5.2.2.9 Liability of Shareholders and Directors

All partners are fully liable for the partnership's debts.

5.2.2.10 Applicable Accounting Standards

As a private partnership normally does not carry on a business, the partnership is not subject to statutory laws for financial statements. However, rarely, exemptions can be made if business entities use a partnership for a project business. In this case, the project could be so large that financial statements and even audit may be applicable.

5.2.2.11 Disclosure Requirements

As a private partnership normally does not carry on a business, the partnership is not subject to audit or disclosure requirements.

5.2.2.12 Employee Participation

As a private partnership normally does not have numerous employees, the personal participation does not apply, but may apply if the private partnership runs an ordinary business.

5.2.3 Commercial Partnership and Private Partnership Company (OHG und Partnerschaftsgesellschaft)

5.2.3.1 Legal Capacity and Power of Disposition

A commercial partnership (OHG) is basically similar to a private partnership (BGB-Gesellschaft) and has at least two partners. The partners may be natural or corporate persons.

The private partnership company (Partnerschaftsgesellschaft) is a special legal vehicle used by consulting firms and businesses, which are regulated on a statutory basis. These special rules, inter alia, apply to legal services, tax services and audit services. The framework of the private partnership is comparable to the statutory rules for commercial partnerships.

5.2.3.2 Process and Requirements for Incorporation

As registration in the commercial register is usually illegal for commercial partnerships, the process of incorporation/formation is quite quick. For private partnership
companies, registration is in compliance with the law, but usually happens within
2–3 weeks.

Registration costs are relatively low. If a special contract or articles of associations are relevant, consultancy fees have to be accounted for.

5.2.3.3 Requirements for Associates/Shareholders and Regulations
Concerning Shareholders' Meetings

Each partner may fully represent the partnership. However, each partner may be
bound by internal rules setting out limits for doing business within the partnership.
This limitation does not work vis-à-vis the partnership's business partners and only
has an internal character. As far as partners' meetings are concerned, it is necessary
to provide for special articles within the articles of association or for special contracts determined by the partners because there are no statutory provisions for this
matter.

5.2.3.4 Articles of Association

As very detailed statutory rules regarding these types of partnerships exist, detailed
articles of association are generally not necessary to set up the entity. However,
a special contract between the partners is normally necessary in order to change
or supplement statutory law, especially in regard to very important matters, such as
powers of attorney, termination of the partnership, rules of termination and the death
of a partner.

5.2.3.5 Minimum Contribution/Initial Capital

The articles of association may also set up a minimum capital, whereas the statutory law has no requirement regarding this aspect. This corresponds with the full
liability of the partners, which may only be limited by special arrangement with
creditors.

5.2.3.6 Commercial Register

A commercial partnership has to be registered in the local commercial register,
whereby this registration is not legitimate. If a commercial partnership does not run
a commercial business, it may still apply for registration and become a legal entity
[as] deemed commercial partnership upon registration. In this case, the registration is
legitimate.

Private partnership companies have to be registered in a special register, called
the partnership register.

5.2.3.7 Regulations Concerning Corporate Name

The partnership must have a trade or brand name or a personal name to be registered accordingly. The partnership acts under this name and is fully subject to all rights and liabilities that may arise from its business.

5.2.3.8 Transfer of Shares/Regulations in the Case of Death of a Shareholder

A partnership interest is normally transferred outside the register to a third party. This change in ownership must then be applied for registration. The old partner will be liable for all liabilities of the partnership incurred until the change of his partnership interest. This liability ceases after 5 years. A change of partnership will also occur if a new partner joins the partnership. In this case, the joining partner becomes liable for all liabilities incurred by the partnership before his entrance. Under normal circumstances, the partners involved in a change of partners or entrance of new partners will settle these questions beforehand.

In the case of death of a shareholder, the remaining partners will continue the partnership unless the articles of association give the heirs the right to become partner.

5.2.3.9 Liability of Shareholders and Directors

The main difference refers to the possibility to limit the liability in regard to debts created by single partners. Within a commercial partnership, each partner is fully liable for all debts of the partnership in respect to the partner responsible for such liability. Within a private partnership company, a partner may limit his liability to debts created by other partners.

5.2.3.10 Applicable Accounting Standards

A commercial partnership or private partnership company is fully subject to compiling financial statements and reporting according to statutory law.

5.2.3.11 Disclosure Requirements

A commercial partnership or private partnership company is not subject to audits.

5.2.3.12 Employee Participation

A commercial partnership or private partnership company may have employee participation in personal matters depending on the number of employees involved. There is no employee participation in business affairs.

5.2.4 Limited Partnership (Kommanditgesellschaft)

5.2.4.1 Legal Capacity and Power of Disposition

A limited partnership consists of at least two partners. One partner possesses unlimited liability ("Komplementär") and one partner has limited liability ("Kommanditist"). First, we take a look at the limited partnership as provided for by statutory purposes. In this case, a general partner is a natural person and not a limited liability company or corporation.

A limited partnership is fully accepted as owner of rights and debtor of liabilities. The general partner, who may have internal limitations stated by a contractual agreement with the limited partners, represents the limited partnership. In very few cases, a limited partner may be given power of attorney to act for the limited partnership on the basis of a special agreement.

5.2.4.2 Process and Requirements for Incorporation

The formation of a limited partnership is relatively simple. Any limited partnership has to be registered in the local commercial register. The rules of a commercial partnership correspondingly apply. Registration usually takes place within 2–3 weeks. Registration costs are relatively low.

5.2.4.3 Requirements for Associates/Shareholders and Regulations Concerning Shareholders' Meetings

There are no statutory rules with regard to shareholder meetings and requirements. Therefore, it is normally useful to provide for the rules on these matters in the articles of association.

5.2.4.4 Articles of Association

The articles of association may determine a minimum capital requirement for each partner and may also render rules on basic questions as right of disposition, distribution of profits, termination, rules of termination and death of partners.

If articles of association are set up to have rules in exchange or in addition to statutory laws, consultancy fees may have to be paid.

5.2.4.5 Minimum Contribution/Initial Capital

As the limited partner is obligated to pay in assets, the amount of these assets is recorded in this register accordingly. However, there is no minimum capital under statutory law. This means that the minimum capital may be EUR 1.

5.2.4.6 Commercial Register

As the limited partnership is fully registered in the local commercial register, any changes in the subject of the entity and its partners have to be reported as soon as possible.

5.2.4.7 Regulations Concerning Corporate Name

The limited partnership may have a personal or brand name. However, the company's name must have a link to at least one person who is fully liable for the partnership's liabilities as general partner.

5.2.4.8 Transfer of Shares/Regulations in the Case of Death of a Shareholder

Shares can be easily transferred, as notarization is not required. Nevertheless, approval from the other shareholders is required. The transfer of shares has to be registered although this is not legitimate.

In the case of death of a limited partner, his heirs will succeed unless the articles of association contain a different regulation. In the case of death of a general partner, the heirs have the right to become a limited partner only if the other partners agree or the articles of association contain this right.

5.2.4.9 Liability of Shareholders and Directors

As the general partners are fully liable, the limited partner is only liable to contribute his minimum capital. If he has deposited these assets, his liability ceases. However, the limited partner becomes liable again if his deposited capital is reduced by distributions or similar events, provided these payments are not covered by outstanding profits from previous years. For businesses done before registration, limited partners are fully liable.

5.2.4.10 Applicable Accounting Standards

The typical limited partnership is fully subject to all statutory laws on financial statements and reporting.

5.2.4.11 Disclosure Requirements

There are no audit requirements.

5.2.4.12 Employee Participation

The limited partnership may be subject to employee participation in personal affairs, but not in business affairs.

5.2.5 Silent Partnership (Stille Gesellschaft)

5.2.5.1 Legal Capacity and Power of Disposition

A silent partnership has no legal capacity with regard to third parties. A silent partnership is considered to be an internal partnership that reflects only the rights and debts between the silent partner and the entity to which the silent partner is related (target company). A silent partner (natural person, partnership or corporation) normally deposits assets into a legal enterprise, e.g. a sole proprietorship or any other business.

A silent partner has no right of disposition, but participates in profits and losses of the target company as defined by the silent partnership agreement.

5.2.5.2 Process and Requirements for Incorporation

There are no special requirements for setting up a silent partnership. However, there are a few statutory laws regulating the basis of such a partnership.

5.2.5.3 Requirements for Associates/Shareholders and Regulations Concerning Shareholders' Meetings

The articles of association may provide for regulations concerning meetings between the silent partner and the target partner.

5.2.5.4 Articles of Association

All necessary regulations are normally provided for in the articles of association, whereby the rules involved are normally comparable to the regulations used within a limited partnership. As far as the interest owed to the silent partner is concerned, the articles of associations can be very flexible.

Economically, the silent partner has the basic rights of a creditor. However, the silent partnership form is often used as a tax vehicle because a silent partnership is regulated under laws similar to a limited partnership; with regards to taxation, it is treated as a limited partnership. This instrument is also used for turning a silent partnership into a corporation.

5.2.5.5 Minimum Contribution/Initial Capital

The articles of association also usually provide for the regulations of depositing capital or services to be rendered by the silent partner.

5.2.5.6 Commercial Register

The partnership is not registered in a commercial register.

5.2.5.7 Regulations Concerning Corporate Name

The partnership has no special name. All business is made in the name and on behalf of the target partner.

5.2.5.8 Transfer of Shares/Regulations in the Case of Death of a Shareholder

Any transfer of the rights from the silent partner is subject to approval by the target partner. If the silent partner dies, his heirs become follow-up partners unless the articles of association have a different guideline for this situation. If the target partner dies or becomes insolvent, the silent partnership ends and is terminated under the rules of the articles of association.

5.2.5.9 Liability of Shareholders and Directors

The silent partner cannot also participate in any losses concerning the business of the target partner. If the target partner incurs losses, the silent partner's liability is normally limited to his deposited capital.

5.2.5.10 Applicable Accounting Standards

The silent partnership itself is not subject to financial statements. The target company fulfils all the requirements.

5.2.5.11 Disclosure Requirements

The silent partnership itself is not subject of disclosure laws or audits.

5.2.5.12 Employee Participation

The rules mentioned above also apply to employee participation. If any, this participation covers the target partners' business and not the silent partner himself.

5.2.6 Limited Commercial Partnership (GmbH & Co. KG)

5.2.6.1 Legal Capacity and Power of Disposition

This legal form is basically the same as a limited partnership (KG). It has sole authority and may act fully as a legal entity itself.

5.2.6.2 Process and Requirements for Incorporation

The process to form a limited commercial partnership is relatively easy, as only two partners are required. The distinctive feature of this legal form refers to a corporation acting as an unlimited and fully liable partner (GmbH). The formation costs and registration costs are minimal.

5.2.6.3 Requirements for Associates/Shareholders and Regulations Concerning Shareholders' Meetings

As the statutory law has not many rules concerning technical items, such as partners' meetings, etc., these items are addressed and regulated by the articles of association.

5.2.6.4 Articles of Association

Articles of association have to be defined in detail; they may be necessary to regulate the internal relationship of the partners. These articles of association are not applied for in the commercial register, but may create consulting costs.

5.2.6.5 Minimum Contribution/Initial Capital

There is practically no minimum capital necessary to form the limited commercial partnership, as the limited partner ("Kommanditist") requires no capital contribution. The same applies to the general partner, a limited commercial corporation (GmbH). Under normal circumstances, the shares of this corporation are wholly owned by the limited partners thus creating a concentrated limited liability company, in effect owned by one person.

5.2.6.6 Commercial Register

The limited commercial partnership has to be registered.

5.2.6.7 Regulations Concerning Corporate Name

The limited commercial partnership may use a trade name, brand name or a name consisting of the partners' names. However, the trade name of the partnership has to affiliate the unlimited partner (GmbH) in order to show the public that there is no natural person liable for partnerships debts.

5.2.6.8 Transfer of Shares/Regulations in the Case of Death of a Shareholder

The interest of a limited partner ("Kommanditist") will be transferred outside the partnership by a contractual agreement between the old partner and the new partner or by transferring the interest of the leaving partner to one or all of the remaining partners. Consequently, the same applies to a change of the unlimited partner's share. However, such a change is relatively rare as the assurance of liability for partnerships debts by using a corporation as unlimited partner is one of the most important features of this legal form.

In case of death of a limited partner his heirs will succeed unless the articles of association contain a different regulation. As the general partner is a limited liability corporation, it cannot cease to exist.

5.2.6.9 Liability of Shareholders and Directors

The unlimited partner (GmbH) itself acts as sole director of the partnership. The director of the unlimited partner (GmbH) himself is not liable unless he is involved in a criminal case or similar events.

5.2.6.10 Applicable Accounting Standards

The limited commercial partnership is fully subject to financial statement requirements for legal and tax purposes. Unless it is a small company, audit of financial statements is compulsory.

5.2.6.11 Disclosure Requirements

The unlimited liability partnership is also deemed to be a corporation for disclosure purposes.

5.2.6.12 Employee Participation

The limited partnership may be subject to employee participation in internal matters and, depending on its size, in external matters.

5.2.7 Limited Liability Corporation (GmbH)

5.2.7.1 Legal Capacity and Power of Disposition

This legal entity is seen as a "small" corporation under German law. It has full legal authority as a corporation and full power to act for itself.

5.2.7.2 Process and Requirements for Incorporation

The requirements for incorporation and information are laid down in a special statutory law (GmbH-Gesetz). The formation costs currently amount to approximately EUR 500.

5.2.7.3 Requirements for Associates/Shareholders and Regulations Concerning Shareholders' Meetings

The statutory law has no requirements concerning who can become shareholder of a limited liability corporation. As far as shareholders meetings are concerned, the statutory law lays down certain minimum requirements. Normally, the articles of association have more details on the subject and also provide details as to who may represent a shareholder.

5.2.7.4 Articles of Association

Articles of association (Gesellschaftsvertrag = Satzung) are obligatory and binding for all shareholders. They have to be registered with the commercial register upon formation. Any change of the articles of association is subject to a shareholder's resolution, conducted before a notary and registered accordingly.

5.2.7.5 Minimum Contribution/Initial Capital

Under current law, the minimum capital is EUR 25,000. Only half of the minimum share capital has to be paid upon formation. There are supplementary rules in cases of contributing stock through the transfer of goods.

Since November 2008, it is possible for one or more shareholders to form a limited liability corporation by contributing 1 Euro. However, a quarter of the corporation's yearly future profits have to be accrued and netted against outstanding share capital until the minimum share capital of EUR 25,000 is reached.

5.2.7.6 Commercial Register

The limited liability corporation is registered in a special commercial register. As mentioned, the articles of association are registered as well. Furthermore, a list of all shareholders has to be reported to the register at the time of a shareholder change or at the time when it is mandated by the statue to disclose the shareholders' names.

5.2.7.7 Regulations Concerning Corporate Name

A limited liability corporation has its own name, which may contain a fantasy name or a name linked to the shareholders.

5.2.7.8 Transfer of Shares/Regulations in the Case of Death of a Shareholder

A transfer of shares has to be done before a notary. Any change in shares must be reported to the directors of the corporation in due course. The director has to hand in an update list of shareholders at the German Trade Register.

If a shareholder dies, his heirs succeed as shareholder unless the articles of association stipulate differently.

5.2.7.9 Liability of Shareholders and Directors

The shareholders are only liable to the extent of their capital stock. If the capital is fully contributed, the shareholders are not liable for the company's debts.

The directors (Geschäftsführer) are not personally liable for debts or events regarding the corporation. However, they may become liable to the shareholders if they act without the shareholders' approval, according to a general agreement. The shareholders of a limited corporation can give binding orders to its directors regardless of the item involved. The directors also are liable for criminal acts and negligent behaviour if special laws apply (insolvency, etc.).

5.2.7.10 Applicable Accounting Standards

The limited liability corporation is fully subject to all applicable commercial, legal and tax requirements of financial statements, reporting, audit and disclosure.

5.2.7.11 Disclosure Requirements

Basically there are three types of corporations in regard to audit and disclosure. Small corporations are not subject to audit, but to disclosure at a minimum level. Medium-sized corporations are subject to audit and disclosure at a higher level. Large corporations are also subject to audit and disclosure, but at a much higher level.

5.2.7.12 Employee Participation

Limited liability corporations may be subject to employee participation in internal and external situations. This depends on the conducted business and the number of employees on the payroll.

5.2.8 Corporation (Aktiengesellschaft)

5.2.8.1 Legal Capacity and Power of Disposition

This legal form is the typical corporation used for running a large business in Germany. The corporation has full authority and power to act for itself.

5.2.8.2 Process and Requirements for Incorporation

The formation requirements are different from those used for a limited liability corporation (GmbH). There are additional formalities to form a corporation by contributing capital with goods or similar items. The forming shareholders may use a small form of this type of corporation, which makes it very similar to a limited liability corporation (GmbH). However, this small version has not had much publicity and has no practical impact.

The formation costs are somewhat higher than the costs for forming a limited liability corporation (GmbH). The standard cost could reach EUR 2,000.

5.2.8.3 Requirements for Associates/Shareholders and Regulations Concerning Shareholders' Meetings

There are no special requirements for shareholders as any natural persons or corporate entities may hold a corporation share. Moreover, any partnership may be shareholder.

The statutory law has very detailed rules governing the relationship between the corporation and its shareholders. This also includes shareholders' meetings, etc.

5.2.8.4 Articles of Association

These statutory laws are very proficient, so it may not be necessary to have additional or supplementary articles of association. If such articles of associations are agreed upon, they must be applied for with the commercial register.

5.2.8.5 Minimum Contribution/Initial Capital

The minimum contribution to share capital is EUR 50,000. The shares may be issued as individual share certificates (Stückaktien) or as par value shares (Nennbetragsaktien). The shares may be anonymous or in shareholders' names (Namensaktien).

It is possible to form a corporation as a sole shareholder. All shareholder capital must be deposited upon formation. As the corporation must have a board (Aufsichtsrat) and directors (Vorstand) by law, the formal shareholders must nominate the originating board, which nominates the originating directors alone. If a capital contribution by transferring goods is involved, the whole process of formation is subject to a special audit (Gründungsprüfung).

5.2.8.6 Commercial Register

Deviating from the rules for partnerships, the corporation (AG) as well as the limited liability company (GmbH) are deemed to become effective as existing legal entities upon registration, and not upon formation.

The articles of association are part of the commercial register as well as the formation documents and any subsequent change of the directors, etc.

5.2.8.7 Regulations Concerning Corporate Name

There are no special rules governing the use of a business name by the corporation. Normally, the name of the corporation is associated to its business or the forming shareholders.

5.2.8.8 Transfer of Shares/Regulations in the Case of Death of a Shareholder

A transfer of shares is made outside the commercial register and does not require certification by a notary. In case of shares issued in the name of the shareholder, any change has only legal effect after registration in a special register maintained for this purpose by the corporation itself (Aktienregister).

A change in shareholders may include his death and does not need approval or similar certificates to be issued by the corporation itself or its directors. The heirs are full shareholders in regard to the shares held by the predecessor. There may be rules available concerning a conflict of interest if the heirs form a community owning the respective shares (Erbengemeinschaft).

5.2.8.9 Liability of Shareholders and Directors

Shareholders are generally not liable for agreements made on behalf of the corporation. The directors (Vorstand) are also not liable unless criminal offences, fraud or negligent behaviour are involved. There are very specific and difficult liability issues regarding the board (Aufsichtsrat) whose function is to oversee the directors on behalf of the shareholders.

5.2.8.10 Applicable Accounting Standards

The corporation has to meet all applicable legal and tax requirements for financial statements.

5.2.8.11 Disclosure Requirements

Audit and disclosure are required. In general, the same rules as for limited liability companies apply. In particular, any listed corporation is subject to audit, even if it does not exceed the limits of a small business.

5.2.8.12 Employee Participation

Corporations may be subject to workers' participation in internal and external issues. This depends on the business run and the number of employees on the payroll.

5.3 Summary

5.3.1 Advantages and Disadvantages of the Different Legal Forms

All partnership forms including the sole proprietorship have the disadvantage of full liability for the partners or unlimited partners. The limited partnership and the limited liability partnership have the effect that the liability is personally reduced or hedged by a partner having a small underlying net worth. For this reason, the limited commercial partnership (GmbH & Co. KG) is now found very often in German businesses.

The limited partnership (KG) may be useful if some of the partners are to be fully liable and some only in a limited form.

The private (non-commercial) partnership (BGB-Gesellschaft) has full liability for each partner and is therefore only used if the partnership does not have debts or it can reduce these debts to the extent of the assets owned by the partnership.

The sole proprietorship may be an effective instrument if the silent partner intends to avoid his own debts. This legal form, however, has the disadvantage that a silent partner is not involved in managing the partnership and cannot also act towards third parties.

The limited liability corporation (GmbH) is very flexible and may be able to avoid shareholder debts. However, changes of ownership in shares or of the articles of association are subject to a notary certificate and other formalities. For a long time, the GmbH had the disadvantage of a minimum capital, which does not apply to partnerships. Since November 2008, it has been possible to form a special type of GmbH (Unternehmergesellschaft) with no minimum capital.

The corporation (AG) is a very difficult commercial form from a formation standpoint and requires additional manpower, who form the managing departments (directors, board). The AG also has a high minimum capital requirement. In comparison to the GmbH, the AG is costly, time-consuming and formal.

5.3.2 Recommendations Depending on the Individual Case

Each legal entity in Germany has its own area and business, which needs to be addressed; the issue as to which type of entity form can then be decided.

The sole proprietor is used for small business units formed by a natural person, who runs the business on his own liability. As an alternative, he may use a limited liability corporation (GmbH), which however, does not work in his favour if he is still liable for business debts personally, and creditors (especially banks) often demand this.

A non-commercial partnership should only be used in cases that do not include personal liability.

The commercial partnership (OHG) should be run by persons who work together personally within a business that directly reflects the full liability of each partner.

The limited partnership (KG) may be used in certain situations when a senior partner, who formally worked as a sole proprietor sets up a partnership with other persons, who are not fully involved in the daily business or will become successors in business in the future. In the latter situation, the limited commercial partnership (GmbH & Co. KG) becomes an interesting alternative, unless the full liability of the existing general partner is the basis for running the business.

The limited commercial partnership (GmbH & Co. KG) is a very flexible instrument combining the basics of a partnership with limited liability. However, this legal form has to meet many commercial requirements typical for corporations. It is therefore partly deemed to be a corporation.

A silent partnership is very flexible and has different variations. As a silent partnership can be formed in addition to a partnership or corporation, this legal entity constitutes an alternative to participate in a special project for a limited period of time.

The limited liability corporation (GmbH) has a very simple structure and may also be used in connection with a limited partnership. The formalities involved are relatively low and are virtually non-existent if the corporation is wholly owned by one person.

The corporation (AG) has a very high reputation under German legal entities. The level of requirements for the formation of an AG is relatively high and it requires experience and expertise in order to be managed properly. The corporation normally is needed if the company intends to create capital by issuing shares or convertible debts.

Chapter 6
Hungary

Attila Kovács

Abstract In the chapter on Hungary, the author Attila Kovacs starts with a short introduction into the possible legal forms in Hungary. He uses the general analysis framework for the handbook on legal forms in Europe to analyse four different legal forms: the limited liability company (Kft.), the company limited by shares (Rt.), the unlimited partnership (Kkt.) and the limited liability partnership (Bt.).

The author concludes his discussions with a summary where he provides exemplary recommendations based on individual requirements.

Contents

6.1 Introduction

The Hungarian law allows the establishment of the following legal forms:

- Unlimited partnership ("közkereseti társaság", Kkt.)
- Limited partnership ("betéti társaság", Bt.)
- Limited liability company ("korlátolt felelösségû társáság", Kft.)
- Company limited by shares ("részvénytársaság", Rt.)
- Joint venture ("közös vállalat", Kv.)

A. Kovács (✉)
Kovács Réti Szegheő Attorneys-at-Law, Bimbó út 143, H-1024 Budapest, Hungary
e-mail: kovacs.attila@krs.hu

M.J. Munkert et al. (eds.), *Founding a Company*, DOI 10.1007/978-3-642-11259-1_6,   89

With the passage of Act Nr. IV., from 2006, the law no longer allows joint enterprises to be established:

- Association ("egyesülés"), a cooperation in the form of judicial persons, which is covered by law for traditional reasons
- Acknowledged group of companies ("elismert vállalatcsoport"), a new legal form for companies, which is comparable to a conglomerate.

An acknowledged group of companies registered in the commercial register does not result in the creation of a separate legal entity apart from the business associations that belong to the group.

Additionally, the European limited company (Societas Europaea, SE) is acknowledged by Hungarian law. All of the business entities mentioned above are capable of holding rights, able to close contracts, to acquire property and to incur debts. Furthermore, they are enabled to act as a party in a lawsuit. For some forms of companies, the Hungarian law demands special legal forms. For example, banks can only be established as a limited company or as a cooperative society. In addition, further approval by the responsible authority might be required. The limited liability company and the limited company are most common.

In the following, we lay an emphasis on the limited liability company and the limited company, as these are the two most common legal forms for companies in Hungary. Furthermore, we include the unlimited liability partnership and the limited partnership because the financial requirements for the first two of the above-mentioned legal forms can exceed the financial capabilities of a newly established company.

6.2 Description of Relevant Legal Forms

6.2.1 The Limited Liability Company (Kft.)

6.2.1.1 Legal Capacity and Power of Disposition

The Kft. is a company that is a legal person, and the organization itself is a judicial entity. Business on behalf of the Kft. is conducted by the managing director(s).

The Kft. has two compulsory corporate bodies: the managing director(s) and the board members. The supervisory board must also be established in four cases as listed below:

1. for public limited companies, except for any public or private limited company that is controlled by the one-tier system;
2. for private limited companies, if requested by founders or members (shareholders), who control at least 5% of the total number of votes;
3. regardless of the form and operational structure of the company, when prescribed by law with an aim of protecting public assets or concerning the activities in which the company is engaged;

4. if the annual average of the number of full-time employees employed by the business association exceeds 200, the employees have the right to take part in the supervision of the company. In this case, the representatives of the employees comprise one-third of the members of the supervisory board.

The Kft. may have one or several managing directors. The appointment of the managing directors is the responsibility of the board. The managing directors represent the Kft. to third parties. They can be assigned joint authority to sign on behalf of the Kft. only together with another managing director (or authorized employee) or they can be assigned authority to sign solely on behalf of the Kft.

6.2.1.2 Process and Requirements for Incorporation

A Kft. is set up by way of articles of association created by all founding members in the form of a notarized deed or a deed countersigned by an attorney. The company will legally exist upon its entry into the commercial register held by the county or metropolitan court acting as the Court of Registration in the territory where the company's corporate headquarters is located.

The statutory deadline for the registration procedure is 15 working days from the date of submission of application in the normal process, one hour in the simplified process. There are two ways to establish a new company. There is a simplified way and the normal court proceedings. The simplified one is cheaper and faster than the normal proceedings. The registration fee for the simplified proceedings amounts to HUF 15,000, while the fee for the normal proceeding amounts to HUF 100,000. Furthermore, the publication charge for the simplified proceeding amounts to HUF 5,000, while the charge for the normal proceeding amounts to HUF 25,000. (The Spring 2009 EUR/HUF exchange rate is approximately 235 HUF/1 EUR.)

If documents necessary for registration have not been filed with the Court of Registration along with the application for registration or if the processing fee has not been paid in full, the application for company registration can be rejected within three working days following the date of submission. This also holds true if the company did not meet the formal requirements set forth by the relevant legal act (in the simplified proceeding, this deadline is one hour). Eight days after the rejection, the documents can be submitted again for registration. The Court of Registration has 8 days following the date of receipt to examine the application and the other corporate documents as to whether they are in compliance with the relevant statutory provisions (in the simplified proceeding, this deadline is one working day).

If the company fails to apply for its registration within 30 days after signing the articles of association or fails to report any change in the data registered within the same deadline, the person responsible for these acts is penalized with an amount between HUF 50,000 and 500,000 (between EUR 200 and 2,000).

A newly registered company must also register with the local municipality, State Taxation Office, Central Statistical Office and Social Security Authorities. Branch offices and commercial representation offices should also be registered with the Court of Registration and may only start their activities after doing so.

6.2.1.3 Requirements for Associates/Shareholders and Regulations Concerning Shareholders' Meetings

The ultimate power in a limited liability company rests with the shareholders. The Kft.'s board meeting must be held at least once a year.

Further meetings must be held: when losses exceed 50% of the capital, at the request of members holding 5% of the shares, the company is on the brink of insolvency or has stopped making payments and its assets do not cover its debts, and when capital has fallen below the required minimum (HUF 500,000). The most important strategic decisions fall within the exclusive rights of the board members. The board decides, for example, on election, removal and replacement of managing directors or capital increase or reduction. For the validity of the decision, it is necessary that at least half of the initial capital or the majority of eligible votes are represented. The articles of association may specify a higher rate of participation, but should not specify a quorum that is less than a simple majority. This is linked to the general rule that the resolutions of the board members are passed by a simple majority of votes. In certain cases, either specified by law or by the articles of association, higher thresholds could be required to pass a board member resolution.

Special rules apply for a one-member Kft., or if one member holds more than 75% of shares.

The supervisory board of a Kft. must consist of at least three or a maximum of 15 persons. It is not involved in the management of the company and its only role is the controlling and monitoring of the Kft. Members of the supervisory board are appointed by the board members. Further rights can be assigned through the articles of association.

6.2.1.4 Articles of Association

The articles of association are to be signed by all members and countersigned by an attorney-at-law. The following items must be included: company name; registered seat; registered office or company register number; members of the company indicating – unless otherwise provided by law – their name (corporate name) and address (registered office); for legal persons and business associations lacking the legal status of a legal person, their company registration number; the main business activity and all other activities of the company, which the company intends to indicate in the register of companies; registered capital including cash and/or in-kind contribution and date/source of contribution; company representation and method for acting on behalf of the company (individual/joint); first executive officers; duration of the company (in case of time limit) and the number, amount and type of shares.

Other details can be included in the articles of association, as needed, for instance, regarding rights attached to specific shares, particulars concerning business locations, etc.

6.2.1.5 Minimum Contribution/Initial Capital

The Hungarian law provides security to a Kft.'s creditors in the form of "minimum share capital". The registered capital must be available to the Kft. and is under no circumstances paid back to the members.

The minimum share capital is HUF 500,000. Members who act fraudulently during the foundation bear unlimited, joint and a great amount of liability for all resulting damages.

A company can only be registered if at least half of each cash contribution is paid to the order of the company. If the full amount of cash contributions is not paid at the time of the foundation of the company, the method and due date of the payment of the remaining amounts are to be specified in the articles of association. All cash contributions are to be paid up within a period of 1 year following the registration of the company. If the value of in-kind contributions at the time of foundation amounts to at least half of the initial capital, it shall be made available to the company in its entirety at the time of foundation. If the in-kind contribution is not made available to the company in its entirety at the time of foundation, it shall be provided within 3 years from the company's registration.

In the case of a one-member company, all in-kind contributions shall be made available to the company before the application for registration is submitted to the Court of Registry. In regard to the cash contributions, the above-mentioned regulations could be applied with one exception: the Articles of Association claim it sufficient to pay HUF 100,000 to the order of the company.

The basic rule for Kft. capital funding is that if a Kft. does not have equity equal to at least half of the minimum amount of registered capital demanded by law for two consecutive financial years, and the members (shareholders) of the business association fail to provide for the necessary funds within a period of 3 months after approval of the annual report for the second year, it must be transformed into another form of company within 60 days or the company is required to pass a resolution about its termination without succession. For this reason, board members must be called in immediately after the equity falls below one-half of the registered capital set out in the articles of association or below the minimum registered capital set out by law.

Accordingly, no dividends are to be paid out if, as a result of such a payment, the equity of a Kft. falls below its registered capital. If this is not the case, then dividends can be paid out in proportion to a member's capital contribution subsequent board member resolution.

6.2.1.6 Commercial Register

The commercial register and the documents filed with the Court of Registration are publicly available and anyone can review them or request a copy. Third parties can rely on data or documents registered in the commercial register if that data has been published in the company report until the contrary is proved, the good faith of the person acquiring any right for compensation by relying on the data registered in the commercial register or published in the company report must be presumed.

Furthermore, the Kft. must submit everything related to the annual report (e.g. also the auditor's statement of approval or the resolution on the appropriation of the after-tax profit) to the Court of Registration within 30 days of the date of the balance sheet. If the company does not fulfil this obligation, the Court of Registration is entitled to declare the company as terminated within 15 days counted from the electronic information of the Tax Authority.

6.2.1.7 Regulations Concerning Corporate Name

The designation "Kft." must be indicated in the company name. The company name must also differ from the names of all other companies in the same or similar line of business.

6.2.1.8 Transfer of Shares/Regulations in the Case of Death of a Shareholder

Business shares in a Kft. are transferred by way of a business share transfer agreement to which the provisions of civil law apply. There are statutory pre-emption rights established by law and the members are also entitled to set out restrictions on the transfer of business shares in the articles of association. Once a business share transfer has been conducted, the managing director of the Kft. is to be informed of the event by way of a notification from the acquirer to which strict formality requirements apply. The managing director then files the amended board members' list with the Court of Registration. A business share, if so provided for in the articles of association, can have different rights attached. As there is no share certificate issued for business shares in a Kft., a public offering of the shares in a Kft. is not possible and the collection of members from the public is expressly prohibited. The only cost attached to the transfer of business shares is a fee for the registration of the change of members in the commercial register.

An acquisition of own shares is allowed upon a resolution of the board members. The Kft. may then acquire a maximum of one-third of its business shares from its assets in excess of its registered capital provided that the business share to be acquired by the Kft. has been paid in full. This business share does not entitle the Kft. to exercise voting rights. The Kft. must have its own business shares or must transfer it to its members without compensation. A further alternative is the withdrawal of the acquired business shares. A one-member Kft. may not acquire its own business shares.

6.2.1.9 Liability of Shareholders and Directors

Managing directors, as mentioned above, represent and sign on behalf of the Kft. Furthermore, they exercise the employer's rights towards the employees of the company. In the relationship with the board members, several tasks are assigned to the directors: holding of the board members' meeting; maintenance of the company's register of members; and the reporting of the required data and information to the Court of Registration.

Managing directors are obliged to act in the best interest of the company. Therefore, they are liable to the company according to the rules of Hungarian civil law for the damages that they cause the company if they break the law or exceed their managerial duties, disregard the articles of association or the resolutions made by the board members. Any claims against (former) managing directors must be made within 5 years of the occurrence of damage.

If the company has assigned managing directors only the right to sign jointly then the directors are jointly and severally liable. The company is liable for damages that are caused by the managing directors to third parties.

The liability of the members in a Kft. is limited only to providing capital contribution undertaken in the articles of association. In general, the members are not liable for the obligations of the Kft. Certain circumstances may lead to full and unlimited liability for the obligations of the Kft. The relevant legal provisions define the following exceptions from the general rule:

- if a member holds more than 50% or 75% of the votes and uses his influence in a way in which the company pursues a constantly detrimental business policy, which leads to the liquidation of the Kft;
- if the members of the Kft. pass a resolution, which they knew would be against the company's interest;
- if the members of the Kft. pass a resolution that they should have known would be against the company's interest; if they would have applied reasonable care, they knew or should have known with due care that the business association would not be able to satisfy its obligations towards third parties as a result thereof;
- if the members have abused the limited liability provision to the detriment of the creditors.

6.2.1.10 Applicable Accounting Standards

The Hungarian accounting system has been brought in line with the EU Accounting Directives and the International Accounting Standards.

Annual reports must be put together according to valid law. The annual report is comprised of the balance sheet, the income statement, and the notes on the accounts. A business report needs also to be prepared concurrently with the annual report. Relief is granted to parent companies, which fulfil two out of three of the following criteria for two consecutive years:

1. the balance sheet total does not exceed HUF 2,700 million;
2. annual net sales revenues do not exceed HUF 4,000 million;
3. the average number of employees in the financial year does not exceed 250 persons.

Before determining the indices defined above, for a consolidated parent company, the subsidiary companies and joint undertakings, need to be taken into consideration first.

Companies who fulfil two requirements do not have to file a management report and can also draw up less detailed accounts. The approval of the annual report falls within the exclusive authority of the board members. All companies are required to undergo audits if their net sales proceeds exceed an average HUF 50 million (approximately EUR 200,000) for two consecutive years.

6.2.1.11 Disclosure Requirements

The register of official company records consists of the commercial register and any enclosures for the verification of data contained in the commercial register, as well as other documents that the company is required to submit by law. All data (current and past) from the commercial register, as well as from the previously mentioned documents, must be made available to the public. The annual report is submitted to the Court of Registry and is published for public distribution.

6.2.1.12 Employee Participation

Kft.s that have an annual average of more than 200 employees have to allow employees to take part in the supervisory board. In such cases, one-third of the supervisory board needs to be composed of employees' representatives.

6.2.2 Company Limited by Shares (Rt.)

6.2.2.1 Legal Capacity and Power of Disposition

The Rt. is a company that bears legal personality, and the organization itself is a judicial entity. Business on behalf of the Rt. is conducted through one of the three compulsory bodies, namely the board of directors. The other bodies are the shareholders' meeting and the supervisory board.

6.2.2.2 Process and Requirements for Incorporation

An Rt. may operate as private or public Rt. The foundation of an Rt. may take place by means of private or public foundation.

When establishing a private Rt., the founders attempt to subscribe for all the shares of the Rt. A private Rt. is established by a deed of foundation signed by all the founding shareholders. A public Rt. is established by way of subscription of its shares in a public foundation procedure. The statutes of a public Rt. are approved by its founding general meeting.

The Rt. comes into existence on the date of registration with the Court of Registration. The deadline for the registration of an Rt. in the commercial register corresponds to the deadline applicable. HUF 600,000 (about EUR 2,400) is payable in the case of a public Rt. and HUF 100,000 (about EUR 400) in the case of a private Rt. as stamp duty. In both cases, a publication fee of HUF 25,000 (about EUR 100) must be paid.

The simplified proceedings can be applied to the private Rt. similar to the Kft. In the simplified procedure, the registration fee amounts to HUF 15,000 and the disclosure fee amounts to HUF 5,000.

A newly registered company must also register with the local municipality, State Taxation Office, Central Statistical Office and Social Security Authorities. Branch offices and commercial representation offices should also be registered at the Court of Registration and can start their activities only after doing so.

6.2.2.3 Requirements for Associates/Shareholders and Regulations Concerning Shareholders' Meetings

An Rt. is required to have three corporate bodies: the shareholders, the board of directors, and the supervisory board (Supervisory board is only mandatory for the public Rt.). The details of an Rt.'s organizational structure are outlined in the founding documents and in the bylaws of the corporate bodies. The board of directors is the managing body of the Rt. and consists of three to eleven individuals. The members of the board of directors represent the company towards third parties. The management board exercises its rights and performs its duties as an independent body. The rules of procedure approved by the management board provide for the division of tasks and competences among the members of the management board.

Members of the board of directors are appointed by the shareholders. Only the private Rt. is entitled to provide authorization to the supervisory board in the deed of foundation in order to be able appoint directors. The independence of the members of the board of directors is similar to the managing directors of a Kft. A private Rt. may decide that no board of directors is elected, rather that the rights and obligations of the board of directors shall be carried out by a sole executive officer. The shareholders are the supreme body of the Rt., consisting of all shareholders in the company. A shareholders' meeting must be convened at least once a year as set out in the deed of foundation. As a general rule, the shareholders' meeting passes its resolutions by a majority of votes; however, in certain matters specified by law and the deed of foundation, a majority of 75% of votes is required for passing a resolution.

The establishment of a supervisory board is mandatory for the public Rts. The duties correspond with those of a Kft. supervisory board. The members of the supervisory board are appointed by the shareholders' meeting.

6.2.2.4 Articles of Association

See Sect. 6.2.1.

6.2.2.5 Minimum Contribution/Initial Capital

The minimum share of (registered) capital for the private Rt. is HUF 5,000,000; the capital of the public Rt. amounts to HUF 20,000,000.

A private Rt. may be registered only if, prior to the submission of the application for registration,

- the founders who have agreed to provide contributions in cash have paid at least 25% of the face value or issue price of the shares, which they have committed to subscribe for in the articles of association;
- in-kind contributions have been made available to the company, with the exception that the value of in-kind contributions is less than 25% of the share capital.
- the articles of association may prescribe the minimum amount of cash contributions to be paid or may specify the value of the in-kind contributions to be provided before registration at a higher percentage of the share capital.

In the case of providing in-kind contributions, the auditor's evaluation of the contribution in kind must be attached to the deed of foundation.

If an Rt. does not have equity that is at least equal to the minimum registered capital set out by law for two consecutive years, it must be transformed into another business entity. The capital can be rendered in cash or in kind. In the case of contributions in kind, an auditor's report that describes and evaluates the contribution must be prepared. Except for the reduction in share capital, shareholders are not exempt from the obligation of rendering their contributions and they cannot, during the existence of the Rt., reclaim the contributions they have made.

The prior approval of the shareholders is required for any agreement on the transfer of property to be concluded within 2 years of the date of the Rt.'s registration between the Rt. and one of its founders or between the Rt. and one of its shareholders holding at least ten percent of the voting rights, where the value of the compensation to be provided by the Rt. equals at least one-tenth of its share capital.

The Rt. is allowed to make any disbursements from its own funds to a shareholder on the basis of its shareholding in the Rt., in cases outlined by law and only if the conditions set out by law are satisfied, allowing for the exception of the reduction in the share capital. No disbursement can be made if the company's equity capital is less than its registered capital or, if the payment were made, it would be reduced to less than the registered capital. Any payment made in breach of these provisions must be repaid to the Rt., provided the Rt. can prove the bad faith of the shareholder.

If a shareholder receives any payment on a basis other than its shareholding in the Rt., which is not permitted by law and which is otherwise incompatible with the prudent management of the Rt., the payment must be repaid to the Rt. provided that the Rt. can prove the bad faith of the shareholder.

Shareholders are entitled to dividends in cash or in kind. Shareholders are entitled to receive dividends only in proportion to their deposited capital contributions.

The shareholders can, between the approvals of two consecutive annual reports, make a decision on the payment of interim dividends if the deed of foundation provides for such and if conditions set forth by law are met.

6.2.2.6 Commercial Register

Generally, the requirements for an Rt. correspond with the requirements set for a Kft. A public Rt. faces additional disclosure and filing requirements as demanded by Hungarian laws and regulations relating to the public trading of shares.

6.2.2.7 Regulations Concerning Corporate Name

The designation "Rt." must be indicated in the company name. The company name must also differ from the names of all other companies in the same or similar line of business.

6.2.2.8 Transfer of Shares/Regulations in the Case of Death of a Shareholder

Shares in a private Rt. may be either printed shares or dematerialized shares. Printed share certificates are negotiated by means of the full or empty endorsement drawn up on the reverse side of the share or the sheet (allonge) attached to the share. If the shares are dematerialized, the shares are to be registered shares that are transferred upon the debiting and crediting of the security accounts from the contracting parties. The shares of a public Rt. can only be of the dematerialized type.

In the case of the transfer of a printed share, the selling shareholder must notify the private Rt.'s board of directors of the share sale. This has to happen within 8 days after the date of the transfer in order to correct the register accordingly.

The transfer of printed shares is to be validated through the private limited company, and shareholders can exercise their shareholders' rights in respect to the company only if such shareholders have been entered into the register of shareholders.

The following persons may not be entered into the register of shareholders:

1. persons who requested such without legal right;
2. persons who have acquired their shares in violation of the regulations on the transfer of shares set forth by law or the articles of association.

The shares issued by an Rt. can have different rights attached to them, e.g. voting rights, dividend rights, etc.

6.2.2.9 Liability of Shareholders and Directors

The duties of the members of the board of directors of an Rt. are similar to those of managing directors of a Kft. Also, the same qualification and liability rules are applicable.

As a general rule, the obligation of shareholders to the Rt. is limited to the provision of the face value or issue price of the shares.

6.2.2.10 Applicable Accounting Standards

Generally, the requirements for an Rt. correspond with the requirements set for a Kft. Additional financial reporting obligations applicable to public Rt.s are set out by Hungarian laws and regulations relating to the public trading of shares.

6.2.2.11 Disclosure Requirements

The register of official company records consists of the commercial register and any enclosures for the verification of data contained in the commercial register, as well as other documents that the company is required to submit by law. All data (current and past) from the commercial register, as well as from the aforementioned documents, must be made available to the public. The annual report is submitted to the Court of Registry and is disclosed for public distribution.

6.2.2.12 Employee Participation

The rules regulating employee participation in the supervisory board for an Rt. correspond with the requirements applicable to a Kft.

6.2.3 Unlimited Partnership (Kkt.)

6.2.3.1 Legal Capacity and Power of Disposition

Kkt. does not have the legal status of a legal person, but a Kkt. also has legal capacity under its corporate names; it can obtain rights and take on commitments, such as acquiring property, making contracts, and can sue and be sued.

6.2.3.2 Process and Requirements for Incorporation

The registration application must be filed with the Hungarian Court of Registration within 30 days of the conclusion of the articles of association. If the applicable laws require any official licence for the establishment of the company, it must accompany the application. Once the registration is submitted, the company can start its operations as a pre-company until the registration is approved or declined. A pre-company can pursue business activities, but may not conduct business activities requiring an official licence.

The Court of Registration must decide on the registration within one hour in the case of business entities submitting registration using the model articles of association annexed to the new Company Procedure Act (simplified proceeding) or otherwise within 15 days (normal proceedings). These periods commence at the delivery of the application to the Court of Registration. If the Court fails to meet these deadlines, the company is considered to be automatically registered in the simplified proceedings on the second working day and in the normal proceedings on the 19th day following the application submission.

Registration fee: HUF 50,000, in the simplified proceedings HUF 15,000; publication fee: HUF 14,000, in the simplified proceeding amounts HUF 5,000; legal fees: approximately EUR 1,500 to EUR 2,500; notary certification fee: HUF 15,000 per signature (about EUR 60).

A newly registered company must also register with the local municipality, State Taxation Office, Central Statistical Office and Social Security Authorities. Branch offices and commercial representation offices should also be registered at the Court of Registration and are only able to start their activities after doing so.

6.2.3.3 Requirements for Associates/Shareholders and Regulations Concerning Shareholders' Meetings

The supreme body of the unlimited partnership is the general meeting, where all members take part in person. The general meeting has no formal rules concerning the appointment of members and the way of deciding on company issues. At the general meeting, members have the power to resolve all matters that the law or the articles of association grant as being under the competence of the partnership's supreme body. Members may tender the decision of any matter under the competence of the general meeting by a three-quarters majority of the votes.

In the course of passing resolutions, each member has equal voting rights. The articles of association can contain provisions deviating from this general rule, but each member must have at least one vote. Unless otherwise specified, all members are entitled to management of the partnership. The entitled members represent the unlimited partnership and sign on its behalf. Each manager (or executive officer) can act independently. If other managers object to intended measures, with the exception of urgent measures, they may not be taken until the general meeting passes a respective resolution.

In general, the general meeting passes its resolutions by a simple majority of votes, calculated by the number of all eligible votes. The resolution is passed by a unanimous vote of all members in order to modify the articles of association, as well as to decide upon issues not belonging to the ordinary business activity of the partnership. Similarly, a unanimous resolution is required for termination without legal successor or for transformation of the partnership.

6.2.3.4 Articles of Association

See Sect. 6.2.1.

6.2.3.5 Minimum Contribution/Initial Capital

No minimum capital is required to found and operate an unlimited partnership.

6.2.3.6 Commercial Register

The commercial register and the documents filed with the Court of Registration are publicly available and anyone can review these or request a copy. Third parties can rely on data or documents registered in the company register if that data is published in the company gazette. Until the contrary is proved, the good faith of the person acquiring any right for compensation by relying on the data registered in the commercial register or published in the company gazette must be presumed.

6.2.3.7 Regulations Concerning Corporate Name

The designation "Kkt." must be indicated in the company name. The company name must also differ from the names of all other companies in the same or similar line of business.

6.2.3.8 Transfer of Shares/Regulations in the Case of Death of a Shareholder

A unanimous resolution is required for termination without a legal successor or for transformation of the partnership. The heir of a member who has died may join the partnership only based on an agreement with the other members.

6.2.3.9 Liability of Shareholders and Directors

Partners in an unlimited partnership bear a joint and great deal of liability in respect of the unsettled obligations of the company and at least two partners are required for the formation and operation of such an entity. Any company, with the exception of partnerships, may become a partner in an unlimited partnership. Individuals may also become partners; however, minors and individuals already bearing much joint liability in another company are excluded.

Active participation of the partners in the conduct of the partnership's business is legally required. Only the members of the company may carry out the function of executive officer; no third parties are permitted to do so.

The creditors of a member cannot make use of the assets that have been transferred to the partnership by that member. Only the member's business share may cover the claim of the creditor.

6.2.3.10 Applicable Accounting Standards

See Sect. 6.2.1.

6.2.3.11 Disclosure Requirements

The register of official company records consists of the commercial register and any enclosures for the verification of data contained in the commercial register, as well as other documents that the company is required to submit by law. All data (current and past) from the commercial register, as well as from the before-mentioned documents, must be made available to the public. The annual report is submitted to the Court of Registry and is published for public distribution.

6.2.3.12 Employee Participation

Employee participation is not required.

6.2.4 Limited Liability Partnerships (Bt.)

6.2.4.1 Legal Capacity and Power of Disposition

A Bt. does not have the legal status of a legal person, but a Bt. does have legal authority under its corporate names. It can obtain rights and take on commitments, such as acquiring property, making contracts, and can sue and be sued.

6.2.4.2 Process and Requirements for Incorporation

See Sect. 6.2.3.

6.2.4.3 Requirements for Associates/Shareholders and Regulations Concerning Shareholders' Meetings

In general, the requirements are similar to the Kkt. requirements. However, the limited partners are not entitled to manage the partnership unless the members agree otherwise in the articles of association or there is no member who is entitled to manage the partnership due to the termination of membership, in which case an external member can be considered to be entitled to manage and represent the company. The limited partners (external members) may also take part in the activity of the meeting of members; thus, they can vote, initiate measures, view the books of the company, etc.

6.2.4.4 Articles of Association

See Sect. 6.2.1.

6.2.4.5 Minimum Contribution/Initial Capital

No minimum capital is required to found and operate a limited partnership.

6.2.4.6 Commercial Register

See Sect. 6.2.3.

6.2.4.7 Regulations Concerning Corporate Name

The designation "Bt." must be indicated in the company name. The company name must also differ from the names of all other companies in the same or similar line of business.

6.2.4.8 Transfer of Shares/Regulations in the Case of Death of a Shareholder

A unanimous resolution is required for termination without a legal successor or for transformation of the partnership.

If all general or limited partners withdraw from the partnership, the partnership terminates unless a new partner is acquired and reported to the Court of Registration within 6 months of withdrawal of the previous general or limited partner, or the remaining partners decide to continue operation as an unlimited partnership (transformation into Kkt.) and report to the Court of Registry the admission within the said deadline.

6.2.4.9 Liability of Shareholders and Directors

In a limited partnership, the minimum number of members is two, of which at least one, the general partner, bears unlimited liability. The other partners' liability is limited to the amount of their capital contribution.

One of the key differences, as compared to a Kkt., is that in a Bt. at least one of the members (the external member) has limited liability, while in an unlimited partnership, all members have unlimited liability.

6.2.4.10 Applicable Accounting Standards

See Sect. 6.2.1.

6.2.4.11 Disclosure Requirements

The register of official company records consists of the commercial register and any enclosures for the verification of data contained in the commercial register, as well as other documents that the company is required to submit by law. All data (current and past) from the commercial register, as well as from the before-mentioned documents, must be made available to the public. The annual report is submitted to the Court of Registry and is published for public distribution.

6.2.4.12 Employee Participation

Formal employee participation is not required.

6.3 Summary

According to prevailing laws, no special permit is required to establish a commercial enterprise in Hungary. Companies can be founded by natural or legal entities, Hungarians and foreign nationals alike. Even a single person can found a joint-stock company or a limited liability company; the only requirement is that the headquarters of such companies must be located within Hungary.

When deciding upon the legal form to choose, every entrepreneur has to consider the above-mentioned points in order to identify the right legal form for the company. This chapter focused on the four primary legal forms of companies in Hungary – Kft., Rt., Kkt., and Bt., all of which strongly resemble the German legal forms GmbH, AG, OHG and KG, respectively. Although there are additional legal forms that are used, their share is insignificant for the scope of this book.

The Rt. and the Kft. are the most common legal forms for businesses in Hungary. Since both are limited liability companies, the risk of entrepreneurs setting up a Kft. or Rt. is limited to the minimum capital requirements if they act according to the laws. This risk reduction comes along with higher requirements in terms of disclosure and accounting standards. In addition, employee participation is enforced by law once a certain limit (200 employees) is reached. To sum up, it can be stated that the reduction in risk is associated with higher complexity when running a business in one of the two forms.

The Kkt. and the Bt. have different risk distributions among managers and owners. In the Kkt., the manager is identical with the owner, therefore, bearing the entire entrepreneurial risk. An entrepreneur choosing this legal form must be aware of this fact. Therefore, the Kkt. can only be recommended for rather small businesses that do not require a lot of capital or for companies that consist of only few investors with sufficient capital. If many investors are needed, the Kkt. would not be recommended. Because all partners are entitled to do business on behalf of the company, the risk rises dramatically. The Bt. would be a good alternative. The managing directors still bear the entire risk, but they are able to raise money by winning limited partners for the company to secure the capital base of the company.

If an entrepreneur does not want to bear the entire risk and wants to limit his liability, then the Rt. or the Kft. should be chosen. The limitation of risk, as mentioned above, comes along with higher requirements for the company. However, especially the private Rt. makes it easy to raise sufficient money while limiting the risk of shareholders and managers at the same time.

There is no clear recommendation for a legal form to choose in Hungary. Several factors have to be taken into account to capture the complexity of the decision. Important criteria could be size of the business, number of managers, capital to be raised, complexity of the business model, risk of the business model, etc. In the end, the legal form should match the risk profile of the owner and the capital requirements of the business.

Chapter 7
Italy

Sergio Finulli and Michael J. Munkert

Abstract In the chapter on Italy, the authors Sergio Finulli and Michael J. Munkert start with a short introduction into the general laws and regulations with regard to setting up and running a business. They use the general analysis framework for the handbook on legal forms in Europe to analyse six legal forms: the informal partnership (Società semplice – S.s.), the general partnership (Società in nome collettivo – S.n.c.), the limited partnership (Società in accomandita semplice – S.a.s), the limited liability company (Società a responsabilità limitata – S.r.l.), the joint-stock company (Società per azioni – S.p.A.) and the Partnership limited by shares (Società in Accomandita Per Azioni – S.a.p.a.).

The authors conclude their discussions with an evaluation of the advantages and disadvantages of the different legal forms.

Contents

S. Finulli (✉)
Studio Bianchi Finulli, Via Morozzo della Rocca, 3, 20123 Milan, Italy
e-mail: sergio.finulli@bianchifinulli.it

M.J. Munkert et al. (eds.), *Founding a Company*, DOI 10.1007/978-3-642-11259-1_7,   107
© Springer-Verlag Berlin Heidelberg 2010

7.1 Introduction

7.1.1 Overview

Italy is characterized by a broad-based, mixed economy divided between state holdings, major corporations and small to medium-sized businesses.

Italian law places no restrictions on foreign investment. This general principle can be limited on reciprocity basis. There are no reciprocity problems for European Union countries, but reciprocity has to be carefully verified for other countries.

Foreigners may usually control and manage 100 percent of the equity capital in an Italian business and are free to transfer, either in whole or in part, any activities that they have acquired or established. In fact, the country has proved fertile ground for acquisitions, and statistics indicate that several hundred transactions have been concluded over the past few years alone.

All companies established in Italy are governed by the provisions of the Italian Civil Code whether they are owned by Italian citizens or foreigners. Special laws also apply to banks, insurance companies as well as investment and trust firms. New enterprises must register with the Italian Registrar of Companies (through the Chamber of Commerce), notify the tax authorities and register employees with the relevant social security authorities. Companies that intend to import or export goods subject to licensing must register with the Ministry of Foreign Trade and retailers must receive licensing from municipal or regional authorities.

Until the Reform of Company Law, which was introduced by Legislative Decree January 19th, 2003, No. 6 (hereafter the reform), many of the rules governing a "Società per azioni" (Joint-Stock company) were also applicable to a "Società a responsabilità limitata" (Limited).

With the Reform, the legislature has clearly manifested its intention to regulate smaller enterprises in a totally different manner by stressing the importance of the personal contribution provided to the company by shareholders. To a certain extent, this type of company has been equalled to a limited liability partnership, but it is still characterized by its capital being divided into intangible shares, "quotas", which are not represented by certificates.

In a recent research study conducted by the Italian Chambers of Commerce, such reform has been praised for its positive results on the creation of new companies limited by share (with a particular increase in the creation of small Limited Liability Companies).

Furthermore, the numbers shown in the study reveal that corporations currently established in Italy are divided as follows:

- Limited liability companies (Srl) = 87%
- Limited liability companies with sole shareholder (Srl socio unico) = 7%
- Joint-stock companies (SpA) = 5.2%
- Joint-stock companies with sole shareholder (SpA socio unico) = 0.7%
- Limited partnership with share capital (Sapa) = 0.1%

7.1.2 Legal Framework

The Italian Constitution's Section III is entirely written for and based on "economic relationships". As provided for by Art. 41 (Business Freedom), "private economic initiatives are free" given that, with no doubts, "they should not interfere and be against social utility".

The Italian Civil Code, Section V, is dedicated to Labour and Commerce. Of particular interest to our chapter are the Articles about the entrepreneurs, businesses and companies.

7.1.3 Entrepreneur/Business

As provided for by Art. 2082 of the Civil Code, an entrepreneur is someone who professionally carries on an economic activity with the aim of producing and selling goods or services.

Under current regulations, either a person or a legal entity can, under particular circumstances, be considered an entrepreneur. Not only persons, but also legal entities such as public companies, limited liability companies or partnerships are indeed allowed, under our regulations, to carry on business activities.

As provided for by Arts. 2135–2187, business activities can be divided into commercial activities or agricultural activities.

7.1.3.1 Commercial Register

As provided for by Art. 2195, all entrepreneurs conducting the following activities

1. industrial activities aiming at the production of goods or services;
2. activities dealing with the exchange of goods;
3. activities dealing with air, land or water transport;
4. activities in the finance and insurance industries; or
5. other activities auxiliary to the ones above

must register with the local commercial register (through the local Chamber of Commerce).

Registration should be made, as set forth by Art. 2196 of the Civil Code, within 30 days of set-up indicating, in the provided form, names and details of the entrepreneur/s (generally founders) and of those carrying representation, type of activity, address/es, etc. All modifications occurring after the first registration also have to be registered with the commercial register. The registration with the commercial register is compulsory for all commercial activities and also for cooperatives (Art. 2200) and state-run companies conducting a commercial activity. Small entrepreneurs (Art. 2202) and activities in the farming industry are not subject to registration with the Registrar of Companies.

7.1.3.2 Accounting Requirements

All entrepreneurs are subject to accounting requirements provided for by current regulations. Beyond what the current tax laws require, all entrepreneurs should keep and update a journal (account book) and an inventory book. More documents might be required, but this depends on the activity carried out by the entrepreneur.

7.1.3.3 Bankruptcy and Insolvency Proceedings

As provided for by Art. 2221, in Italy, bankruptcy is limited only to entrepreneurs conducting commercial activities. State-owned companies and small entrepreneurs are not subject to bankruptcy.

7.1.3.4 L'azienda

The Italian Civil Code (Art. 2555) considers the "azienda" to be the resources (factors of production) organized by the entrepreneur in order to carry on his business activity. Art. 2556 establishes that all registered businesses should deposit, in the same register and in a written form only, all contracts regarding the transfer of "azienda" use rights. Other articles in the same section of the Civil Code are related to the "non-competition clause", transfer of contracts, rent of the business, etc. Current regulations protect business names and trade marks.

7.1.4 Partnerships/*Companies*

7.1.4.1 Partnership Deed

Parties wishing to set up a company must enter into a contract. As stated in Art. 2247, a company agreement (by means of articles of association) is a contract under which two or more persons transfer assets or services for doing business jointly with the goal of sharing the ensuing profits.

The three essential requirements for entering a partnership deed are as follows:

1. contributions;
2. jointly carrying out a business activity;
3. sharing the earnings.

7.1.4.2 Requirements While Conducting Business

Among those requirements established by law, the following requirements are considered a form of protection for third party interests when dealing with the firm. Every partnership/company has to be clearly identified in any contract or mailing by writing the full name, kind of company, address and, what is most important, the name of the commercial register it belongs to (usually the registrar of the city where the registered offices of the company are) and the identification number given by the registrar, which is the same identification number for tax purposes (Codice Fiscale).

Further information that should be written includes the following:

- for all limited liability companies, the amount of the share capital as reported in the last approved financial statement;
- whether the company is under liquidation;
- in case of a limited liability company with shares owned by one person only, this should be stated clearly in all documents.

7.1.4.3 Types of Companies

From an organizational point of view and as provided for under current regulations, companies can be distinguished into the following types:

1. Partnerships

   - informal partnerships (Società semplice)
   - general partnerships (Società in nome collettivo)
   - limited partnerships (Società in accomandita semplice)

2. Companies limited by share

   - limited liability companies (Società a responsabilità limitata)
   - Joint-stock companies (Società per azioni)
   - limited partnership limited by shares (Società in acomandita per azioni)

All the above companies are for profit; they are set up and run to make profits, which subsequently will be distributed among the partners.

The type of company to be set up is decided upon by the partners; companies with the purpose of carrying out a commercial activity can only take the form of an informal partnership. This is the only restriction with which they must comply. There is also the possibility of setting up other types of entities in the form of cooperatives and mutual insurance companies based on the principle of mutuality. Their aim is to provide their members with goods, services and job opportunities at better conditions than those offered in the marketplace. The provisions that govern joint-stock companies can also apply to cooperatives and, when this is envisaged in the company bylaws, the provisions governing limited liability companies apply. Mutual societies are governed by the rules that govern cooperatives.

Finally, all companies, except for informal partnerships, can have the aims of a consortium, i.e. coordinate the economic activities of several entrepreneurs who do similar business or who contribute to specific steps in the overall business cycle.

Though not covered in this chapter, it is important to point out that state-owned companies, foundations or associations (registered or non-registered) can perform economic activities.

7.1.4.4 Merger, Demerger or Transformation

Strategic and organizational choices taken in the articles of association might be subject to modification during the existence of a company. The current law regulates such modifications in the following articles:

- transformations (Arts. 2498–2500)
- mergers (Arts. 2501–2504/6)
- demerger (Arts. 2504/7–2504/10)

Choices made during the set-up of a partnership/company are to be considered changeable. It is always possible to adapt the organizational and economical structure of a business in accordance with the market or in accordance with the partners' decision.

7.2 Description of Relevant Legal Forms

7.2.1 Informal Partnership (Società semplice – S.s.)

7.2.1.1 Legal Capacity and Power of Disposition

The Società semplice (informal partnership) is the most elementary form of enterprise.

The fundamental characteristic of an informal partnership is that the scope of its activities is limited to non-commercial, profit-making economic activities. The legal capacity of the Società semplice (S.s.) is identical to that of a sole proprietor, who leads the individual enterprise. General rules for the Società semplice are given by Art. 2249 Section 2 c.c. and from Art. 2251–2290 c.c.

7.2.1.2 Process and Requirements for Incorporation

It is extremely simple to set up an informal partnership.
In fact

- the contract need not be of any special type, except where special types of assets are involved (and except for specific limitations);
- all that is needed to set up an informal partnership is the mutual agreement by the partners to jointly carry out a non-commercial profit-making activity;
- informal partnerships must be entered into the commercial register (but the registration has only a declaratory effect);
- informal partnerships need to register with the tax authority and, only with limited exclusions, to register with the Social Security National System (INPS) and with the Workers Compensation Authority (INAIL).

7.2.1.3 Requirements for Associates/Shareholders and Regulations Concerning Shareholders' Meetings

Current regulations do not fix any limit or criteria on the number of partners, except when special laws apply.

7.2.1.4 Articles of Association

There is no need for articles of association.
A written agreement is however required, when

- real estate or real estate rights are transferred to the partnership;
- the right to use property is granted to the partnership for an unlimited time or for a period of time more than 9 years.

7.2.1.5 Minimum Contribution/Initial Capital

Minimum contributions and fixed assets are not required for a Società semplice.

7.2.1.6 Commercial Register

The registration with the commercial register is compulsory for Società semplice and is part of the incorporation process.

7.2.1.7 Regulations Concerning Corporate Name

The company name of a Società semplice has to include the family name or at least the initials (first name and family name) of the partners or of a partner.

7.2.1.8 Transfer of Shares/Regulations in the Case of Death of a Shareholder

An associate cannot transfer his share without the approval of the other partners, both during the lifetime and after the death of the partners. Indeed, if one of the partners dies, except for shares of the inactive partner, no other shares are automatically transferred to his heirs.

Transferring the share may be agreed upon beforehand by including a clause in the articles of association stating that shares may be sold and that partners who die can be succeeded by their heirs.

However, the death of a partner does not influence the existence of the company (Art. 2284 c.c.). That does not mean that the heirs automatically become associates of the company, but they receive the right to be paid out at the level of their shareholding. This is concluded by receiving the monetary value of the shares (Art. 2282 c.c.).

7.2.1.9 Liability of Shareholders and Directors

Unless there is an agreement to the contrary, associates are personally liable on the basis of the solidarity principle (in solido) for the debts and obligations of the company.

Special agreements can be reached whereby partners without powers of representation have no liability.

Generally, the management is confronted with extensive duties concerning agency (Art. 2260 Section 1 c.c.). More important, due care has to be taken in the discharge of management duties (Art. 1710 c.c.). If the management duties (in accordance with the law or the company bylaws) are violated, Section 2 of Art. 2260 describes the judicial consequences.

7.2.1.10 Applicable Accounting Standards

In conducting a business activity, the company needs to keep a journal following double-entry bookkeeping and an inventory book; the following registers are also required for taxation purposes:

- the depreciable assets' register, containing a complete list of every asset of the company together with their costs of purchase, depreciation charged ,and net value;
- VAT purchases' register; and
- VAT sales' register.

For tax purposes only, the company has the obligation to follow either double-entry bookkeeping or the option to follow a simpler system. The limits of revenues applicable are less than EUR 309,874.14 for service-oriented companies or craft-oriented companies, and with revenues of less than EUR 516,459.90 for all other companies.

7.2.1.11 Disclosure Requirements

Public disclosure is limited to the articles of association, partners and directors.

In accordance with Art. 2261, non-managing partners have a wide range of rights to make inquiries.

7.2.1.12 Employee Participation

Board of directors with employee representatives is not necessary.

7.2.2 General Partnership (Società in nome collettivo – S.n.c.)

If the parties wish to set up a general partnership, they must respect the specific rules laid down by the Civil Code, bearing in mind in any case that, for many aspects, the law refers the reader to the provisions regulating informal partnerships, which consequently apply equally to general partnerships.

7.2.2.1 Legal Capacity and Power of Disposition

The legal requirements within the Civil Code for non-incorporated firms such as the Società semplice are also applicable for the Società in nome collettivo (Art. 2293 c.c.). Therefore, the legal capacity is identical to the proprietors running the company.

The design of the Società in nome collettivo is set forth by Art. 2291 and the c.c. that follows.

7.2.2.2 Process and Requirements for Incorporation

General partnerships are all companies that show, according to Art. 2249 Section 1 c.c. and Art. 2195 c.c., all relevant trade characteristics. The incorporation process is characterized by a company agreement (through articles of association and company bylaws) in a notary act (two or more members). The Società in nome collettivo has to be registered with the commercial register and, although not a condition for the existence of this type of company, registration is a condition for its regularization. This type of company should also be registered with the tax authorities. The tax authorities give the company a tax number (Codice Fiscale) and a VAT number. Moreover, it has to be registered with INPS (Social Security) and with INAIL (Workers Compensation Authority).

The details of the articles of association provided by Art. 2295 c.c. are the following:

- First and last name, date and place of birth, permanent residence and nationality of shareholder;
- Name of the company

- Name(s) of the partners who have the power of management and representation of the company
- Liaison of the company
- Business model of the company
- Deposit
- Delegation of profits and losses
- Timeframe
- Obligations of partners

7.2.2.3 Requirements for Associates/Shareholders and Regulations Concerning Shareholders' Meetings

The Società in nome collettivo has to consist of at least two partners.

Current regulations do not fix any limit or criteria on the number of partners, except when special laws apply.

7.2.2.4 Articles of Association

The articles of association have to be submitted within 30 days after the notary act to the office of the commercial register of the district in which the company's headquarters are situated. Therefore, the articles of association are obligatory. Given the case that nothing else is stated in the articles of association, each partner has the right, but not the obligation to lead and represent the association.

If the partnership contract makes no provision on how the power of management is to be exercised, then the notion of separate management shall apply: each partner is a director. That means, he has the power of managing the company and may carry out any transaction included in the corporate purpose by himself, without the obligation of requesting the consent or the opinion of the other directors or of informing them in advance of any transactions he has planned.

Separate management offers the advantage of making decisions rapidly, but is not without pitfalls, as the individual director may carry out transactions that are not profitable for the company, without the others being aware of what is going on.

For this very reason, joint management is seen as advantageous. Joint management must be explicitly agreed upon by the partners in the partnership deed (articles of association) or by amending the latter if this is not allotted for, since, unless explicitly specified, separate management is the rule.

Furthermore, joint management may be based either on unanimity or on a majority vote. Where unanimity is required, the consent of all the partner-directors is required in order to carry out business transactions. In majority-based companies, a majority of the directors is sufficient and is calculated on the basis of the profits attributed to each partner.

Both separate management and joint management may be entrusted to all the partners, or only to some of them. Finally, the management of the company may be entrusted to only one of the partners. Informal partnerships and general partnerships could also possibly be managed by third parties who are not partners. If a company, whether it is a stock company or a partnership, is a member of a partnership, it can legitimately be appointed manager of the latter. In this case, the manager is the stock company or a shareholder of the latter, and not a person appointed by the latter.

7.2.2.5 Minimum Contribution/Initial Capital

There are no requirements in terms of minimum deposits and fixed assets for a Società in nome collettivo. This is governed by Art. 2295 Section 6 c.c.

7.2.2.6 Commercial Register

The registration with the commercial register is compulsory for the Società in nome collettivo and part of the incorporation process.

7.2.2.7 Regulations Concerning Corporate Name

The company name of the Società in nome collettivo has to be constituted with at least one name of the partners. Moreover, it is required that the legal form S.n.c. is included in the company name. Both Arts. 2292 Section 1 c.c. and 2564 Section 1 c.c. are relevant.

7.2.2.8 Transfer of Shares/Regulations in the Case of Death of a Shareholder

The transfer of shares is only possible when all associates approve the request (if not stated differently in the company bylaws). If no succession plan is available, legal heirs only have claims on the liquidation of the inherited share. Divergent arrangements for share transfer or what to do in the case of the death of a partner can be integrated in the articles of association. In general, they are relatively comparable with the regulations of the Società semplice.

7.2.2.9 Liability of Shareholders and Directors

A partner's liability in the Società in nome collettivo is unlimited (Art. 2291 c.c.) and joint. This means that every partner is liable with all the business assets as well as all of his private property. It is important to consider that each partner is liable for the total sum of liabilities of the company. However, if the partner pays the total sum of liabilities, he is allowed to recover his money from the other partners. This concept is called the solidarity principle.

   In first place, the company is liable with its company assets in accordance with Art. 2293 in association with Art. 2267 Section 1. Only if the company assets are insufficient to meet a creditor's claims, can he request payment by any one of the partners.

7.2.2.10 Applicable Accounting Standards

The company is to keep a journal following double-entry bookkeeping and an inventory book; the following registers are also required for taxation purposes:

- the depreciable assets' register, containing a complete list of every asset of the company, together with their costs of purchase, depreciation charged and net value;
- VAT purchases' register; and
- VAT sales' register.

For tax purposes only, the company has the obligation to follow either double-entry bookkeeping or the option to follow a simpler system. (The limits of revenues applicable are less than EUR 309,874.14 for service-oriented companies or craft-oriented companies, and with revenues less than EUR 516,459.90 for all other companies).

7.2.2.11 Disclosure Requirements

Public disclosure is limited to articles of association, partners and directors.

In accordance with Art. 2261, non-managing partners have a wide range of rights to make inquiries.

7.2.2.12 Employee Participation

The same standards as for the Società semplice are applicable.

7.2.3 Limited Partnership (Società in accomandita semplice – S.a.s)

7.2.3.1 Legal Capacity and Power of Disposition

The legal requirements within the Civil Code for non-incorporated firms such as the Società semplice are also applicable for the Società in accomandita semplice. Therefore, the legal capacity is identical to that of the proprietors running the company.

The design of the Società in accomandita semplice is listed out in Art. 2313 and the c.c. that follows.

7.2.3.2 Process and Requirements for Incorporation

The incorporation process is similar to that of general partnerships. The articles of association must comply with the same requirements, in form and content, as those laid down for the general partnerships. It is characterized by a company agreement in a notary act (two or more partners). The articles of association for the S.a.s. are to be registered with the commercial register. If this is not done, the partnership is irregular and the provisions that apply are less favourable for partners, as already described in the paragraph on general partnerships (S.n.c.). Registration ensures disclosure and the protection of third parties that have nothing to do with the company, as pointed out for the general partnership.

This type of company should also be registered with the tax authorities. The tax authorities give the company a tax number (Codice Fiscale) and a VAT number. Moreover, it has to be registered with INPS (Social Security) and with INAIL (Workers Compensation Authority).

7.2.3.3 Requirements for Associates/Shareholders and Regulations Concerning Shareholders' Meetings

The Società in accomandita semplice consists of at least two legal types of partners. Therefore, a minimum of two partners is required. One is called the general partner (soci accomandatari). This general partner has unlimited liability. The other is called the limited partner (soci accomandanti) and is only liable to a fixed amount of money.

7.2.3.4 Articles of Association

The articles of association have to be submitted within 30 days after the notary act to the office of the commercial register, in the district in which the company's headquarters are situated. Therefore, the articles of association are obligatory. Given the case that nothing else is stated in the articles of association, each general partner (soci accomandatari) has the right, but not the obligation, to lead and represent the association.

General partners have the same rights and duties as partners in general partnerships. Moreover, partners with limited liability (limited partners) are not allowed to actively contribute to the management of the association. In doing so, they would lose the benefit of limited liability. The article of association must include the names of the general partners as well as those of the limited partners.

7.2.3.5 Minimum Contribution/Initial Capital

There are no requirements in terms of minimum deposit and fixed assets for a Società in accomandita semplice.

7.2.3.6 Commercial Register

The registration with commercial register is compulsory for the Società in accomandita semplice and an important part of the incorporation/formation process.

7.2.3.7 Regulations Concerning Corporate Name

The company name of the Società in accomandita semplice has to be constituted with at least one name of the general partners. Moreover, it is required that the legal form S.a.s. is included in the company name. In no case, the name of one of the limited partners may be shown.

7.2.3.8 Transfer of Shares/Regulations in the Case of Death of a Shareholder

The transfer of shares is only possible if all general partners (soci accomandatari) approve the request (unless stated differently in the company bylaw). If no succession plan is available, legal heirs only have claims on the liquidation of the inherited share. Divergent arrangements for share transfer or what to do in the case of the death of a general partner can be integrated in the articles of association.

Unless the articles of association provides otherwise, partners with limited liability can transfer their shares without approval from the other partners and in the case of death, to the legal heirs, because they are not actively involved in the management of the company. However, they have no right to participate in day-to-day business.

7.2.3.9 Liability of Shareholders and Directors

The general partners' (soci accomandatari) liability is unlimited. Therefore, they are liable with all their private property. In contrast, limited partners (soci accomandanti) with limited liability are only liable to the extent of their share of the capital. Furthermore, the partners with limited liability act as loaners with additional rights such as an allowance to look into the accounts, profit participation, etc. According to jurisdiction, the limited partner participates with the relative percentage of his ownership.

7.2.3.10 Applicable Accounting Standards

The company shall keep a journal following double-entry bookkeeping and an inventory book; the following registers are also required for taxation purposes:

- the depreciable assets' register, containing a complete list of every asset of the company together with their costs of purchase, depreciation charged, and net value;
- VAT purchases' register;
- VAT sales' register.

For tax purposes only, the company has the obligation to follow either double-entry bookkeeping or the option to follow a simpler system. The limits of revenues applicable are less that EUR 309,874.14 for service-oriented companies or craft-oriented companies, and with revenues of less than EUR 516,459.90 for all other companies.

7.2.3.11 Disclosure Requirements

Public disclosure is limited to the articles of association, partners and directors.

In accordance with Art. 2261, non-managing associates have a wide range of rights to make inquiries.

7.2.3.12 Employee Participation

The same standards as for the Società in nome collettivo are applicable.

7.2.4 Limited Liability Company (Società a responsabilità limitata – S.r.l.)

7.2.4.1 Legal Capacity and Power of Disposition

The S.r.l. (Civil Code, Art. 2472 ff.) is well suited for a limited number of partners. In general, this is the kind of structure used by small to medium-sized enterprises, where limited liability is required. This is by far the most common type of company used by Italian entrepreneurs and that is chosen most frequently by foreign parent companies when setting up their subsidiaries in Italy.

With the inscription in the commercial register, an S.r.l. acquires a legal personality.

7.2.4.2 Process and Requirements for Incorporation

The Società a responsabilità limitata can be incorporated via a contract or a legal act according to Art. 2463 Section 1 c.c. In line with Art. 2463 Section 2 c.c., the articles of association need a public or notary deed and the following minimum statements:

1. Name, surname or firm name of the shareholders
2. Company name with legal form
3. Purpose of the company
4. Amount of capital
5. Shareholder contributions
6. Number of shares for every shareholder
7. Management and representation rules
8. Managing directors and auditors if necessary
9. Costs of incorporation

According to Section 3, the corporation law regulations from Arts. 2329–2332 and Art. 2341 c.c. must be used in the incorporation process.

Following these steps, the company must be registered with the commercial register (Ufficio del registro delle imprese) within 30 days and the articles of association must be also be presented. All partners have to be explicitly named (Art. 2475

Section 1 Nr. 7 c.c.). After the registration with the commercial register (about 4 weeks), the enterprise receives its entity with limited liability. Upon formation, each shareholder is to deposit one-fourth of his money contribution and the full premium.

The contributions include money and, depending on the articles of association, any items of economic value including services supplied by shareholders if adequately guaranteed (it is possible to substitute the deposit through a certificate of insurance or a bank guarantee). Publication is not required.

Extreme flexibility is given, as provided for by current regulations, to the management governing such kind of company. It is possible to have a sole director or a board of directors (which can decide without complying with the "board method" provided the bylaws allow for this, and except for cases where a board decision is required by the law), but in addition, now there are also forms of joint administration (under which the directors have to act jointly) or separate (under which each director can work on his own); mixed forms are available for some acts and/or categories of acts, and separate for remaining acts.

This type of company should also be registered with the tax authorities, where it is given a tax number (Codice Fiscale) and a VAT number. Moreover, it has to be registered with INPS (Social Security) and with INAIL (Workers Compensation Authority).

7.2.4.3 Specific Feature: Limited Liability Company with Sole Shareholder

A sole shareholder S.r.l. requires a unilateral deed, full payment of the capital contribution and certain disclosure requirements. Should a sole shareholder acquire an existing, non-sole shareholder S.r.l., he has to cover outstanding debts and make the changes of shareholders public.

During insolvency, sole shareholders are liable without limitation if contributions remain unpaid or disclosure requirements are incomplete.

7.2.4.4 Requirements for Associates/Shareholders and Regulations Concerning Shareholders' Meetings

According to Arts. 2475 and 2490 Civil Code, the incorporation can be conducted with one or more partners.

7.2.4.5 Articles of Association

The articles of association will be set forth by shareholders in accordance with their needs. Therefore, they will be less formal and most likely be drawn up in the form of contracts.

The appointment of the internal board of auditors (Collegio Sindacale) is mandatory when provided by the articles of association, when the capital is not below EUR 120,000 and if for two subsequent years, two of the limits set forth in Art. 2435-bis (total of balance sheet's capital assets EUR 4,400,000, net revenue EUR 8,800,000, average number of employees 50) have been exceeded. Besides the appointment of an internal board of auditors, shareholders can appoint an external auditor for accounting audits.

7.2.4.6 Minimum Contribution/Initial Capital

The minimum contribution has to amount to at least EUR 10,000 (Art. 2474 Civil Code). A minimum of 25 percent of that amount usually has to be acquired in the foundation process. In the case of a single partner-executive model (one-person S.r.l.), the whole sum (Art. 2476 c.c.) has to be deposited. The shares of the associates can be differently sized, but may not be less than EUR 1. If the amount is larger than the minimum amount, it has to be a euro-multiple amount.

An expert estimates the in-kind contributions and renders sworn statements regarding their value.

7.2.4.7 Commercial Register

The registration of the Società a responsabilità limitata is compulsory according to Art. 2331 Civil Code.

7.2.4.8 Regulations Concerning Corporate Name

The company name has to include the term "S.r.l." (Art. 2473 c.c.). If the name used by the business is similar to existing ones and creates confusion, the commercial register can decline the registration of such company.

7.2.4.9 Transfer of Shares/Regulations in the Case of Death of a Shareholder

The deed of transfer for shares, duly authenticated by a notary, must be filed within 30 days with the commercial register.

The company cannot purchase its own shares, grant guarantees or loans enabling third parties to purchase shares. If the bylaws forbid transferring shares, including transfers upon death, shareholders may withdraw. The bylaws, however, can prohibit withdrawal before completion of 2 years of company formation or subscription of the relevant share.

Shares can normally be freely transferred, but the company bylaws may provide limitations. If the transfer is forbidden or subject to approval of directors, partners or third parties, or if it is otherwise impossible, partners or their heirs may choose to withdraw from the company. The commercial register must be notified about the transfer of shares. If provided for in the company bylaws, the transfer is effective towards the company only after its inscription on the shareholders' register. This renders the transfer enforceable against the company and third parties.

The shares of the dead shareholder are, according to Art. 2469 – subject to other agreements in the company bylaws – freely transferable in the case of death.

7.2.4.10 Liability of Shareholders and Directors

In case of insolvency, only sole shareholders are liable without any limitation if debts remain unpaid or disclosure requirements about them are incomplete.

7.2.4.11 Statutory Books

The following statutory books are required by the Civil Code:

- the register of shareholders if provided for by the company bylaws;
- the register of shareholders' decisions including minutes of shareholders' meetings and decisions held via written consultations or on the basis of shareholders' written consent;
- the register of directors' decisions (if appointed); and
- the register of Collegio Sindacale's and/or auditors' decisions (if appointed), containing minutes of inspections carried out during the year and the annual report.

7.2.4.12 Applicable Accounting Standards

The following accounting books are required by the Civil Code:

- the journal containing day-to-day entries of all transactions undertaken by the company that are relevant to the accounts and
- the inventory register containing a complete listing of all balances that make up the annual financial statements including detailed stock, receivables and payables listings, but excluding any detail of the profit and loss account.

Moreover, the following registers are required for taxation purposes:

- the depreciable assets' register containing a complete list of every asset of the company, together with their costs of purchase, depreciation charged and net value;
- VAT purchases' register; and
- VAT sales' register.

Accounting standards are stated by Italian Civil Code and by national standards issued by OIC (Organismo Italiano di Contabilità).

Companies using ordinary accounting and controlled by a listed company can adopt IFRS international standards.

The draft financial statements for the financial year are drawn up by the director(s) for formal presentation to the shareholders' meeting. The director's report and the Collegio Sindacale (if appointed) report are prepared at this point. The annual financial statements are drawn up in accordance with the rules established by the Civil Code, including the following general principles:

1. the company is presumed to be a going concern;
2. prudence – unrealized profits should not be included, whereas all foreseeable losses should be reflected in the financial statements;

3. consistency – accounting principles and valuation criteria must be applied without variations to ensure the comparability of financial statements with those of the past; and
4. accrual – income and expenditure must be accounted for in the period in which they are earned or incurred, and not in the period in which the cash payments occur.

The draft accounts must be preliminarily approved by the director(s) and signed by the chairman of the board or the sole director. In accordance with the EU Fourth Directive, the financial statements comprise a balance sheet, a profit and loss account and an explanatory note (companies applying IFRS must additionally prepare a financial report).

At least 30 days before the date of the shareholders' meeting, the draft accounts and the directors' report must be given to the Collegio Sindacale, if appointed, so that it can prepare its report. The complete set of accounts must be deposited at the company's registered office at least 15 days before the meeting that will approve the accounts.

Smaller companies (total of balance sheet's capital assets: EUR 4,400,000, net revenues: EUR 8,800,000, average number of employees: 50) have the option of preparing their accounts in a simplified form. In this case, there is no need for a directors' report; the balance sheet and profit and loss account are less detailed and the explanatory note contains less information.

7.2.4.13 Disclosure Requirements

Full disclosure has to be made in regard to articles of association bylaws, directors, shareholders, financial statements with annual reports from management and auditors and minutes of ordinary meetings of shareholders approving the financial statement and all extraordinary meetings of shareholders.

7.2.4.14 Employee Participation

Board of directors with employee representatives is not necessary.

7.2.5 Joint-Stock Company (Società per Azioni – S.p.A.)

7.2.5.1 Legal Capacity and Power of Disposition

The S.p.A. (Civil Code, Section 2325 ff.) is the normal form for larger companies (joint-stock companies). An S.p.A. can be listed on the stock exchange, although the absolute majority is not. However, it is necessary for a company to be an S.p.A. in order to be listed.

With the inscription in the commercial register, as provided for by Art. 2331 Section 1 c.c., an S.p.A. acquires legal personality.

7.2.5.2 Process and Requirements for Incorporation

As provided for by Art. 2328 c.c., it is possible to incorporate a Società per Azioni by means of an agreement or of a legal unilateral act.

The requirements in order to set up a joint-stock company are stated in Art. 2329 Code Civil. The incorporation process of an S.p.A. starts with a contract (or unilateral act) with the articles of association and bylaws, in the form of a notary public deed. In the articles of association, the first members of the board of directors and chief executives have to be named. Depending on the management system, which also has to be stated, sole proprietors and/or legal persons who/which are responsible for the auditing (including financial statements) have to be named as well.

The total equity capital of the company must be fully underwritten and 25 percent of the financial contribution (according to Art. 2342 Code Civil) has to be deposited at a registered bank account at the time of the signing of the articles of association until the registration with the commercial register. The Company Law Reform provides that an S.p.A. can also be incorporated with a sole shareholder, who may be a company or an individual. The sole shareholder has unlimited liability for the company obligations only if proper information has not been provided to the commercial register or for non-compliance with rules on contributions. In the case of this unilateral formation, the entire contribution must be deposited at a registered bank account.

The next requirement is to check for special legal requirements, e.g. government authorization for activities envisaged by the company. Following this, the founders have to check with the notary public about other essential conditions required by law to form the company. The final step of the procedure for the establishment of the company and the recognition of its legal personality is the formal registration of the company within 20 days in the commercial register, under the supervision of the Ministry of Productive Activities pursuant to Art. 2330 Section 1 c.c. Registration has the practical value of giving legal publicity to third parties of the existence of the company and of its characteristics.

On the basis of the provisions in force as of January 1, 2004, the administration of joint-stock companies may be organized according to three separate models: the traditional model, the monistic model (of Anglo-Saxon origin) and the two-tier model (of German origin).

This type of company should also be registered with the tax authorities, where it is given a tax number (Codice Fiscale) and a VAT code. Moreover, it has to be registered with INPS (Social Security) and with INAIL (Workers Compensation Authority).

7.2.5.3 Requirements for Associates/Shareholders and Regulations Concerning Shareholders' Meetings

Incorporation of the S.p.A. can be conducted through the signing of the articles of association or by means of unilateral act of a single shareholder.

7.2.5.4 Articles of Association

Articles of association will be set forth by shareholders in accordance with current regulations and business needs. The appointment of the internal board of auditors (Collegio Sindacale) is mandatory. Besides the appointment of an internal board of auditors, shareholders can appoint an external auditor for accounting audits.

Current regulations allow, among shareholders, specific agreements, which can have a duration of up to 5 years. Such agreements are meant to regulate relationships and voting rights among shareholders. If the duration is unlimited, participants may withdraw, giving a 6-month prior notice.

7.2.5.5 Minimum Contribution/Initial Capital

The minimum equity capital required is EUR 120,000. The contributions can be in money, in kind, and/or by assignment of credits, of which, the last two must be paid in full when underwriting the corresponding shares. A designated expert of the competent territorial court estimates the contributions and renders sworn statements regarding their value.

7.2.5.6 Commercial Register

The registration with the commercial register terminates the incorporation process. If the inscription is not undertaken within 90 days after the closing of the articles of association, the foundation charter becomes inoperative.

7.2.5.7 Regulations Concerning Corporate Name

The name of the company (denominazione sociale) must include the legal form of the company "S.p.A." as provided for by Art. 2326 c.c.

If the name used by the business is similar to existing ones and creates confusion, the commercial register can decline the registration of such company.

7.2.5.8 Transfer of Shares/Regulations in the Case of Death of a Shareholder

The company's bylaws can set limitations to the right to transfer shares. If the transfer of the shares is subject to the approval of directors, partners or third parties, and if the transfer is denied or is otherwise impossible, partners or their heirs must have the right to withdraw from the company.

7.2.5.9 Liability of Shareholders and Directors

In case of insolvency, only sole shareholders are liable without any limitation if contributions remain unpaid or disclosure requirements about them are incomplete.

7.2.5.10 Statutory Books

The following statutory books are required by the Civil Code:

- the register of shareholders giving names of all shareholders, their participation share, the part of capital nominal value paid, and all changes to this information;
- the register of shareholders' decisions including minutes of shareholders' meetings;
- the register of directors' decisions (if appointed);
- the register of Collegio Sindacale's and/or auditors' decisions, containing minutes of inspections carried out during the year, and the annual report; and
- the register of bondholders.

7.2.5.11 Applicable Accounting Standards

The following accounting books are required by the Civil Code:

- the journal containing day-to-day entries of all transactions undertaken by the company that are relevant to the accounts and
- the inventory register, containing a complete listing of all balances that make up the annual financial statements including detailed stock, receivables and payables listings, but excluding any detail of the profit and loss account.

   Moreover, the following registers are required for taxation purposes:

- the depreciable assets' register, containing a complete list of every asset of the company together with their costs of purchase, depreciation charged and net value;
- VAT purchases' register; and
- VAT sales' register.

Accounting standards are stated by the Italian Civil Code and by national standards issued by OIC (Organismo Italiano di Contabilità).

Listed companies and companies controlled by a listed company can adopt IFRS international standards. The draft financial statements for the financial year are drawn up by the director(s) for formal presentation at the shareholders' meeting. The director's report and the Collegio Sindacale report are prepared at this point. The annual financial statements are drawn up in accordance with the rules established by the Civil Code, including the following general principles:

1. the company is presumed to be a going concern;
2. prudence – unrealized profits should not be included, whereas all foreseeable losses should be reflected in the financial statements;
3. consistency – accounting principles and valuation criteria must be applied without variations to ensure the comparability of financial statements with those of the past; and

4. accrual – income and expenditure must be accounted for in the period in which they are earned or incurred and not in the period in which the cash payments occur.

The draft accounts must be preliminarily approved by the director(s) and signed by the chairman of the board or the sole director. In accordance with the EU Fourth Directive, the financial statements comprise a balance sheet, a profit and loss account and an explanatory note (companies applying IFRS must additionally prepare a financial report).

At least 30 days before the date of the shareholders' meeting, the draft accounts and the directors' report must be given to the Collegio Sindacale so that it can prepare its report. The complete set of accounts must be deposited at the company's registered office at least 15 days before the meeting that will approve the accounts. Smaller companies have the option of preparing their accounts in a simplified form.

According to Art. 2435 c.c., the preparation of a shortened annual report is only permissible with the absence of a stock exchange listing if in two following annual reports, two of the following three limits were not exceeded:

- total of balance sheet's capital assets: EUR 4,400,000,
- net revenues: EUR 8,800,000, or
- average number of employees: 50.

In this case, there is no need for a directors' report. The balance sheet and profit and loss account are less detailed and the explanatory note contains less information.

7.2.5.12 Disclosure Requirements

Full disclosure is required for articles of association bylaws, directors, shareholders, financial statements with annual reports of management and auditors, minutes of ordinary meetings of shareholders approving the financial statement and all extraordinary meetings of shareholders.

7.2.5.13 Employee Participation

Board of directors with employee representatives is not necessary.

7.2.6 Partnership Limited by Shares (Società in Accomandita Per Azioni – S.a.p.a.)

7.2.6.1 Legal Capacity and Power of Disposition

Limited partnership with share capital is a modified form of a joint-stock company (S.p.A.) in which general partners manage the company that has unlimited liability as permanent directors, with contingent liability for social security liabilities as well.

The provisions that are specific for this type of a company are reduced to a few, which above all concern the management of the company by the unlimited partners. The legal requirements within the Civil Code for Società per Azioni are also applicable for the Società in Accomandita Per Azioni (Art. 2454 c.c.). Therefore, the S.a.p.a. possesses legal capacity.

7.2.6.2 Process and Requirements for Incorporation

The articles of association have to be legalized in a notary act (with two or more partners). Additionally, a registration in the respective commercial register has to be confirmed. This type of company should also be registered with the tax authorities, where it is given a tax number and a VAT number. In addition, it has to be registered with INPS (Social Security) and with INAIL (Workers Compensation Authority).

7.2.6.3 Requirements for Associates/Shareholders and Regulations Concerning Shareholders' Meetings

The characteristic of this type of company consists of two different groups of shareholders: limited partners, who are not involved in the management of the company and are liable only for their contribution and general partners, who are directors and thus, personally and unlimitedly liable.

All other aspects are the same as those of the joint-stock company (S.p.A.).

7.2.6.4 Articles of Association

The general provisions referring to the articles of association for the Società in accomandita per azioni are identical to that of the joint-stock company (S.p.A.). The names of general partners must be indicated. The unlimited partners are directors of the company and have the same duties as directors of the joint-stock company (S.p.A.).

Amendments to the articles of association have be approved by the shareholders by the same majority as prescribed for resolutions of the extraordinary general shareholders' meetings in the joint-stock company and should also be approved by all general partners. The appointment of the board of auditors (Collegio Sindacale) is mandatory. Besides the appointment of an internal board of auditors, shareholders can appoint an external auditor for accounting audits.

7.2.6.5 Minimum Contribution/Initial Capital

The minimum equity capital required is EUR 120,000 and the other provisions are the same like those of the joint-stock company (S.p.A.).

7.2.6.6 Commercial Register

The provisions are the same as those for the joint-stock company (S.p.A.).

7.2.6.7 Regulations Concerning Corporate Name

The provisions are the same as those for the joint-stock company (S.p.A.).

7.2.6.8 Transfer of Shares/Regulations in the Case of Death of a Shareholder

The provisions are the same as those for the joint-stock company (S.p.A.).

7.2.6.9 Liability of Shareholders and Directors

General partners are liable in solido and without limitation for the partnership obligations, and limited partners are liable within the limit of the portion of the capital invested.

7.2.6.10 Applicable Accounting Standards

The provisions are the same as those of the joint-stock company (S.p.A.).

7.3 Summary

7.3.1 Informal Partnership (Società semplice (S.s.))

The set-up costs for a Società semplice are very low. This company structure perfectly suits small to medium-sized enterprises as no minimum capital is required. Entrepreneurs have a high degree of flexibility and the option of simplified accounting rules.

The company can only carry out a non-commercial profit-making activity. Partners, with the exception of those without powers of representation only if previously stated, are completely liable with their private money and also in a solidly united way. Therefore, it is very important to trust the other partners.

7.3.2 General Partnerships (Società in nome collettivo (S.n.c.))

Again, set-up costs for a Società in nome collettivo are low. Moreover, the management and organizational demands are low. This structure also suits small to medium-sized companies. No minimum capital is required as well as no company bodies. The disclosure requirements are very low, meaning that the balance sheet does not have to be published and moreover, the joint and unlimited liability enlarges the creditworthiness. Partners are completely liable with their private money – also in a solidly united way. Partners cannot exercise a business activity on their own in competition with that of the partnership without consent of the other partners. Partners have the obligation to take their decisions together. If a partner takes a decision on his own without any other partners' consent, the whole corporation can be at stake. Therefore, it is very important to trust the other associates.

7.3.3 Limited Partnership (Società in accomandita semplice (S.a.s.))

Set-up costs are low. Again, requirements for the management and organization are low in monetary terms. No minimum capital is required and therefore is perfectly suitable for small to medium-sized enterprises. Company bodies are not a prerequisite and the management is strongly transferred to the general partner.

The limited partner is not allowed to take part in the decision-making management process within the company. If allowed, he loses all his rights as a limited partner and becomes a general partner.

7.3.4 Limited Liability Company (Società a responsabilità limitata (S.r.l.))

The shareholders are only liable up to their contribution. The directors of the company can be either shareholders or outsiders, even non-residents. This company form is an independent legal entity and can sue or be sued under its name. Due to its low equity capital (EUR 10,000), this type of company is suitable for small to medium-sized businesses. Additionally, there is an option to use transparency taxation.

Compared with other company forms, the set-up costs are relatively high as are the complexities in incorporation. If the equity capital is more than EUR 120,000, a board of internal auditors must be appointed. Furthermore, the limited company has to submit a financial statement to the commercial. If, due to loss, the capital falls below the minimum, the directors become personally liable. Full disclosure has to be made to third parties in respect of the articles of association, shareholders and financial statements of the company. Repayment of loans granted by shareholders is postponed to repay all other debts and liabilities.

7.3.5 Joint-Stock Company (Società per Azioni (S.p.A.))

The shareholders are only liable for their contribution. The directors of the company can be either shareholders or outsiders, even non-residents. This company form is an independent legal entity and can sue or be sued under its name.

The joint-stock company represents the most cost-intensive form of company incorporation. It also has the highest disclosure and auditing requirements. If, due to loss, the capital falls below the minimum, the directors become personally liable.

Full disclosure has to be made to third parties in respect of the articles of association, shareholders and financial statements of the company.

7.3.6 Partnership Limited by Shares (Società in Accomandita Per Azioni (S.a.p.a.))

S.a.p.a. guarantees that the business is preserved. The unlimited partners are by law directors, and the rules on the appointment of new directors during the lifetime of the company give the directors the right to veto on the choice of new directors, thus ensuring that the leading group is safe from attempts of hostile takeovers.

S.a.p.a. has the same cost and highest disclosure and auditing requirements of the joint-stock company (S.p.A.).

Chapter 8
The Netherlands

Pietia C. van der Laarhoven Mark and Johan F. Langelaar

Abstract In the chapter on the Netherlands, the authors John F. Langelaar and Pietia C. Laarhoven van der Mark start with a short introduction into the general laws and regulations with regard to setting up and running a business. They use the general analysis framework for the handbook on legal forms in Europe to analyse six legal forms: the joint stock company/corporation (Naamloze Vennootschap – N.V.), the limited Liability Company (Besloten Vennootschap – B.V.), the limited commercial partnership (Commanditaire Vennootschap – C.V.), the partnership (Vennootschap onder Firma – V.O.F.), the civil partnership (Maatschap – Mts.) and the individual enterprise/sole proprietorship (Eenmanszaak).

The authors conclude their discussions with an evaluation of the advantages and disadvantages of the different legal forms and provide exemplary recommendations depending on the individual case of the founders.

Contents

P.C. Laarhoven van der Mark (✉)
TeekensKarstens Attorneys-at-Law & Civil Law Notaries, Vondellaan 51, 2332 AA Leiden, The Netherlands
e-mail: laarhoven@tklaw.nl

M.J. Munkert et al. (eds.), *Founding a Company*, DOI 10.1007/978-3-642-11259-1_8,
© Springer-Verlag Berlin Heidelberg 2010

8.1 Introduction

Foreign firms and/or individuals can found a business in the Netherlands generally without restrictions. Domestic financial participation or management is not required. The choice of location and real estate is unrestricted. Due to the Netherlands' trade law, each enterprise must be registered in the trade register with the chamber of commerce. This can be done at every office, though formally the registration is controlled by the office within whose jurisdiction the registered place of business (or the registered address) falls. The data required for registration depend on the selected form of business organization. A copy of the partner contract is to be attached to the request for entry into the commercial register.

During formation, the choice of the legal form is of crucial importance, as depending upon legal form, corresponding obligations result (adhesion, employment of capital, tax, etc.). In addition, a difference between unincorporated firms and legal entities is made in the Netherlands. By law, a legal entity is a body with its own rights and obligations.

The two most important legal entities are

- Naamloze Vennootschap (N.V.) – corporation (the German AG)
- Besloten Vennootschap (B.V.) – limited liability company (the German GmbH).

Additionally, there are four important types of unincorporated firms:

- Vennootschap onder firma – General partnership (the German OHG)
- Commanditaire Vennootschap – Limited partnership (the German KG)
- Eenmanszaak – Sole proprietorship (the German EU)
- Maatschap – Limited liability partnership (the German GbR).

The legal framework regulating the corporate activities area comprises a set of basic laws that cover all the aspects of a business set-up and operation in the Netherlands. The most relevant laws are

- Wetboek van Koophandel (WvK) – Trade Law
- Burgerlijk Wetboek (BW) – Dutch Civil Code
- Handelsregisterwet (HRGW) – Trade Register Law.

In the following, we describe the different characteristics of Dutch legal forms and their respective establishment formalities from an entrepreneurial perspective. Thus, other legal forms such as Vereniging (association) and Stichting (foundation) are not taken into consideration.

8.2 Description of Relevant Legal Forms

8.2.1 Joint Stock Company/Corporation (Naamloze Vennootschap – N.V.)

8.2.1.1 Legal Capacity and Power of Disposition

Naamloze Vennootschap is the Dutch version of a public limited liability corporation. It is an independent legal entity and therefore, independently legally responsible for its actions. This is a fundamental legal concept and it means that the company is a legal person, which carries its own rights and duties independent of natural persons, e.g. the shareholders.

This legal form is usually selected by large-scale enterprises or by medium-sized enterprises that would like to take up public capital. The capital stock is divided into shares, which are owned by members; where these shares are not registered to certain owners, they can be traded on the stock market (freely transferable). The shareholders are liable only for their portion of the capital.

Dutch corporate law is based on the so-called "two-tier system", which means a distinction between management and supervision in separate organs – the management board and the supervisory board. Generally, within Dutch companies, one can opt for a supervisory board. Only in the case of a so-called "large company" do the articles of association have to provide for a supervisory board.

A company is a large company (or "structure company") if, over a continuous period of 3 years, it meets the statutory definition of a structure company. This is the case when the company

- has an issued capital plus reserve (including retained earnings) of at least EUR 16 million,
- is required to establish, and has established a works council based on legal obligations,
- regularly employs, together with its dependent companies, at least 100 employees in the Netherlands.

Upon expiration of the 3-year term and assuming proper registrations have been filed with the commercial register in the Netherlands, the articles of the association must be amended to incorporate certain mandatory provisions relating to the large company. The most important legal consequences are that a company must have a supervisory board with at least three members and important powers within the company, such as the appointment and dismissal of the management, are transferred to the supervisory board. In addition, major management decisions require the approval of the supervisory board.

A one-tier board system as in the United States is not possible, but an N.V.'s articles of association can provide for a similar system, where executive and non-executive directors serve on the same board to a certain extent. If there is a two-tier board structure, the supervisory board supervises and advises the management board. The articles of association may provide for a more extensive role, for example, by requiring prior approval of the supervisory board for certain managerial actions. Both boards must act in the interest of the N.V. as a whole, which includes all stakeholders.

A company is subject to the dual-board regime if it has more than 100 employees in the Netherlands, a works council and the amount of issued capital exceeds EUR 16 million. The dual-board regime was established because the Dutch legislators did not consider the control of the general meeting very effective in a large company with many shareholders. As a result, the supervisory board has more powers within dual-board companies.

Unless the articles of association or law provide otherwise, the power to represent the company is unlimited and each individual managing director is authorized to represent the company. The articles often determine that the company can only be represented by a particular number of directors. Usually, the articles also prescribe that certain major management decisions are subject to the prior approval of the general meeting or the supervisory board.

8.2.1.2 Process and Requirements for Incorporation

Setting up an N.V. is subject to a formal procedure. Incorporation occurs by performing a notarial deed of incorporation before a Dutch civil law notary. A notary in the Netherlands is officially appointed by Royal decree, whose legally prescribed functions include drawing up articles of association and deeds for the transfer of property and mortgages. He may also act as legal advisor in certain matters. One shareholder is enough to incorporate the company, whereas there are a few things required to conduct the incorporation. For the registration of joint stock companies in the Netherlands, the following are required:

- EUR 45,000 capital stock (minimum). At least 20 percent of the N.V.'s authorized capital must be issued during incorporation by the founders.
- A notarial deed. Each founder is party thereto. The costs for this notarial deed of incorporation amount to approx. EUR 1,750. This deed must contain the articles of association, the amounts of issued and paid-in share capital and the names of the (first) managing (and supervisory) directors.
- A ministerial declaration of no objection (Ministry of Justice) after examination of the founders as the providers of capital, the members of the supervisory board and the managing directors for any bankruptcy and fraud. This declaration will be provided as soon as the credentials of the founder have been verified. This procedure can take anywhere from 2 to 10 weeks.
- Entry in the commercial register at the chamber of commerce.

The funds used to pay the shares issued on incorporation (EUR 18,000 minimum) must be paid into a bank account in the (future) company's name opened in the Netherlands or elsewhere within the European Union. It is generally more expedient to open an account in the Netherlands or at least with a Dutch bank, as the formalities required for opening bank accounts in these circumstances are minimal and banks accept the opening of accounts for companies not yet in existence. The shares issued on incorporation may also be paid by a contribution in kind. For the contribution in kind to be valid the incorporators must make a description of the assets to be contributed and they must mention the value of the contribution. The value must be stated per a date no longer than 5 months prior to the date of incorporation. In addition, an expert must have issued a statement certifying that the value of the assets to be contributed is at least equal to the amount (in cash) to be paid on the shares.

It is also recommended search be conducted in order to find out whether the intended company name or a similar name has already been registered with the chamber of commerce. Due to intellectual property regulations, prior registrations of a similar trade name could result in an obligation to change the company's name. After execution of the deed of incorporation, the company can be registered at the chamber of commerce, which finalizes the incorporation procedure.

The duration for an incorporation of an N.V. depends on the underlying conditions of the ministry, the chamber of commerce and the notary. In general, it is between 11 days and up to 1 month.

8.2.1.3 Requirements for Associates/Shareholders and Regulations Concerning Shareholders' Meetings

The members of the management and supervisory board are usually appointed, suspended and dismissed by a general meeting of shareholders. Generally, the general meeting also decides on the adoption of the annual accounts, issue of shares, distribution of profits, amendments to the articles of association as well as (de-)mergers or dissolution of the company. There is also a statutory requirement of shareholder approval for any board resolution, which fundamentally alters the company's identity or character. In practice, the power of the general meeting may be limited to a significant extent. For instance, the articles of association may stipulate that matters such as the issue of shares, amendments to the articles of association or dissolution can only be decided following the proposal of another body, such as the supervisory board. An N.V. may also be subject to the so-called "structure regime", under which the powers of corporate bodies are allocated differently. The structure regime is mandatory for an N.V. meeting certain specific (mostly size-related) criteria. Such an N.V. may, however, be fully or partially exempted from the structure regime in specific circumstances, notably if it is a group holding company and the majority of the group employees are based outside the Netherlands.

One key feature of the structure regime is the mandatory institution of a supervisory board, which has the power to appoint and dismiss members of the management board (rather than the general meeting having that right). In addition, under the structure regime, a number of significant managerial actions require the approval of the supervisory board. Moreover, the general meeting can only dismiss the supervisory board in its entirety and although the power to appoint supervisory directors is still vested in the general meeting, the supervisory board has the exclusive right to nominate candidates.

An annual general meeting of shareholders must be held within 6 months of the end of each fiscal year. Extraordinary general meetings may be convened whenever appropriate. Meetings are convened by the management and/or supervisory board and these boards also prepare the meeting agenda and documentation. Shareholders or depository receipt holders representing individually or collectively either a minimum of one percent of issued capital or a market value of EUR 50 million are generally entitled to put items on the agenda of a meeting (provided the issues to be raised do not jeopardize vital company interests).

8.2.1.4 Articles of Association

After the deed of incorporation is complete, the articles of association must be filed with the commercial register of the chamber of commerce.

The articles of association contain, among other things, the name of the company, the company's registered office and the authorized capital of the company. The articles of association are important because they contain the initial regulations regarding the statutory organization of the company. In comparison to the B.V., the articles of association of the N.V. do not need to contain share transfer restrictions. This is not compulsory for the N.V.

An N.V.'s articles of association may stipulate the formation of a supervisory board in addition to the board of management. In the case of large companies, the law requires the establishment of a supervisory board. A large company is a company, whose issued share capital and reserves amount to at least EUR 11.3 million, that which qualifies for the establishment of a work council and employs 100 or more employees in the Netherlands (including those employed through subsidiaries). If a small company decides to establish a supervisory board, it may attribute to this board whatever powers and duties it may decide. In the case of large companies, a number of decisions spelled out by law, which may influence the continuity of the company, need approval from the supervisory board.

8.2.1.5 Minimum Contribution/Initial Capital

The minimum capital/capital stock amounts to EUR 45,000 in cash or other assets. The founders must draw at least 20 percent of the initial stock. Shareholder liability is restricted to the capital on the bearer shares.

8.2.1.6 Commercial Register

Immediately following incorporation, the company must be registered with the commercial register of the chamber of commerce and with the Dutch tax authorities. Registration in the trade register is automatically reported in the Official Gazette (Nederlandse Staatscourant). Each managing director of the company must sign a form to be registered at the commercial register. If the company has only one shareholder, this fact and the identity of the shareholder will be referred to in the appendix of the company's registration details, which is publicly available. In order to register a non-Dutch company as sole shareholder or managing director of a Dutch company, an extract of the commercial register with respect to the non-Dutch company, which may not be older than 1 month, or a "Certificate of Good Standing" of that company has to be provided to the commercial register. Entry in the trade register (Art. 2:69 BW) works right justifying.

8.2.1.7 Regulations Concerning Corporate Name

The corporate name must end with the initials "N.V."

Furthermore, the proposed name must not be misleading or too general or too similar to an existing business.

8.2.1.8 Transfer of Shares/Regulations in the Case of Death of a Shareholder

Trading shares of a listed N.V. are transferred often depending on the activity of the capital market. There are no special hereditary legal successor rules.

8.2.1.9 Liability of Shareholders and Directors

In the case of an established N.V., the liability of a shareholder is restricted to the amount of issued share capital.

In principle, there is no shareholder liability; only the entity is liable. However, the managing director is personally liable if

Personal external liability of the directors applies only in case of

- Tort (6:162 BW)
    - damages were caused due to a misleading (re)presentation in the annual accounts (2:139 BW); or
    - the director accepted a debt on behalf of the company, while he knew or should reasonably have known that the company would not be able to or is not able to fulfil its obligation and shall offer no financial means to reimburse the damages caused by its non-performance, except if he can prove circumstances that justify his acts;
    - the director willingly and knowingly ignored the fair treatment of creditors.
- Evident improper management
- Violation of laws (e.g. tax and social security laws and anti-trust laws).

8.2.1.10 Applicable Accounting Standards

The annual accounts must be drawn up in accordance with Generally Accepted Accounting Principles (GAAP) and detailed statutory requirements. If listed on a stock exchange in the EU, the N.V. must draw up the accounts under International

Accounting Standards/International Financial Reporting Standards (IAS/IFRS) as approved by the European Commission.

8.2.1.11 Disclosure Requirements

Within 6 months from the end of the N.V.'s fiscal year, the management board must prepare the annual report (jaarverslag) and the annual accounts (jaarrekening) consisting of the balance sheet, profit and loss account and explanatory notes.

The annual accounts consist of the following:

- financial statements (balance sheet, profit & loss account and the notes thereto);
- annual report;
- other information.

The presentation of the financial statements differs with each type of company. "Small companies" only need to present limited information, while "large companies" need to present full information (see Table 8.1).

Section 9 of Book 2 of the Dutch Civil Code distinguishes between "small-", "medium-", and "large-" sized companies. Arts. 2:396 and 2:397 provide for certain exemptions in Section 9 of Book 2 of the Dutch Civil Code for small and medium-sized companies. These exemptions apply to a company if it satisfies at least two of the requirements set out below on two consecutive balance sheet dates and, without interruption, on two consecutive balance sheet dates thereafter. These exemptions apply automatically unless the general meeting of shareholders decides otherwise (no later than 6 months after commencement of the financial year).

For the purpose of these requirements, the value of the assets, the net revenue and the number of employees shall be aggregated, as if the company is required to prepare consolidated annual accounts. This does not apply if the company applies Art. 2:408 BW (see below).

The exemptions of Arts. 2:396 and 2:397 shall also apply in respect to the company's first and second financial years: that satisfy the requirements concerned in its first financial year. As a company's circumstances change, it may find that it meets the criteria for a different category. Sometimes these changes are the result of only modest fluctuations in status that may even be temporary. In order to eliminate the

Table 8.1 Overview on company size criteria

	Small	Medium	Large
Value of assets in accounts	≤EUR 3,650,000	> EUR 3,650,000 ≤EUR 14,600,000	>EUR 14,600,000
Annual net revenue	≤EUR 7,300,000	> EUR 7,300,000 ≤EUR 29,200,000	>EUR 29,200,000
Annual average number of employees	<50	> 50 < 250	≥250

administrative burden of constantly changing requirements, a company cannot move from one category to another for two consecutive years.

Moreover, a company moving from one category to another generally remains subject to the requirements of its former category for the year in which it changes category. For example

	Conditions satisfied	Subject to requirements for
Year 1	Small company	Small company
Year 2	Medium company	Small company
Year 3	Medium company	Medium company

This example serves only as an illustration. Please note that the circumstances of every N.V. are unique and that each individual situation should be reviewed separately.

Certain documents must be prepared by the board of directors each year and made available for inspection by the general meeting of shareholders at the offices of the company. These documents must be prepared within 5 months after the end of the company's financial year. In special instances, the general meeting of shareholders may extend this period by a maximum of 6 months.

The required documents are

(a) Large companies

1. consolidated and unconsolidated balance sheets, profit and loss accounts and notes;
2. annual report and certain other information;

(b) Medium companies

3. consolidated and unconsolidated balance sheets and notes;
4. limited consolidated and unconsolidated profit and loss accounts and notes;
5. annual report and certain other information;

(c) Small companies

6. summary balance sheets and notes (consolidated and unconsolidated);
7. limited profit and loss accounts and notes (consolidated and unconsolidated);
8. annual report and certain other information.

The annual accounts need to be signed by all (current) managing directors and the members of the supervisory board (if applicable). If one or more of their signatures is missing, the reason for the omission has to be stated.

The publication requirements differ considerably according to the size of the company. They can be summarized as follows (Table 8.2).

A company must publish its annual report within 8 days following the completion and approval of its annual accounts. If these have not been determined and approved

Table 8.2 Publications requirements by company size

	Small company	Medium-sized company	Large company
Balance sheet and notes	Condensed	Condensed	Full disclosure
Profit and loss accounts and notes	Disclosure not required	Condensed	Full disclosure
Special provisions concerning the notes and principles of valuation and determination of financial results	Full disclosure related to the balance sheet only, except for minor exemptions	Full disclosure except for minor exemptions	Full disclosure
Management report	Disclosure not required	Full disclosure	Full disclosure
Additional information	Disclosure not required	Full disclosure except for minor exemptions	Full disclosure

in the manner prescribed by law within 7 months (under certain conditions, a post-ponement of 13 months is possible) after the financial year-end, management must publish them without delay. In that case, they must clearly disclose that they have not yet been determined or approved. Publication occurs by filing a copy of the required information with the chamber of commerce.

The company must ensure that its annual accounts as prepared, the annual report and the supplementary information are all available at the company's offices from the day notice is given of the general meeting of shareholders at which the accounts are to be considered. The shareholders (or – if applicable – of depository receipts issued with the company's co-operation) are entitled to inspect the documents at the company's offices and to obtain a copy free of charge.

Art. 2:403 BW provides for certain exemptions on the provisions of Section 9 of Book 2 of the Dutch Civil Code for companies that are part of a group.

Provided that the conditions stated in Art. 2:403 Subsection 1 are met, such a company does not need to present its annual accounts in accordance with the accounting and auditing provisions laid down in Arts. 2:391–2:394 BW.

Under Article 2:408 of the Dutch Civil Code, intermediate holding companies may be excluded from the consolidation requirements.

8.2.1.12 Employee Participation

When a company employs more than 50 people, a workers council must be formed. This council has an advisory say in the general aspects of the business, especially on working conditions, mergers, investments, etc.

The appointment of workers on the corporate board or the establishment of joint employer/worker councils, as found in some other European countries, is common in the Netherlands and is a matter of negotiation between management and the union. Such councils are found in larger firms and are considered to be a forum or means of communication. Dutch legislation provides for employee participation on the boards.

To protect the interests of employees during mergers, Dutch law provides a specific merger "law": the SER Fusiegedragsregels (the Merger Code of the SER). The Sociaal-Economische Raad (the Social and Economic Council) is the main advisory body to the Dutch government on national and international social and economic policy.

The SER Merger Code is not a law. It provides rules of conduct that are relevant to the preparation and realization of a merger or a public offer for shares. The SER Merger Code is applicable if the merger involves an enterprise that is established in the Netherlands and that (regularly) employs at least 50 employees.

Before the parties involved agree on a merger, they will have to notify the relevant trade unions (associations of employees) about the preparation, the consideration for and the consequences of the merger. The union must be able to present its opinion on the proposed merger from the viewpoint of the interests of the employees in such a way that these opinions can have substantial influence on the effectuation of the merger and/or on the stipulations thereof. Informing the unions is often considered a problem, because the parties involved usually aim at maximum confidentiality. If (one of) the merger parties or the union(s) are of the opinion that the preparation of the (proposed) merger is not in accordance with the SER Merger Code, they can submit a complaint with the SER Committee for Merger Affairs. This committee can decide that merger proceedings are not in line with the SER Merger Code. Moreover, the committee can qualify this as "seriously imputable", which can result in claims based on non-performance in case the SER Merger Code is part of a collective labour agreement or unlawful act.

8.2.2 Limited Liability Company (Besloten Vennootschap – B.V.)

8.2.2.1 Legal Capacity and Power of Disposition

Being a legal entity, a B.V. acquires full legal capacity as of the date of its registration with the commercial register. Starting with this date, the company may enter into any commercial transaction, if it is within the declared object of activity of the firm.

The B.V. is allowed to start up its activities before the actual incorporation takes place, but must signify this by adding the initials i.o. (for "in oprichting": in incorporation) to the initials B.V. after its name. During this period, founders are fully liable for the debts and obligations of the B.V. incorporation. After its incorporation, the company will have to confirm all acts performed on its behalf during the formation period. By this confirmation, the company takes over the full liability of the founders during the period of incorporation.

8.2.2.2 Process and Requirements for Incorporation

Incorporation by one or more individuals or companies occurs through the taking out of a notarial deed of incorporation before a Dutch civil law notary. That deed must contain

(a) the company's articles of association;
(b) details on the shares issued at incorporation and on the incorporator(s)/shareholder(s);
(c) the appointment of the first managing and (as the case may be) supervisory directors; and
(d) the determination of the first financial period of the company.

Incorporation (i.e. execution of the deed of incorporation) can take place only after

1. the Netherland's Ministry of Justice has been provided with the relevant information on the incorporator(s) and the first managing director(s), set out in paragraphs 4.8 and 4.9 below;
2. the Ministry has granted the approval on the documents submitted to it by means of a declaration of no objection; and
3. the civil law notary has received a statement from a bank established in the Netherlands or elsewhere in the European Union indicating that the share capital to be issued at incorporation has been paid into a bank account in the company's name.

A founder does not need to be present at the signing meeting if he has given a power of attorney to a representative or acts through a nominee. A founder also does not need to be a Dutch resident or citizen. Initial shareholders have to pay in a minimum capital of EUR 18,000. Payment on shares can – like shares in the capital of an N.V. (§ 2.1.2). – be made in cash or in other assets. If payment is made in other assets than cash, an auditor's report has to certify that the assets do not represent less value than required. Each method of payment has its special formal requirements.

For foreign corporations setting up a Dutch B.V., the following information is required:

- full corporate name of the founder;
- name of the country where and under whose laws the founder has been incorporated;
- place of registered office and full business address of the founder;
- legal proof of the existence of the founder, e.g. statement of good standing issued by a lawyer or registration documents including articles of association.

If the founder is a private person, then instead of information of the founding company details of the private person are required, such as

- surname and forenames in full;
- full residential address;
- place and date of birth;
- nationality;

- occupation;
- marital status.

Furthermore, the following information is needed in both cases:

- copies of the proposed directors' and founders' passports;
- proposed name of the B.V.;
- proposed objectives of the B.V.;
- authorized capital of the B.V.;
- issued and deposited capital of the B.V.;
- par value of the B.V.'s shares;
- the first financial year – the first year may be longer or shorter than 12 months;
- registered office and place of business of the B.V. in the Netherlands;
- founders have to state by writing that they do not have the intention to sell the shares within the first year after formation of the B.V.;
- a letter of good standing for every founder provided by a bank or a notary.

The share capital and shareholders must be registered in a shareholders register.

The process of B.V. incorporation takes a minimum of 2 weeks if the proper applicant documents are immediately available. Normally, the whole process takes at least 4–8 weeks. The costs for the notarial deed of incorporation are about EUR 1,350. Total incorporation costs are estimated to be EUR 3,000.

Corresponding clause: Art. 2:175 lid 2 BW.

8.2.2.3 Requirements for Associates/Shareholders and Regulations Concerning Shareholders' Meetings

As stated above, a B.V. may be created by one or more individuals or legal entities. All founders of a B.V. will be examined by the Dutch Ministry of Justice and have to pass the declaration of no objection. A founder does not need to be a Dutch resident or citizen. A B.V. issues registered shares to its shareholders.

A B.V. has to comply with the annual obligations of holding a general meeting of shareholders. For B.V.'s with only one shareholder, all decisions made by the general meeting of shareholders have to be reported in written minutes, which have to be filed at the office of the company.

If a B.V. has only one shareholder, the name of the shareholder has to be filed at the chamber Of commerce.

Corresponding clause: Art. 2:175 lid 2 BW.

8.2.2.4 Articles of Association

The company's articles of association need to contain at least the following information to be incorporated:

- name and registered seat;
- the objective of the company's business;
- a provision regarding limitation or transferability of the shares (either a right of first refusal for the other shareholders if shares are offered for sale or prior approval from a corporate body for any proposed share transfer (or for a combination of both));
- sole or joint signatory powers for members of the board of directors;
- whether the company will have a board of supervisory directors;
- financial years and first reporting date.

The articles of association have to be drawn up by a civil notary.

A B.V.'s articles of association may stipulate the formation of a supervisory board in addition to the board of management. For large companies, the law requires the establishment of a supervisory board. A large company is a company of which the issued share capital and reserves amount to at least EUR 11.3 million, that which qualifies for the establishment of a work council and employs 100 or more employees in the Netherlands (including those employed through subsidiaries). If a small company decides to establish a supervisory board, it may attribute to this board whatever powers and duties it may decide. In the case of large companies, a number of decisions spelled out by law, which may influence the continuity of the company, need approval by the supervisory board (see Chapter Limited Liability Company 82.2. for more detail).

8.2.2.5 Minimum Contribution/Initial Capital

The minimum share capital is EUR 18,000 in cash or other assets (accountant's statement compulsory). At least 25 percent of the authorized capital must be issued and paid in.

8.2.2.6 Commercial Register

Immediately following incorporation, the company must be registered with the commercial register of the chamber of commerce and with the Dutch tax authorities. Corresponding clause: Art. 2:175 BW
   (see Sect. 8.2.1 for more detail).

8.2.2.7 Regulations Concerning Corporate Name

The corporate name must end with the initials "B.V." Furthermore, reference is made to 2.1.7.
   Corresponding clause: Art. 2:175 BW.

8.2.2.8 Transfer of Shares/Regulations in Case of Death of a Shareholder

Shares of the B.V. can be transferred without affecting the continued existence of the company, although the shares of a B.V. may not be offered for public subscription or trading. The transfer has to take place before a Dutch notary. A B.V. does not issue share certificates. There are no general regulations in case of death/inheritance.

8.2.2.9 Liability of Shareholders and Directors

If a B.V. starts up its activities before the actual incorporation takes place, the founders are fully liable for its debts and obligations in incorporation. After its incorporation, the company will have to confirm all acts performed on its behalf during the formation period. By this confirmation the company takes over the full liability of the founders during the period of incorporation.

With its incorporation, a B.V. receives legal capacity and thus liability. In principle creditors can only make claims on the assets of the B.V. and not on the assets of the director(s) or shareholder(s). The liability of shareholders is restricted to the capital on the issued shares.

(See Sect. 8.2.1 for more detail on personal external liability of the directors; correspondent clause regarding misleading (re)presentation in the annual accounts is 2:149 BW.)

8.2.2.10 Applicable Accounting Standards

The annual accounts must be drawn up in accordance with Generally Accepted Accounting Principles (GAAP) and detailed statutory requirements. Alternatively, International Accounting Standards/International Financial Reporting Standards (IAS/IFRS) as provided by the European Commission might be used.

8.2.2.11 Disclosure Requirements

The accounting principles in the Netherlands are described in Section 9 of Book 2 of the Dutch Civil Code, jurisprudence of the Supreme Court, International Accounting Standards Committee (IASC) and the guidelines drawn up by the Raad voor de Jaarverslaggeving.

See Sect. 8.2.1 for more detail.

8.2.2.12 Employee Participation

Reference is made to this for the joint stock corporation (see Sect. 8.2.1).

8.2.3 Limited Commercial Partnership (Commanditaire Vennootschap – C.V.)

8.2.3.1 Legal Capacity and Power of Disposition

A limited partnership ("commanditaire vennootschap") or "CV" is not a legal entity, such as an N.V. and a B.V. Under Dutch legislation, a CV is a legal relationship pertaining to the law of obligations between one or more managing partners (beherende vennoten) and one or more limited partners (commanditaire vennoten). Parties to a CV intend to establish a CV in order to practice a business under a common name for a joint account.

8.2.3.2 Process and Requirements for Incorporation

There are no specific requirements for the establishment of a CV. However, normally parties to a CV enter into a written contract in which the essentials of the CV are stipulated. For instance, in the CV contract, parties decide for which joint objectives the CV will be established. The CV contract can also be drawn up before a Dutch civil law notary.

No notarial deed of incorporation is needed, however, it is recommended to have a contract or agreement in place between the partners in which the internal legal relations are defined. Preferably, this should be on paper and notarially certified. There are no personal requirements, only that the partners must be at least 18 years old. Within 1 day, the incorporation of a CV can be established. There are no fixed costs for the incorporation of a CV. Costs may vary significantly depending on the complexity of the circumstances.

8.2.3.3 Requirements for Associates/Shareholders and Regulations Concerning Shareholders' Meetings

The CV consists of at least two or more partners, of whom one is the partner and the other is the limited partner. Regarding the control over the CV, a distinction should be made between internal and external control.

Only the managing partner is authorized, within the objects of the CV, to represent the CV in external affairs, to act on behalf of the CV and to sign commitments to third parties and vice versa. If there are two (or more) managing partners to the CV, the CV contract can contain a provision that the authorization of another managing partner is required for specific matters as described in the contract. A limited partner shall not act as a managing partner or transact any business for or in the name of the CV, nor has the right, power of authority to act for, execute any document or instrument on behalf of or otherwise bind the CV in any manner.

Internally, each partner basically has equal votes unless the CV contract determines otherwise. The number of voting rights may be linked to the capital contribution of the partners; however, under Dutch law, it is possible to separate the capital contribution of the partners from the voting rights.

Compared to a B.V., CV partners are in principle both "the shareholders" as well as "the management board" of the company, provided that a limited partner is not authorized to represent the CV in external affairs. The contract usually contains rules regarding the meetings of the partners.

8.2.3.4 Articles of Association

There are no formal requirements. It is recommended that members draw up a contract between the partners. In the articles of association, the distribution of profits between the managing partners and the limited partners is specified.

8.2.3.5 Minimum Contribution/Initial Capital

There are no minimum requirements for a capital contribution. In order to realize the objectives' of the CV, each of the parties is obliged to make a contribution consisting of an amount in cash and/or goods and/or rights to the CV. A managing partner may also contribute its labour or management activities. According to Dutch law, a CV can have a separate equity. This implies that only business creditors to the CV can make claims against the CV. Private creditors may recover their claims from the CV's assets. The principle of separate equity pertains only to the position of private and business creditors and not to CV ownership matters.

Since a CV is not a legal entity, it cannot legally acquire property in its own name. Property acquired by a CV shall be the joint ownership (undivided co-ownership) of all CV partners, unless otherwise agreed upon by all the partners. For practical reasons, the managing partner may represent the other partners of the CV in the event of a transfer of assets. Of course, the managing partner needs to be duly authorized to do so.

8.2.3.6 Commercial Register

The CV should be registered with the commercial register of the chamber of commerce in the event activities are carried out in the Netherlands. However, this registration is not a constitutive requirement for establishing a CV under Dutch law. The names of the limited partners (they are only involved in the profit) may not appear.

8.2.3.7 Regulations Concerning Corporate Name

Reference is made to this for the joint stock corporation (see Sect. 8.2.1).

8.2.3.8 Transfer of Shares/Regulations in Case of Death of a Shareholder

According to the Dutch law, the CV ends if one of the acting partners withdraws or dies. In this case the CV is shut down, the capital gets dissolved and is divided among the partners.

8.2.3.9 Liability of Shareholders and Directors

A managing partner of a CV is in its capacity jointly and severally liable. A limited partner is in its capacity limited liable. A limited partner is only liable to the extent of its capital contribution in the CV. Pursuant to the Dutch trade code, two circumstances bring along a joint and several liability for the limited partner for all debts and obligations of the CV:

1. if a limited partner is involved in management (directly or by proxy) and/or;
2. if the name of the limited partner is used in the name of the CV.

8.2.3.10 Applicable Accounting Standards

Reference is made to this for the limited liability company (see Sect. 8.2.2).

8.2.3.11 Disclosure Requirements

Under Dutch law, a CV is obliged to keep proper books, records and accounts of its business. Except for the exemption as mentioned hereunder, there are no statutory requirements for drawing up the annual accounts. However, the CV contract normally contains provisions in respect thereof.

In general, no annual accounts need to be published with the chamber of commerce except, however, if all managing partners are capital companies under foreign law. In that case, all statutory provisions in the Dutch civil code, in respect to the annual accounts and annual report, also apply to a CV.

8.2.3.12 Employee Participation

Reference is made to this for the joint stock corporation (see Sect. 8.2.1). The partners may choose to establish such bodies in order to delegate certain tasks and responsibilities. These tasks and responsibilities are laid forth in the CV contract.

8.2.4 Partnership (Vennootschap onder Firma – V.O.F.)

8.2.4.1 Legal Capacity and Power of Disposition

A general partnership ("vennootschap onder firma" or "VOF") is not a legal entity, such as an N.V. and a B.V. and thus, has no legal capacity by itself. Under Dutch legislation, a VOF is a legal relationship pertaining to the law of obligations between two or more managing partners. Parties to a VOF intend to establish a VOF in order to practice a business under a common name for a joint account.

Each partner is authorized, within the objectives of the VOF, to represent the VOF in external affairs, to act on behalf of the VOF and to sign and to commit the VOF to third parties and vice versa. If there are two (or more) partners to the VOF, the VOF contract can contain a provision that the authorization of another partner is required for specific matters as described in the contract.

8.2.4.2 Process and Requirements for Incorporation

There are no specific requirements for the establishment of a VOF. However, normally VOF parties enter into a written contract in which the essentials of the VOF are stipulated. For instance, in the VOF contract, parties decide the joint objectives for which the VOF will be established. The VOF contract can also be executed before a Dutch civil law notary. Costs of incorporation are flexible and thus, vary significantly depending on the complexity of the circumstances.

8.2.4.3 Requirements for Associates/Shareholders and Regulations Concerning Shareholders' Meetings

A VOF is to be created by two or more individuals or legal entities. All parties are required to bring in money or other assets. The company should be managed under a joint name and joint assets. In regards to the control over the VOF, a distinction should be made between internal and external control.

Each partner is authorized, within the objectives of the VOF, to represent the VOF in external affairs, to act on behalf of the VOF and to sign and to commit the VOF to third parties and vice versa. If there are two (or more) partners to the VOF, the VOF contract can contain a provision that the authorization of another partner is required for specific matters as described in the contract.

Internally, each partner basically has equal votes unless the VOF contract determines otherwise. The number of voting rights may be linked to the capital contribution of the partners; however, under Dutch law, it is possible to separate the capital contribution of the partners from the voting rights.

Under Dutch law a management board or supervisory board is not a statutory body. Compared to a B.V., the partners to a VOF are in principle both "shareholders" as well as "the management board" of the company. However, the partners may choose to establish such bodies in order to delegate certain tasks and responsibilities. These tasks and responsibilities are laid down in the VOF contract.

8.2.4.4 Articles of Association

A partnership contract is not compulsory, but is in fact essential. There are no formal foundation requirements (preferably a contract on paper and executed before a civil law notary). An agreement should state the length of the limited partnership, the contribution, authority, share of profits and the arrangements for resignation of the partners. Profits are allocated in line with a formula set out in the partnership contract.

Corresponding clause: Art. 22 WvK.

8.2.4.5 Minimum Contribution/Initial Capital

There are no minimum requirements for a capital contribution. In order to realize the objectives of the VOF, each of the parties in the VOF is obliged to make a contribution consisting of an amount in cash and/or goods and/or rights and/or its labour or management activities to the VOF. According to Dutch law, a VOF can have separate equity. This implies that only business creditors to the VOF can make claims against the CV. Private creditors of the partner may not recover their claims from the assets of the VOF. The principle of separate equity pertains only to the position of private and business creditors and not to ownership matters of the VOF.

Since a VOF is not a legal entity, it cannot legally acquire property in its own name. Property acquired by a VOF shall be the joint ownership (undivided co ownership) of all VOF partners, unless otherwise agreed upon by all the partners.

8.2.4.6 Commercial Register

The VOF should be registered with the commercial register of the chamber of commerce in the event that activities are carried out in the Netherlands. However, this registration is not a constitutive requirement for establishing a VOF under Dutch law. Corresponding clause: Art. 23 WvK and Art. 3 / Art. 5 HRGW.

8.2.4.7 Regulations Concerning Corporate Name

A VOF has to conduct its business under a joint corporate name. Further reference is made to this for the joint stock corporation (see Sect. 8.2.1).

Corresponding clause: Titel 3 WvK.

8.2.4.8 Transfer of Shares/Regulations in Case of Death of a Shareholder

Shares are transferable, but for a transfer the agreement of all other shareholders is needed. There are no general regulations defined for transfer of shares in the event of death/inheritance of a shareholder. Shareholders should define regulations, in the articles of association, for transfer of shares in the event of the death of a shareholder. The admission of a new partner requires the consent of the other partners to the extent specified in the partnership agreement.

8.2.4.9 Liability of Shareholders and Directors

The partners are jointly and severally responsible and liable to third parties for partnership debts.

There is a distinction between private and corporate assets, but partner's liability includes private property. In the case of bankruptcy, all partners have unlimited liability. When a partner retires, he remains responsible for all liabilities incurred before his retirement.

Corresponding clause: Art. 18 WvK.

8.2.4.10 Applicable Accounting Standards

The annual accounts must be drawn up in accordance with Generally Accepted Accounting Principles (GAAP) and detailed statutory requirements. Alternatively, International Accounting Standards/International Financial Reporting Standards (IAS/IFRS) as proved by the European Commission can be used.

8.2.4.11 Disclosure Requirements

Under Dutch law, a VOF is obliged to keep proper books, records and accounts of its business. Except for the exemption as mentioned hereunder, there are no statutory requirements for drawing up the annual accounts. However, the VOF contract normally contains provisions in respect thereof.

In general, no annual accounts need to be published with the chamber of commerce except, however, if all partners are capital companies under foreign law; in which case, all statutory provisions in the Dutch civil code in respect of the annual accounts and annual report also apply to a VOF.

8.2.4.12 Employee Participation

Reference is made to this for the joint stock corporation (see Sect. 8.2.1). The partners may choose to establish such bodies in order to delegate certain tasks and responsibilities. These tasks and responsibilities are laid down in the VOF contract.

8.2.5 Civil Partnership (Maatschap – Mts.)

8.2.5.1 Legal Capacity and Power of Disposition

The civil partnership is a venture without legal personality. Thus, only the partners are personally liable and legally capable.

8.2.5.2 Process and Requirements for Incorporation

No particular requirements apply to the establishment of a civil partnership. Costs of incorporation are flexible and thus, vary significantly depending on the complexity of the circumstances.

8.2.5.3 Requirements for Associates/Shareholders and Regulations Concerning Shareholders' Meetings

The civil partnership is a collaboration between two or more natural and/or legal persons.

8.2.5.4 Articles of Association

The mutual appointments are laid down in a civil partnership contract. In this contract, agreements are made concerning the input of the partners, profit sharing and the partitioning of the power. However, contract restrictions exist: it is, for example, not possible to exclude one of the partners in profit sharing; this is, however, possible with loss sharing. When the partners have not made any agreements concerning profit and loss sharing, it is divided on the basis of the value of investment made by the partners in the company.

8.2.5.5 Minimum Contribution/Initial Capital

There are no capital requirements.

8.2.5.6 Commercial Register

On July 1, 2008, the new Trade Register Law (Handelsregisterwet) became effective. On the basis of the aforementioned law, all companies and legal persons in the Netherlands need to be registered at the chamber of commerce.

8.2.5.7 Regulations Concerning Corporate Name

There are two different forms of civil partnerships: the silent civil partnership and the public civil partnership. The silent partnership is a partnership where the partners each have their own practice and under their own name, but may jointly acquire personnel or specialized equipment. The public partnership is a partnership where the partners work together under a common name. Further reference is made to this for the joint stock corporation (see Sect. 8.2.1).

8.2.5.8 Transfer of Shares/Regulations in Case of Death of a Partner

There are no general regulations in case of death/inheritance.

8.2.5.9 Liability of Shareholders and Directors

The partners are liable each for equal parts. A partner may only enter into obligations towards third parties on his or her own behalf. The other partners are not jointly and severally liable for obligations. However, each partner is liable for the partnership obligations.

8.2.5.10 Applicable Accounting Standards

All companies must comply with the Dutch statutory requirements for book and record keeping.

8.2.5.11 Disclosure Requirements

Reference is made to this for the Partnership (VOF), see Sect. 8.2.4. The same requirements apply to the civil partnership.

8.2.5.12 Employee Participation

Reference is made to this for the joint stock corporation (see Sect. 8.2.1).

8.2.6 Individual Enterprise/Sole Proprietorship (Eenmanszaak)

8.2.6.1 Legal Capacity and Power of Disposition

A sole proprietorship itself has no legal capacity. The legal capacity is provided through the natural person owning the proprietorship.

8.2.6.2 Process and Requirements for Incorporation

There are no special incorporation/formation requirements. Starting up the activities of the firm is decisive for its foundation. Additionally, an official legal registration is possible.

8.2.6.3 Requirements for Associates/Shareholders and Regulations Concerning Shareholders' Meetings

The owner of a sole proprietorship can only be a natural person, not a legal entity.

8.2.6.4 Articles of Association

There are no articles of association applicable.

8.2.6.5 Minimum Contribution/Initial Capital

There are no capital requirements. There is no distinction between business and personal assets.

8.2.6.6 Commercial Register

Reference is made to this for the civil partnership (see Sect. 8.2.5).

8.2.6.7 Regulations Concerning Corporate Name

Reference is made to this for the joint stock corporation (see Sect. 8.2.1).

8.2.6.8 Transfer of Shares/Regulations in Case of Death of a Shareholder

A transfer of ownership is possible through the sale of all proprietorship assets and liabilities. A continuation of the firm in case of the death of the owner is governed by general rules of inheritance.

8.2.6.9 Liability of Shareholders and Directors

The owner has unlimited liability for all debts. As mentioned in the Section "Minimum contribution" (see Sect. 8.2.6.5), there is no separation between the owner's private and business debts and assets.

8.2.6.10 Applicable Accounting Standards

Reference is made to this for the civil partnership (see Sect. 8.2.5).

8.2.6.11 Disclosure Requirements

Reference is made to this for the partnership (see Sect. 8.2.4).

8.2.6.12 Employee Participation

A supervisory board with labour representatives is not possible. Reference is made to this for the joint stock company (see Sect. 8.2.1).

8.3 Summary

If you set up a company in the Netherlands, you have to first choose which type of legal entity would be most suitable with respect to the business operations. To make that choice, knowledge of the different corporate entities is required as well as knowledge of the rules applicable to these different corporate entities. Such a choice may be tax-driven. Furthermore, it is important to realize that the Dutch corporate system is quite different from the Anglo-Saxon system. According to the latter, a company is managed by executives and non-executives. Dutch companies by contrast, can opt for a dual-board system in which the management board is supervised by the supervisory board. For large companies this dual-board system is mandatory. Finally, Dutch corporate law is characterized by detailed rules regarding, among others, good governance, dispute resolution, responsibilities and powers of the different bodies of a company and annual accounts.

8.3.1 Advantages/Disadvantages of Different Legal Forms

8.3.1.1 Corporation (B.V./N.V.)

The main reason for the founding of a B.V. or an N.V. is exclusion of liability. Shareholders in a B.V. or an N.V. are in principle only liable to the amount of their share in the issued share capital. The B.V. as legal form is particularly suitable for small and medium-sized enterprises, which are led by a closed circle of persons or families and do not have the need to raise fresh capital in the capital market. The transferable ownership with the consideration of the restrictions, specified in the articles of association, is also a special advantage of this type of legal form. Creation of a B.V. is less expensive than that of an N.V. The minimum required capital for a B.V. is EUR 18,000 and for an N.V. is EUR 45,000. In principle, the earnings of a B.V. and an N.V. are subject to company taxes (vennootschapsbelast-ing), whereas the dividend payments to the shareholders are subject to dividend taxes.

In the following table, the major advantages and disadvantages are demonstrated (Table 8.3).

Table 8.3 General advantages and disadvantages of a corporation

Advantages	Disadvantages
• Limited liability	• Closely regulated
• Specialized management	• Most expensive form to organize
• Ownership is transferable	• Charter restrictions
• Continuous existence	• Extensive record keeping necessary
• Separate legal entity	• Double taxation
• Possible tax advantages	• Possible development of conflict between shareholders and executives
• Easier to raise capital	–

8.3.1.2 Limited Partnerships (CV / VOF)

There are several advantages in the choice of a C.V. ("Commanditaire Vennootschap") as a tax-deferring vehicle for passive investments by entrepreneurs in all kinds of securities, in real estate (located in countries other than the Netherlands) and, among other things, a CV may maintain bank accounts. The limited partnership tends to develop from a sole trader or a general partnership when a limited partner enters the business to provide extra finance for growth. Additionally, this advantage comes along with low incorporation effort in terms of bureaucracy and the low start-up costs.

However, the authority of the company is divided. Even if the limited partner is not actively involved in operating the business, he also shares interests in the company, as he is the financial backer. Conflicts of interest might arise between the limited partner and the managing partner; therefore, it is crucial for the managing partner to find a suitable partner for the venture. Furthermore, it is not always easy to raise additional capital once the partners have exploited their personal resources. This may however be the same in case of shareholders in a B.V. or an N.V. having fulfilled their payment obligations.

In the following table the major advantages and disadvantages of a CV are demonstrated (Table 8.4):

Table 8.4 General advantages and disadvantages of a CV

Advantages	Disadvantages
• Ease of formation	• Unlimited liability for managing partner. Limited partner to the extent of its capital contribution
• Relatively low start-up costs	• Lack of continuity in business organization in the absence of managing partner
• Additional sources of investment capital	• Divided authority
• Possible tax advantages	• Difficulty raising additional capital
• Limited regulation	• Hard to find suitable partners
• Broader management base	• Possible development of conflict between partners

Table 8.5 General advantages and disadvantages of a VOF

Advantages	Disadvantages
	• Unlimited liability
• No minimum capital required	• High level of trust among the partners needed
• Fast foundation process	• Required for each company. Reference is made in 2.5.6
• Flexible set-up of the articles of association	• Mandatory accounting

The advantages and disadvantages of a VOF are listed in Table 8.5.

8.3.1.3 Sole Proprietorship (Eenmanszaak)

The simplest form of business is the sole proprietorship. Many small businesses operating in the Netherlands are sole proprietorships. A sole proprietor owns and manages the business and is responsible for all business transactions. The owner is also personally responsible for all debts and liabilities incurred by the business. The possible bankruptcy of the entrepreneur means the same as the bankruptcy of the entrepreneur as a private person at the same time. This unlimited liability is of course a disadvantage for this legal form; however, the advantages are numerous. A sole proprietor can own the business for any duration of time and sell it when he or she deems fit. As the owner, an entrepreneur can even pass a business down to his or her heirs and he has complete control and decision-making powers over the business. In this type of business, there are no specific business taxes paid by the company. The owner pays taxes on income from the business as part of his or her personal income tax payments.

The paperwork and formalities for the establishment of a sole proprietorship are substantially less than those of corporations, allowing an entrepreneur to open a business quickly and with relative ease – from a bureaucratic standpoint. Only a registration with the chamber of commerce is required. It can also be less costly to start a business as a sole proprietorship, which is attractive to many new business owners who often find it difficult to attract investors. In addition, the sale or transfer can take place at the discretion of the sole proprietor.

In the following table the major advantages and disadvantages are listed: (Table 8.6).

Table 8.6 General advantages and disadvantages of a sole proprietorship

Advantages	Disadvantages
• Relatively low start-up costs	• Unlimited liability
• Greatest freedom from regulation	• Lack of continuity in business organization when the owner ceases his business
• Owner in direct control of decision making	• Difficulty raising capital
• Minimal working capital required	
• Tax advantages to owner → no corporate tax payments	
• All profits to owner	

Chapter 9
Romania

Roxana Smeu and Adriana Turta

Abstract In the chapter on Romania, the authors Roxana Smeu and Adriana Turta start with a short introduction into the general laws and regulations with regard to setting up and running a business and provide an overview of possible legal forms in Romania. They use the general analysis framework for the handbook on legal forms in Europe to analyse five relevant legal forms: the limited liability company (Societate cu raspundere limitata – SRL), the joint stock company (Societate pe actiuni – SA), the general partnership (Societate in nume colectiv – SNC), the limited partnership (Societate in comandita simpla – SCS) and the limited partnership on shares (Societate in comandita pe actiuni – SCA).

The authors conclude their discussions with an evaluation of the advantages and disadvantages of the different legal forms and provide exemplary recommendations depending on the individual case of the founders.

Contents

R. Smeu (✉)
Dragomir & Associates, Constantin Noica nr. 159, sector 6, 060052 Bucuresti, Romania
e-mail: office@dragomirlaw.ro

M.J. Munkert et al. (eds.), *Founding a Company*, DOI 10.1007/978-3-642-11259-1_9,
© Springer-Verlag Berlin Heidelberg 2010

9.1 Introduction

The legal framework regulating the corporate activities area comprises a set of basic laws that covers all aspects of a business set-up and operation in Romania.

The core laws in that field are the Company Law (Legea no. 31/1990 privind societățile comerciale – "LSC") and the Trade Registry Law (no. 26/1990).

Of these, the Company Law is the most important enactment that expressly regulates the establishment and functioning of all commercial companies in Romania.

Since January 1, 2007, Romania is a full member of the European Union. Therefore, the substantially amended Company Law (by law no. 441/2006) represents an important legislative step in Romania's commitment to align its internal legislation to that of the European Union.

Furthermore, Romanian corporate governance is becoming more and more similar to the European Union, offering a friendly and safe legal background for EU investors seeking to develop businesses in Romania.

The Company Law regulates five types of legal forms:

- Limited liability company (SRL – "societate cu raspundere limitata"),
- Joint stock company (SA – "societate pe actiuni"),
- General partnership (SNC – "societate in nume colectiv"),
- Limited partnership (SCS – "societate in comandita simpla"),
- Limited partnership on shares (SCA – "societate in comandita pe actiuni").

In addition to these common types of legal forms, especially due to the Romanian EU membership, there are some other specific forms of businesses/associations that may be as well established and operated, at various investment levels:

- representative offices of foreign companies – ("reprezentante ale societatilor straine") – their scope is to promote parent company's products or services, identify new business opportunities and/or intermediate international transactions for their parent company,
- branches or subsidiaries of foreign companies ("sucursale ale societatilor straine") – with a slightly similar scope,
- silent partnerships ("asociere in participatiune") – a contractual form of association used by two/more companies to perform a specific commercial activity and
- the European Union's legal forms (EEIG – European Economic Interest Grouping, SE – Societas Europaea, SCE – Societas Cooperativa Europaea).

Except for silent partnerships, the representative offices and the branches, which are not legal entities, all the other types of commercial companies are considered as Romanian legal entities, have legal personality and may acquire land in Romania.

Also, except for the silent partnership, all other types of businesses are subject to the Romanian fiscal and customs legislation. Although silent partnerships are not legal entities and have no legal personality, the members of such silent partnerships are subject to the Romanian fiscal and customs legislation. For example, the provisions of Article 13 of the Romanian Fiscal Code establish the obligation for foreign legal persons that carry on an activity in Romania in an association, such as silent partnership to pay profit tax.

For the general or limited partnership (SNC, SCS) company, law also allows mixed legal forms. When a shareholder of an SNC or an SCS is a legal person by itself, the shareholders' company has to be registered with the SNC or SCS (comparable to a German GmbH & Co. KG).

The most common legal form in Romania is the limited liability company (SRL). In January 2009, the national office for the commercial register stated that 95 percent of all companies registered in Romania between 1999 and 2008 are limited liability companies (SRL). Consequently, the chapter starts with and mainly covers matters affecting limited liability companies.

9.2 Description of Relevant Legal Forms

9.2.1 Limited Liability Company (Societate cu raspundere limitata – SRL)

9.2.1.1 Legal Capacity and Power of Disposition

An SRL acquires full legal capacity beginning the date of its registration in the commercial register. Starting with this date, the company can act as a legal person and may enter into any commercial transaction, as per its declared business purpose.

Up to the final point of the registration procedure, the company has only limited legal capacity provided by law solely for the incorporation activities.

An SRL has one or more directors appointed through the articles of association or at the general meeting. The directors conduct the management activities of the company and bear responsibility for all their debts.

Every director can represent the company alone, unless the articles of association state otherwise (Art. 75 LSC). If the articles of association state that the company can be represented only by all directors, all decisions have to be unanimous. If the directors cannot agree, the decision can be taken by the shareholders representing the absolute majority of the subscribed capital (Art. 76 Para. 1 LSC). The directors are allowed to transfer the right to represent the company to a third party only based on the articles of association or after a decision at the general meeting (Art. 71 Para. 1 LSC).

In regard to third parties, the company is bound through the legal capacity of its directors, even if this legal act crosses the business purpose or the director was not allowed to represent the company at all or alone. If the company can prove that the third party knew or should have known that the business purpose was crossed or the power of representation was misused, or when the legal acts concluded by the director exceed the limits of the mandate provided by law to the director, the company cannot be held liable. The publication of the articles of association alone is not enough to prove the knowledge of misuse (Art. 55 Para. 1 LSC).

The authority of the director can be constrained in the articles of association by a decision at the general meeting, or through an agreement between the company and the director. Constraints are, for example, that certain decisions can be made only at the general meeting or that certain decisions can only be made with the approval of the shareholders. Furthermore, the shareholders can give binding orders anytime.

The regulations of the articles of association or the decisions of the shareholders, which constrain the directors' power of disposition of the, are not effective towards third parties, even when they were published (Art. 55 Para. 2, LSC). The company has to prove that the third party knew about this constraint.

There is no special proof for the power of disposition. However, the content and the limits of the power of agency are established through written documents such as the articles of association, decisions at the general meeting of shareholders or the power of agency agreement. The power of disposition can be seen in the commercial register.

9.2.1.2 Process and Requirements for Incorporation

For the formation of a company, the articles of association that define among other things the relationship of the shareholders is required (Art. 5 LSC). Corporate law specifies that the articles of association must be drawn up in a written form and contain the signatures of all the founders. Corporate law specifies the situations in which the articles of association must be drawn up in front of a public notary. This could be, for example, if real estate is used as a tangible asset for subscribed capital (Art. 5 Para. 5 LSC). A formation that does not fulfil this formality is null and void.

The registration procedure for an SRL consists of the following main steps:

- The desired name of the company has to be checked by the responsible commercial register so that the name does not lead to confusion or disorder with already-existing company names.
- For incorporation, the company needs a Romanian address. In the beginning, it is possible to temporarily choose the address of the lawyer who escorts the formation. Another possibility is to choose the address of an already-existing company, which requires that both companies have at least one joint shareholder or that the building allows, by its structure, more than one company to function at the premises, or that at least one of the shareholders is the owner of the building. (Art. 17 Para. 2 LSC)
- The articles of association (bylaws) must be signed by the shareholders; certain other documents must be signed in front of a public notary or a lawyer.
- In the case of SRL companies, full payment of subscribed share capital is required upon incorporation.
- Capital in cash is required for all types of companies.
- The company is registered with the commercial register by issuance of a registration certificate. This provides a registration code ("cod unic de inregistrare",

abridged as "CUI") valid for both the commercial register and the tax authorities (Art. 8 Law no. 359/2004 on simplifying the formalities for the registration in the trade registry – LSF). An abstract of the registration certificate will be published in the official Romanian journal ("Monitorul Oficial al Romaniei", abridged as MOF). A separate VAT registration is required.

- The registration certificate also includes in the appendix a certificate of status, certifying the registration of the statements that the company meets all the requirements for engaging in the activities listed as the company's objectives. The relevant authorities would subsequently conduct investigations at the registered head offices of the company or at other locations where activity might be carried out, in order to assess the fulfilment of the operating requirements. Likewise, specific authorizations/permits should be obtained if carrying out certain activities provided by the law.
- The company legally exists and has the right to start and run its activities commencing from the date of its registration with the commercial register.

Documents in foreign languages have to be translated into Romanian by translators certified by the Romanian Ministry of Justice.

During the registration procedure, the company has a limited legal capacity – i.e. only for registration purposes.

After incorporation, the company needs a bank account at a commercial bank and a stamp with company and indenture number as stated in the commercial register. Furthermore, it is necessary to register all employees at the responsible agency.

Formation from Abroad

Neither the shareholders, the legal agent, nor the director of the company need to be in Romania at the time of the company formation. The formation is normally supervised by a lawyer. Only specific documents (declaration by the shareholders/directors, decision for the formation of the company, etc.) have to be drawn personally by the shareholders/directors before a notary and/or a lawyer. Documents that are certified by a foreign notary also need to be signed by the certified foreign Romanian representation agency to be accepted in Romania. Exceptions are for countries with which Romania has agreements concerning certificates.

Duration of Incorporation Process

The incorporation procedure takes between 3 and 5 days from the day when the relevant file is submitted to the commercial registry (Art. 8 Para. 3 LSF). However, the usual duration of the registration process can take up to 7 days from the date of the submission. If the company name includes "Roman" or a name of an institution, the process takes longer and special previous authorizations must be obtained. Opening a bank account and creating a stamp takes an additional week. After these processes are finished, the company can start operations.

Costs of Incorporation Process

Apart from lawyer fees, other costs incur during the act of formation. The commercial registration, including the creation of various certificates, publication in the MOF, etc. costs at least EUR 100. The costs for the notary who certifies various translations, authorizations, declarations, etc. add up to about EUR 200. The translation costs are independent from the amount of the text. A capital tax like taxation of equity will not be charged.

9.2.1.3 Requirements for Associates/Shareholders and Regulations Concerning Shareholders' Meetings

The company can be founded by one or more persons. Shareholder of a company can be a domestic or foreign natural or a legal person. The number of shareholders in an SRL is restricted to a maximum of 50 people.

In the case of a one-man company, the sole shareholder cannot be the sole shareholder of another Romanian company. Furthermore, a German person for example, who has a one-man company, cannot be the sole shareholder of another Romanian one-man company (Art. 14 LSC).

Usually, an SRL with a sole shareholder is used as an investment tool when the investors need to launch an SPV (special purposes vehicle) for various preliminary investments purposes (e.g. for buying estate that cannot be directly acquired by foreign legal entities).

There are two types of shareholder meetings – the ordinary meeting of shareholders, which is convened at least once a year within 5 months of the end of the financial year, and the extraordinary meeting of shareholders, which may take place at any time to decide upon a limited list of issues falling in its competencies (Arts. 110 and 113 LSC). The two types of general meetings have different quorum requirements and the competencies of the extraordinary general meeting cannot be exercised by the ordinary general meeting.

The ordinary general meeting is convened to

- discuss, approve or amend the annual balance sheets after listening to the directors' and administrator's report and to determine the dividends,
- to appoint and to revoke the directors and the administrators,
- to appoint and to revoke the financial auditors and to establish the minimum duration of the audit contracts (for companies obligated to have external auditors),
- to establish the proper remuneration for the directors and administrators for the current financial year, unless it was settled by the articles of association,
- to give their opinion on the directors' management of the budget,
- to determine the income and expenditure budget and the activity program for the next financial year as the case may be,
- to decide upon the pledging, renting or dissolving of one or several of the company's units.

The extraordinary general meeting gathers whenever it is necessary to make a decision, for example

- changing the legal form of the company,
- changing the location of the registered office of the company,
- changing the object of activity of the company,
- establishment or dissolution of branches, agencies, representations,
- extending the company's life,
- increasing the registered share capital,
- decreasing the registered capital or its completion by means of issuing new shares,
- merging with other companies or its spin-off,
- early dissolution of the company,
- conversion of the nominative shares into bearer's shares or of bearer's shares into nominative shares,
- conversion of shares from one category into another;
- conversion of one category of bonds into another or into shares;
- issuance of bonds;
- any other modification of the articles of association or any other decision for which the approval of an extraordinary general meeting is requested.

Additional competencies may be stipulated in the articles of association. If the agenda comprises a decision for the amendment of the articles of association, the consent of the entire share capital is necessary, unless the articles of association provide otherwise.

9.2.1.4 Articles of Association

The memorandum of association has to include the following points:

- Shareholder information (family name, forename, social security number (cod numeric personal)), place and date of birth, residence and citizenship of the shareholder, if he is a natural person. If the shareholder is a legal person, the company, headquarter, residence country of the legal person, and entry number at the responsible commercial register have to be declared.
- Legal form, commercial name, headquarter and if available, company logo
- Business purpose of the company with description of the main operational area and the main operations
- The subscribed and deposited registered capital, the number and the nominal value of each share, and also the number of shares held by each shareholder
- Director: Shareholders as well as non-shareholders (externally hired managers) can be announced as director of the company. Competencies and power of agency need to be included in the articles of association. Therefore, the articles of association can state if it is an overall or individual power of agency.

- Share of the shareholders in profits and losses: The exact percentage of share for every single shareholder in the balance sheet profit and loss statement has to be explicitly stated at the articles of association.
- Branches: Further branches or branch offices, factories, agencies and other institutions without own entity. These branches can be started directly with the formation of the company. In this case, they have to be included directly into the act of foundation. If they are included at a later stage, the conditions for branches need to be stated in the articles of association.
- Duration of the company: The duration, for which the company is founded, has to be included into the articles of association. Normally, articles of association are written for an indefinite time.
- Closing/liquidation of the company: The articles of association also have to include a statement about the form of closing and liquidation of the company. A statement about the legal regulations is sufficient.

Business Purpose

According to Romanian law, companies are only allowed to carry out activities that are in line with the business purpose, as stated in the commercial register. The act of foundation has to cite the exact business purpose. The possible operations of Romanian companies are – as in all other Eastern European countries – catalogued. The codes of the National Romanian Bureau of Statistics (CAEN – Codes) have to be used to define the business purpose. It is recommended that the business purpose covers a wide range so there would be no need to change the articles of association in case of an expansion.

Capital Stock

The subscribed and paid capital stock has to be cited with the indication of each shareholder's deposit together with a statement indicating the contribution in cash and/or in kind. If they are tangible assets, the value of the deposit as well as the method of valuation has to be specified. The date of the complete payment must also be cited. The articles of association have to cover the total number of shares, the nominal value of every single share as well as the every single shareholder's number of shares.

Relationship Between the Company and Its Shareholders

Mutual rights and duties between the company and shareholders, which are not already mentioned in the LSC or other related laws, can be mentioned in the articles of association due to the principle of freedom of contract, but have to be within the legal framework. If the articles of association do not contain the demanded information or the clauses of the articles of association are illegal or a legal requirement for the registration of the company is not fulfilled, the commercial register can deny registration if the error is not corrected (Art. 46 LSC).

According to Art. 56 LSC, the registration of the company at the commercial register can be revoked by the responsible tribunal if

- the articles of association are missing or drawn up in the required form;
- the business purpose is illegal or is against public policy;
- all founders were legally incapable at the time when the company was set up;
- there is no decision from the commercial register with regard to the legal capacity concerning the registration of the company;
- important data about the company, address, business purpose, capital stock of the shareholders and subscribed and paid capital stock are missing in the articles of association;
- a previous approval of a public agency is missing;
- the rules about the minimum capital stock are not met; or
- the minimum number of associates provided by the law was not observed.

Facultative Content of the Articles of Association

The facultative parts of the articles of association apply, on the one hand, to the anticipated regulations of the LSC and on the other hand, to regulations which are not mentioned in the LSC, but are allowed, due to the freedom of contract principle still being within the legal framework. An example would be a pre-emption of a shareholder if another shareholder wants to sell his shares of the company to a third party.

Parts of the anticipated regulations can be changed by the shareholders according to the LSC framework, although the law states these regulations differently. But in this context, Art. 192 LSC states that this is only possible with the absolute majority at the general meeting.

Rules about the rights for the general meeting (adunarea generală) are also part of the anticipated regulations and can be expanded by the shareholders during the articles of association according to Art. 194 LSC.

Parts of the anticipated regulations are also rules that demand the arrangement of legal institutions or other specific rights or duties. An example would be the facultative appointment of administrators/Art. 199 LSC), with the observation of the limits provided by law.

Language of the Articles of Association

For registration in the commercial register, the articles of association as well as all other documents that have to be handed in must be in Romanian language. The commercial register takes multilingual versions.

Closing of the Act of Foundation

Shareholders can be substituted at the closing of the articles of association. If a company is founded by an agent, a confirmation of the founder and a special notary authorization is needed. With this template, most of the legal acts can be made under the name and on account of the founder.

9.2.1.5 Minimum Contribution/Initial Capital

According to Art. 11 LSC, the minimum share capital is RON 200 (approximately 50 Euros) and is divided into social parts that cannot have a value less than RON 10. The founders are obliged to integrally pay the subscribed capital stock prior to incorporation. If a director starts working on behalf of the founded company before the registered capital is paid in full, he is liable to be punished with imprisonment (Art. 275 Para. 1 LSC).

Company Share

The equity of a company is divided into several company shares of equal nominal value, not less than RON 10 each (Art. 11 Para. 1 LSC). Company shares cannot be issued in the form of transferable shares (Art. 11 Para. 2 LSC). The articles of association have to include descriptions about the number of shares and their distribution among the particular shareholders. The number of shares is equal to the investment of the shareholders on the equity, as the distribution happens only in exchange for adopted equity. The voting rights, dividend as well as shares on distributed liquidity excess, will be assigned pro-rata on the basis of the size of capital invested (meaning the number of shares) to each shareholder.

9.2.1.6 Commercial Register

A registration certificate (certificat de inregistrare) proves the existence of the company. Every partnership needs to register at the commercial register. The registration is a prerequisite for the formation of the company. Access to the central commercial register is possible via internet (www.onrc.ro).

During a company's operations, some entries must be registered with the commercial register for third parties' information:

- donation, sale, tenancy or trading mortgage funds, as well as any other deeds certifying changes concerning incorporations or providing company or goodwill cessation;
- personal data of the person with power of agency, if the power of agency is limited to a certain branch, the mention will be made only with the register where the branch is registered;
- patents, trade and service marks, brand names, origin names, information regarding the origin, name of the company, emblem or other distinctive signs upon which a company has any rights to;
- opening the proceedings of judicial reorganization or bankruptcy as well as the registering of the respective mentions;

- conviction sentence of the administrator for penal deeds, which make him unworthy to perform this profession; or
- any alteration regarding the registered documents, deeds and mentions.

9.2.1.7 Regulations Concerning Corporate Name

An aspect to be carefully considered prior to incorporation of a company is the legal aspects of the company name.

The company of an SRL needs to possess the trade name as well as the words "societate cu răspundere limitată" or "SRL" according to Art. 36 LRC. The firm has to differentiate from other firms to avoid confusion or disorder with already existing companies. The name of any SRL must be personalized and may contain the name of one or more shareholders.

In any case, insertion of the words scientific ("stiintific"), academy ("academie"), academic ("academic"), university ("universitate" or "universitar"), school ("scoala"), educational ("scolar") or their derivates are forbidden; while insertion of the words national ("national"), Romanian ("roman"), institute ("institut") or derivates to central authorities or institutions is allowed only upon the agreement of the General Secretary of the Government (Secretariatul General al Guvernului) (Art. 39 Para. 2 LRC).

For names containing words of local authorities or institutions, the agreement of the prefect where the company has its residence is required.

9.2.1.8 Transfer of Shares/Regulations in the Case of Death of a Shareholder

a. Conditions

According to Art. 202 LSC, shares can be traded via legal transactions. As the SRL has a restricted number of shareholders, transfer of SRL shares is more restricted than the transfer of SA shares. Shares can be transferred either (1) to another shareholder, (2) to a third party via legal transaction as well as to (3) legitimate or testamentary inheritors.

For the transaction, a contract in terms of a private certificate is necessary. As a transaction of shares changes the articles of association concerning the shareholder structure, an adjustment in the articles of association is also necessary. The new shareholder has to declare that he fulfils the conditions for being a shareholder. The transaction has to be recorded in the internal shareholder booklet and the commercial register (Art. 203 Para. 1 LSC). For third parties, the transaction is only valid after being recorded in the commercial register (Art. 203 Para. 2 LSC).

b. Constraints

The law has no constraints concerning the transfer. The shareholders can state in the articles of association that existing shareholders have an option to buy a share if another shareholder wants to sell his share.

c. Need for approval

The transfer of shares between shareholders needs no approval by the general meeting as it does not change the character of the company. For the other cases, an approval of the shareholders owning three-fourths of the capital stock together is necessary (Art. 202 Para. 2 LSC). The prevailing opinion states that the three-fourths should not include the capital of the shareholder doing the transfer, as this would be acting in his own interest. If the shareholder receives no approval, he can find a new buyer, stay in the company or leave the company with court approval.

Shares of the company are hereditary. If the shares were gained through inheritance, the other shareholders have no right for approval concerning the person who gained the shares. However, a demand for approval can be stated in the articles of association. If the articles of association provide that the company shall not continue with the inheritors as shareholders or that the approval of the associates is necessary, and this is not obtained, the company is committed to pay the inheritors the value of their shares according to the latest approved annual financial statement (Art. 202 Para. 3 LSC).

If the number of shareholders exceeds the legally stated maximum of 50 shareholders due to the added number of inheritors, the inheritors have to announce a number of owners in trust (titulari) to keep the legally acceptable number of shareholders (Art. 202 Para. 4 LSC).

9.2.1.9 Liability of Shareholders and Directors

The founders and the shareholders are not generally liable for liabilities of the company. The founders have an explicit standardized accountability concerning the legal acts of the company prior to registration as long as they have not been taken over by the company.

False Information

For the following damages, the shareholders, the representatives of the company and the first directors are jointly and severally liable without restriction (Arts. 46 and 47 LSC):

- the formation process did not include the legally arranged declarations or
- includes clauses which violate legal regulations or
- does not comply with legal regulations concerning its formation or
- the shareholders did not apply for a record in the commercial register within the time limit (within 15 days after signing the act of foundation) or
- irregularities in the formation process, which were not corrected within 8 days after detection.

A shareholder incurs a penalty if he announces in a dishonest manner false data about the formation of the company or about the economic situation of the company in advertisements, public reports or through statements. He also incurs a penalty if he partly or totally conceals important information by presenting false balance sheets or data about the real economic situation of the company to other shareholders.

Exclusion of a Shareholder

Art. 222 LSC states that a shareholder is excluded from a company if he, after adequate requests of the other shareholders, does not pay his invested capital or at the same time, when he is director, deceives the company or misuses the company or the equity of the company in his own interest or for a third party.

Bankruptcy

The shareholders are liable in the case of company bankruptcy only with their invested capital. According to Art. 138, law on insolvency procedures (Legea privind procedura insolventei nr. 85/2006-LF), members of the executive bodies (managing directors, directors, censors, etc.) are personally liable if the bankruptcy of the company can be traced back to the following events:

- They used commodities or the creditworthiness of the company for their own interest or for the interest of third parties
- They had operational activity in their own interest under the disguise of the company
- They continued with their own operations, which lead to bankruptcy of the company although they knew about the consequences
- They kept fake accounts, hid accounting documents or did not keep the accounts according to law
- They defrauded, disclosed or notionally increased assets of the company
- They collected money in an uneconomical manner for the company to delay the point of bankruptcy
- They paid some creditors 1 month before announcing bankruptcy, which brings disadvantages for other creditors.

Directors incur a penalty if they do not announce bankruptcy within 30 days after insolvency or over indebtedness is known (Art. 143 LF). Furthermore, directors can personally incur a penalty due to dishonest administration, etc.

9.2.1.10 Applicable Accounting Standards

According to Article 5 of the Romanian accounting law, every company is required to adhere to double-entry bookkeeping. It has to create an annual balance sheet and maintain an annual inventory. The company has to keep an account in the Romanian language and currency (RON) (Art. 3 LC). The accounting of the activities done in a foreign currency has to be redone in both the Romanian and the foreign currencies. For internal use, the company can keep an account in a foreign currency or can follow another accounting standard (for example, US-GAAP). Beginning January 1, 2006, Romanian companies and foreign entities doing business in Romania through permanent establishments must apply the newly issued accounting regulations depending on the nature of their business. Trading companies apply the accounting regulations compliant with Fourth and Seventh European Directives, approved by the Order of Ministry of Public Finance of Romania no. 1752/2005 ("OMF 1752/2005"). Companies reaching a specific amount of annual sales, annual net turnover and number of employees in the previous year, are committed to report according to accounting rules based on the relevant EU regulations and the International Financial Reporting Standards (IFRS).

Companies not exceeding the mentioned limits can also make an application to adopt the IFRS standard. Annual balance sheets not committed to be reported after IFRS standards have to be checked by a certified public accountant (CPA).

The fiscal year is the same as the calendar year. The creation of reports for a differing fiscal year is only acceptable for branches of foreign companies, consolidated subsidiaries of the holding company and subsidiaries of the subsidiaries, effective January 1, 2007. Financial institutions, insurance companies and specific financial service companies are excluded from this liberalization (Art. 27 LC).

9.2.1.11 Disclosure Requirements

OMF 1752/2005 specifies companies that should prepare simplified financial statements and the companies that should prepare "complete" financial statements based on three size criteria:

- total assets – EUR 3,650,000
- annual net revenue – EUR 7,300,000, and
- average number of employees during the financial year – 50.

If a company exceeds the limits of two of the three criteria in two consecutive years at its balance sheet date, it must prepare a full set of financial statements comprising balance sheet, profit and loss account statements, statements on changes in equity, cash-flow statement and explanatory notes to the financial statements. Otherwise, it prepares simplified annual financial statements comprising a simplified balance sheet, profit and loss account statements, and explanatory notes to the financial statements. The company can also opt for preparing a statement on changes in equity and/or of cash-flow statement.

The annual balance sheet has to be approved by the general meeting. Within 15 days after the general meeting, copies of the approved annual balance sheet including a report of the director and if applicable, a report by the auditor or the CPA, as well as the decision at the general meeting have to be handed to the responsible tax authorities and deposited at the commercial register (Art. 185 Para. 1 LSC). Annual balance sheets of companies reported after IFRS have to be handed to the tax authorities within 150 days after the end of the fiscal year. Annual business sheets of companies that do not need to report after IFRS have to be handed to the tax authorities within 120 days after the end of the fiscal year (Art. 36 LC).

9.2.1.12 Employee Participation

Employer–employee relations are governed by the Labour Code (effective March 2003), other special laws and the National Collective Agreement. According to Art. 224 of the Romanian employment code, the employees of a company with more than 20 employees can elect an employee representative (reprezentanții salari- aților). The number of employee representatives will be arranged in consultation with the employer and has to be proportional to the number of employees (Art. 225 Par. 3 CM).

The main task of the employee representatives is the supervision of the compli-ance with the rights of the employees based on the valid legislation, the applicable collective bargaining contract, the individual contract of employment and inter-nal regulation. Furthermore, they elaborate internal regulations and foster interests of the employees concerning salaries, working conditions, hours of work and break periods. In addition, the employee representatives can file charges against the employers concerning non-compliance of legal regulations and the clauses of applicable collective bargaining contracts (Art. 226 CM). Employers are under an obligation to invite union representatives to board meetings. Resolutions carried out by the board of directors are required to be reported to the unions within 48 hours of being passed. Elected union representatives cannot be dismissed during their term of office and for a period of 2 years beyond the end of their term.

9.2.2 Joint Stock Company (Societate pe actiuni – SA)

9.2.2.1 Legal Capacity and Power of Disposition

Reference regarding legal capacity is made for the Limited liability company (see Sect. 9.2.1).

The company is administered by a sole director or by a board of directors, each appointed at the general meeting of shareholders. The number of the appointed directors must be an uneven number. The director or the board of directors has the power of disposition. The directors cannot be company employees at the same time, not even for superior executive positions.

Company law provides a specific legal status for the directors of an SA. Thus, the SA's shareholders may choose between two different administration systems: (i) unitary system or (ii) dualist system.

Under the unitary system, the management of the company is entrusted to a single corporate body – either a sole director or a board of directors (should the general meeting of shareholders appoint more than one director). The board of direc-tors (or the sole director) is entitled to take all necessary and appropriate actions towards performing the company's statutory objects, except for any actions specifically entrusted to the general meeting of shareholders. Companies required by law to undergo a financial audit are administered by at least three directors.

The board of directors may delegate the management of the company to one or more executive officers, appointed either from among the members of the board of directors or from outside the board of directors. The executive officers are entitled to take all necessary and appropriate actions regarding the company's management by observing the company's statutory objects and the exclusive competence of the general meeting of shareholders and/or the board of directors. Delegation of responsibilities is mandatory for companies required by law to undergo the financial audit.

Under the dualist system, the management of the company is entrusted exclusively to a directorate ("directorat"), comprising an odd number of directors with the competence to take all necessary and appropriate actions towards performing the company's statutory duties, by observing the exclusive competence of the general meeting of shareholders and/or the supervisory board. In companies that are, by law, required to undergo financial audit, the directorate must comprise at least three directors.

The supervisory board ("consiliu de superaveghere") is entitled only to supervise and control the activity of the directorate. The members of the supervisory board are appointed by the general meeting of shareholders. The members of the directorate are appointed by the supervisory board from persons outside the supervisory board. The number of the members of the supervisory board must be between 3 and 11.

9.2.2.2 Process and Requirements for Incorporation

The registration procedure for a joint stock company is very similar to the one of limited liability company, but differs mainly in the following things:

As a rule, the subscribed capital must be paid upon submission of the incorporation documents. However, in the case of an SA, the shareholders are only obliged to pay at least 30 percent of the subscribed capital upon submission of the incorporation documents. The balance of 70 percent of the subscribed capital must be paid within 12 months of the incorporation of joint stock companies if shares are issued in exchange for cash contributions or within 2 years of the incorporation of joint stock companies if shares are issued in exchange for in-kind contributions.

9.2.2.3 Requirements for Associates/Shareholders and Regulations Concerning Shareholders' Meetings

For the formation of an SA, at least two persons are needed.

The general meeting is the highest body of the SA. It is very similar to the one of the SRL. Additionally, it has to take place after at least 30 days from the convening. The shareholders have to represent at least one-fourth of the subscribed capital. The decisions need the approval of a majority; the articles of association can, however, stipulate the number of votes that are necessary for approval of a decision.

Regulations for attendance of shareholders and vote proportion at an extraordinary general meeting include the following:

- At the first meeting, at least one-fourth of the votes have to attend personally or be represented.
- At the next meetings at least one-fifth of the votes have to attend.
- Exception: decisions about changes of the business purpose, lowering or increasing the subscribed capital, change of legal form, fusion/split/closure need two-thirds of the attended or represented votes.

One or more shareholders who individually or jointly own at least 5 percent of the subscribed capital have the right to post new points on the agenda.

9.2.2.4 Articles of Association

The memorandum of association has to include the following points:

1. if they are natural persons, name and first name, social security number, place and date of birth, addresses and citizenship of the associates; if they are legal persons, the name, the registered office and the nationality of the associates, the registration number in the trade register or the sole registration code according to the national law; in case of a limited partnership by shares, the active partners and the sleeping partners are to be clearly identified;
2. the form, name, the registered office and the logo of the company, if necessary;
3. the company's operational objective, specifying the field of action and its main activity;
4. the subscribed and deposited registered capital. At the time of set-up the subscribed registered capital deposited by each shareholder should be no less than 30 percent of the subscribed capital, except where the law provides otherwise. The remaining of the registered capital is to be deposited within 12 months from the date of the company's incorporation;
5. the value of the assets brought as contribution in kind, the method of evaluation, and the number of shares attributed against them;
6. the number and nominal value of the shares, specifying whether they are registered or on bearer; where there are different categories of shares, the number, nominal value and the rights conferred to each category are to be specified;
7. if they are natural persons, the name and first name, place and date of birth, the address and citizenship of the managers; if they are legal persons, the name, the headquarters and nationality of the managers; the guarantee which the managers are bound to deposit, the powers vested in them and whether they are to act together or separately; the special rights of administration and representation granted to some of them. In a limited partnership by shares, the active partners who represent and manage the company shall be identified;

8. if they are natural persons, the name and first name, the place and date of birth, the address and citizenship of the auditors; if they are legal persons, the name, headquarters and nationality of auditors;

9. clauses regarding the management, functioning and control of administration of the company by the statutory bodies, the controlling of the company by the shareholders as well as the documents to which these shall have access in order to inform themselves and to exert control;

10. duration of the company;

11. method of profit distribution and loss bearing;

12. location of its subsidiaries – branches, agencies, representations or other offices of the same kind without legal personality – when they and the company are set up at the same time, or the conditions to set them up at a later date if such a setting up is considered;

13. special benefits reserved for the founders;

14. the shares for the "sleeping" (silent) partners in a limited partnership by shares;

15. operations concluded by associates on behalf of the company to be set up and which the company is going to take over, as well as the sums of money to be paid for those operations;

16. method of dissolution or liquidation of the company.

9.2.2.5 Minimum Contribution/Initial Capital

An SA-type company must have a minimum share capital of RON 90,000 in cash or in-kind contributions. The Romanian Government may amend the above minimum value of the SA's share capital, not more frequently than once every 2 years, in order to maintain the minimum value of the share capital close to the equivalent of EUR 25,000.

SA capital of an SA is divided into shares; the nominal value of a share must be at least RON 0.1. Shares can either be nominative or bearer shares, as established in the company's constitutive documents. However, shares that are not fully paid up can only be nominative shares.

In general, shares must have equal value and grant equal rights to the shareholders. Corporate law, however, lists the conditions under which preferential shares can be issued (such shares may be issued only in case of a company organized as an SA). Such shares give their holders the right to a preferential dividend and all the other rights granted to the ordinary shareholders (including the right to attend the general meeting of shareholders), but they do not confer any voting rights. However, the holders of the preferential shares acquire voting rights corresponding to the relevant shares in case of (i) the late payment of the dividends, starting with the due payment date of the dividends and (ii) the general meeting of shareholders deciding on non-distribution of the dividends, starting with the publication of the relevant resolution of the general meeting of shareholders, until the effective payment of the dividends.

9.2.2.6 Commercial Register

Reference is made to this for the Limited liability company (see Sect. 9.2.1).

9.2.2.7 Regulations Concerning Corporate Name

The SA has the same name requirements as an SRL. In addition to the trade name, the words "Societate pe actiuni" or "SA" have to be used.

9.2.2.8 Transfer of Shares/Regulations in the Case of Death of a Shareholder

According to Art. 202 LSC, shares can be traded via legal transactions. The transfer of shares is not as restricted as the transfer of shares of an SRL. Shares can be transferred to (1) another shareholder, (2) a third party via legal transaction or (3) legitimate or testamentary inheritors.

The property right over registered shares issued in a material form shall be transferred by the statement made in the shareholders' register and by the mention made on the share, signed by the assignor and the assignee or by their proxies. The property right over registered shares issued in a dematerialized form shall be transferred by the statement made in the shareholders' register, signed by the assignor and the assignee or by their representatives. Other modalities to transfer the property right over registered shares can also be prescribed by the constitutive act.

The property right over the shares issued in a dematerialized form and transacted on the stock market shall be transferred according to Law No. 297/2004.

The subsequent subscribers and assignees shall be jointly liable for the complete payment of the shares for 3 years, starting on the date the assignment mention was made in the register of shareholders.

The property right over the bearer shares shall be transferred by simple assignment.

For the first time in the Romanian law, tender offers of listed companies are extensively regulated. It distinguishes between voluntary take-over bids and (forced) obligatory take-over bids. A voluntary take-over bid is a public offer for the acquisition of at least 33 percent of a listed company's shares. If a natural or legal person owns more than 33 percent of shares, a public offer for the other shares is necessary – an obligatory take-over bid.

Squeeze Out

The regulation of a "squeeze out" is only briefly described in the Romanian law. A shareholder, who owns more than 95 percent of the shares of a company or has purchased at least 90 percent of the existing shares in a public offer procedure, can request other shareholders to sell their shares for a fair price. The exact proceedings as well as precise regulations concerning the "squeeze out" are stated in an embodiment of the law.

Constraints

The law has no constraints concerning the transfer. The shareholders can state in the articles of association that existing shareholders have an option to buy a share if another shareholder wants to sell his share.

Shares of the company are hereditary. If the shares were gained through inheritance, the other shareholders have no right for approval, concerning the person who gained the shares. However, in the articles of association, the founders can include different restraints regarding the transfer of the shares.

9.2.2.9 Liability of Shareholders and Directors

The shareholders are liable in if the company goes bankrupt only with their invested capital. There is no call for additional coverage.

9.2.2.10 Applicable Accounting Standards

It is necessary for an SA to build an auditors' commission with three members and one or more deputies, but the number must be established in such a way that the number of the auditors is always uneven. One of the auditors needs to be an accounting expert ("expert contabil") or accredited in Romania. The main task of the auditors' commission is monthly cash auditing, participation in the general meeting and supervision of the management as well as auditing of the balance sheet, profit and loss calculations, and constructing the audit report. There is no need for auditors if the company is using the IFRS standard and/or employs a CPA or uses the duplicating system.

9.2.2.11 Disclosure Requirements

Corresponding to the SRL, the SA uses the three-size criteria. If two criteria are exceeded, the same duties as with the SRL apply. Additionally, the annual balance sheet has to be checked by the auditor's commission or a CPA. The audit report has to be presented to the shareholders and the Romanian Bond Commission (CNVM). If the CPA has the additional skill "CNCVM" (Authorization to prepare reports for the bond commission), the appointment of one CPA for both reports is sufficient.

9.2.2.12 Employee Participation

Employees working at an SA have at least the same rights as their colleagues at an SRL.

9.2.3 General Partnership (Societate in nume colectiv – SNC)

9.2.3.1 Legal Capacity and Power of Disposition

The SNC is its own entity and receives legal capacity by memorandum of association between two or more natural or legal persons. One or more directors can have the power of agency, whereas the directors do not have to be shareholders.

9.2.3.2 Process and Requirements for Incorporation

The articles of association will be concluded between the shareholders and the company. Afterwards, the company needs to be registered in the commercial register. The steps for the registration are the same for nearly all legal forms. With this step, the company gains its own entity.

9.2.3.3 Requirements for Associates/Shareholders and Regulations Concerning Shareholders' Meetings

The SNC consists of two or more partners, who can be natural or legal persons. To make decisions, such as electing the directors, establishing their powers, duration of their term of office, and remuneration, an absolute shareholder majority is necessary. However, if the directors were appointed through the memorandum of association, the decision to revoke them must be unanimous.

9.2.3.4 Articles of Association

For the foundation, articles of association are necessary.

9.2.3.5 Minimum Contribution

Romanian law does not set a minimum or maximum limit for capital and does not define a mandatory amount for cash or other assets. The capital stock has to consist of cash or tangible assets.

9.2.3.6 Commercial Register

Reference is made to this for the Limited liability company (see Sect. 9.2.1).

9.2.3.7 Regulations Concerning Corporate Name

The company name needs to contain the name of one individual partner and the nature of the partnership. Furthermore, the SNC has the same requirements as an SRL. In addition to the trade name, the words "Societate in nume colectiv" or "SNC" have to be used.

9.2.3.8 Transfer of Shares/Regulations in the Case of Death of a Shareholder

The transfer of the contribution made to the constitutive capital is possible as long as it is allowed by the provisions in the articles of association. However, the transfer of shares does not liberate the assigning associate from the part he owes the company out of his contribution to the capital.

9.2.3.9 Liability of Shareholders and Directors

The owners of a partnership have unlimited and joint personal liability. They can be made responsible with their personal property for all company debts and commitments. The assigning associate shall be held liable against third parties until the day the transfer or the shares or the expulsion or withdrawal decision is definitive.

9.2.3.10 Applicable Accounting Standards

All companies must have their own accounting and reporting procedure and must comply with statutory requirements in the Romanian legislation for book and record keeping. For further information, see Sect. 9.2.1.10, the section on accounting standards applicable for an SRL.

9.2.3.11 Disclosure Requirements

Reference is made to this for the Limited liability company (see Sect. 9.2.1).

9.2.3.12 Employee Participation

Employees working at an SNC have at least the same rights as their colleagues at an SRL.

9.2.4 Limited Partnership (Societate in comandita simpla – SCS)

9.2.4.1 Legal Capacity and Power of Disposition

The SCS has its own entity, but is a legal form that is very rare in practice. It has characteristics of both an SRL and an SA. The SCS gets legal capacity by memorandum of association between at least one general partner and one limited partner and therefore, is its own entity. One or more directors can have the power of disposition and must be necessarily appointed by the company's general partners.

9.2.4.2 Process and Requirements for Incorporation

The company will be founded by one or more shareholders with unlimited liability (general partner) and by one or more shareholders with limited liability (limited partner). The articles of association will be concluded between the shareholders.

Afterwards, the company needs to be registered in the commercial register. The steps for the registration are the same for nearly all legal forms. With this step, the company gains its own entity.

9.2.4.3 Requirements for Associates/Shareholders and Regulations Concerning Shareholders' Meetings

The management tasks have to be executed by the general partners. Company Law no. 31/1990 generally sets out the rights, powers and obligations of limited partners. For example, a limited partner may be held liable as a general partner if the limited partnership legislation is not strictly complied with when a limited partner participates in the management of the partnership's business without having been mandated to that effect by the company's representatives, by means of a special power-of-attorney, registered with the trade register, or allows his or her name to be used in the name of the limited partnership.

9.2.4.4 Articles of Association

No information available.

9.2.4.5 Minimum Contribution/Initial Capital

There is no minimum contribution for this legal form. Deposits can be made as money deposits or tangible assets.

9.2.4.6 Commercial Register

Reference is made to this for the Limited liability company (see Sect. 9.2.1).

9.2.4.7 Regulations Concerning Corporate Name

The company name needs to contain the name of the general partners. Furthermore, an SCS has the same requirements as an SRL. In addition to the trade name, the words "Societate in comandita simpla" or "SCS" have to be used.

9.2.4.8 Transfer of Shares/Regulations in the Case of Death of a Shareholder

Reference is made to this for the General partnership (see Sect. 9.2.3).

9.2.4.9 Liability of Shareholders and Directors

The general partners have unlimited and joint personal liability, unlike the limited partners, who only have a liability of their deposit.

9.2.4.10 Applicable Accounting Standards

All companies must have their own accounting and reporting procedure and must comply with statutory requirements in the Romanian legislation for book and record keeping. For further information, see the chapter on SRL.

9.2.4.11 Disclosure Requirements

Reference is made to this for the Limited liability company (see Sect. 9.2.1).

9.2.4.12 Employee Participation

Employees working at an SCS have at least the same rights as their colleagues at an SRL.

9.2.5 Limited Partnership on Shares (Societate in comandita pe actiuni – SCA)

9.2.5.1 Legal Capacity and Power of Disposition

The SCA has its own entity, but is a legal form that is also very rare in practice. It has characteristics of both SRL and SA. The SCA receives legal capacity by memorandum of association between at least one general partner and one limited partner and therefore, its own entity. One or more directors, appointed from the general partners, can have the power of disposition.

9.2.5.2 Process and Requirements for Incorporation

Like the SCS, the SCA gets legal capacity by memorandum of association between at least one general partner and one limited partner and therefore, its own entity. The main difference is that the capital stock of the SCA is divided into shares. To found an SCA, at least two shareholders are necessary.

9.2.5.3 Requirements for Associates/Shareholders and Regulations Concerning Shareholders' Meetings

Articles of association will be concluded between the shareholders and a memorandum of association will be written. Afterwards, the company needs to be registered in the commercial register. The steps for the registration are the same for nearly all legal forms. With this step, the company gains own entity.

9.2.5.4 Articles of Association

Reference is made to this for the Joint stock company (see Sect. 9.2.2).

9.2.5.5 Minimum Contribution/Initial Capital

An SCA company must have a minimum share capital of RON 90,000, in cash or in-kind contributions. The Romanian government may amend the above minimum value of the SCA's share capital, not more frequently than once every 2 years, in order to maintain the minimum value of the share capital close to the equivalent of EUR 25,000.

Under certain conditions, a limited liability company may be set up by a sole shareholder. The capital stock is divided into shares (unlike the SCS). The shares have registered value of no less than RON 0.1.

9.2.5.6 Commercial Register

Reference is made to this for the Limited liability company (see Sect. 9.2.1).

9.2.5.7 Regulations Concerning Corporate Name

The company name needs to contain the name of the general partners. Furthermore, the SCA has the same requirements as an SRL. In addition to the trade name, the words "Societate in comandita pe actiuni" or "SCA" have to be used.

9.2.5.8 Transfer of Shares/Regulations in the Case of Death of a Shareholder

Reference is made to this for the Joint stock company (see Sect. 9.2.2).

9.2.5.9 Liability of Shareholders and Directors

The general partners have unlimited and joint personal liability, unlike the limited partners, who only have a liability of their deposit.

9.2.5.10 Applicable Accounting Standards

All companies must have their own accounting and reporting procedure and must comply with statutory requirements in the Romanian legislation for book and record keeping. For further information, see the chapter on SRL.

9.2.5.11 Disclosure Requirements

Reference is made to this for the Limited liability company (see Sect. 9.2.1).

9.2.5.12 Employee Participation

Employees working at an SCA have at least the same rights as their colleagues at the SRL.

9.3 Summary

9.3.1 Advantages and Disadvantages of Different Legal Forms

9.3.1.1 Limited Liability Company – SRL

Advantages

The paid subscribed capital can work for the company directly from the start. The SRL is the most common of the Romanian legal forms; it is highly accepted in Romania and abroad. The set-up process is fast and cheap, the liability is limited and the minimum capital is only RON 200. For the formation, only one person is required. An SRL has flexible articles of memorandum and can be easily formed from another country.

Disadvantages

Not more than 50 shareholders are allowed. The transfer of shares is not easy.

9.3.1.2 Joint Stock Company – SA

Advantages

The joint stock company allows more than 50 shareholders and can be traded on a stock exchange market. This brings good access to capital markets. The structure allows shares to be traded easily.

Disadvantages

The minimum contribution of RON 90,000 ($\sim$ EUR 25,000) is quite high compared to other legal forms, making it unattractive for start-ups. Furthermore, banks and insurance companies have no choice other than to choose an SA as their legal form. The SA requires higher bureaucratic effort then other legal forms.

9.3.1.3 General Partnership – SNC

The main advantage is the lack of minimum contribution required.

9.3.1.4 Limited Partnership – SCS

Advantages

The main advantage is the lack of minimum contribution required. In Romania, the SCS is seen as a partnership, but in Germany the SCS is classified as a capital company. In some cases, this can lead to tax savings if the parent company has its headquarters in Germany and founds an SCS in Romania. Limited partners have no risk except losing their deposit.

Disadvantages

Only general partners have rights, can manage the company and make decisions regarding the internal affairs of the company. Furthermore, general partners have unlimited and joint personal liability. The company name has to include the name of one shareholder and the nature of the partnership.

9.3.1.5 Limited Partnership on Shares – SCA

Advantages

Shares make it easier to segment the shareholders. Limited partners have no risk except losing their deposit. The general partners are the only ones that can be elected as directors of the company and adopt decisions regarding the internal affairs of the company, making processes easier and more flexible than in an SA.

Disadvantages

The minimum contribution of RON 90,000 (~EUR 25,000) is quite high compared to other legal forms, making it unattractive for start-ups. Furthermore, general partners have unlimited and joint personal liability. The company name has to include the name of one shareholder.

9.3.2 Recommendations Depending on the Individual Case

Apart from the purpose of the business and the general circumstances of the formation, there are three important factors for the selection of a legal form:

- the minimum contribution
- the liability as a shareholder
- the complexity of incorporation.

Although Romania has many different legal forms, an SRL seems to be the most adequate for most of the companies. As all legal firms have legal entity and nearly the same incorporation process, a recommendation cannot be made on this point – apart from the SA, which has the most complex incorporation process and a very bureaucratic administration.

Looking at the minimum contribution, the SA is also not very favourable. Although there are forms that have no minimum contribution at all, the amount for the SRL is still not very high. If the shareholder liability is now taken into consideration, SRL stands out with the limited liability on the low deposit. In general, the formation of an SRL in Romania is recommended; still, the individual needs have to be analysed.

Bibliography

ONRC (2009) http://www.onrc.ro. Accessed 5 June 2009.
Carpenaru S (2007) Romanian commercial law, 7th edn. Universul Juridic, Bucarest
Carpenaru S et al (2006) Company law, comments, 3rd edn. C.H. Beck.

Chapter 10
Spain

Astrid Dorfmeister and Michael J. Munkert

Abstract In the chapter on Spain, the authors Astrid Dorfmeister and Michael J. Munkert start with a short introduction and overview on the contribution. They use the general analysis framework for the handbook on legal forms in Europe to analyse six relevant legal forms: the stock corporation (Sociedad Anónima – S.A.), the limited company (Sociedad Limitada – S.L.), the sole proprietorship (Trabajador Autónomo), the general partnership (Sociedad Colectiva – S.C.), the limited liability partnership (Sociedad comanditaria – S. Com.) and the branch office (Sucursal). In addition, they also provide an overview of some more legal forms in Spain.

The authors conclude their discussions with an evaluation of the advantages and disadvantages of the different legal forms.

Contents

A. Dorfmeister (✉)
Dr. Frühbeck, Abogados & Economistas y Cía. S.C., C/Balmes, 368, pr. 2ª,
08006 Barcelona, Spain
e-mail: barcelona@fruhbeck.com

M.J. Munkert et al. (eds.), *Founding a Company*,
DOI 10.1007/978-3-642-11259-1_10, © Springer-Verlag Berlin Heidelberg 2010

10.1 Introduction

Setting up a company in Spain can be a long and complicated task especially if the person intending to start a business is not familiar with the local legal system or with ways to confront the peculiar Spanish bureaucracy. The success of the whole business depends not only depend on internal factors such as the business concept or management, but also on external factors such as the legal system and, to a certain extent, the prevailing level of bureaucracy.

The high impact of these external factors makes it mandatory for the person or the company to understand the legal requirements associated with starting up and running a business in Spain. A special licence is needed for many businesses, and legal requirements may vary from one region to another. Therefore, it is generally advisable to seek some kind of professional legal and fiscal advice when setting up a business.

The following section outlines all relevant legal forms in Spain as a first step. Subsequently, the individual legal forms are characterized and described in greater detail. The last section summarizes the main findings and discusses the most significant advantages and disadvantages of most relevant legal forms.

10.2 Description of Relevant Legal Forms

There are several different legal forms to choose from when either an individual or a company aims at starting up a business in Spain. The most suitable legal form for any intended venture in Spain depends on the size of the company, the owners and a number of other factors that are elaborated in the sections to follow.

Today, the two most common legal forms in Spain are the Sociedad Limitada (S.L.), which is similar to a limited company in other countries, and the Sociedad Anónima (S.A.), which is the counterpart to a stock corporation in other countries. From a foreigner's perspective, who plans to establish a business in Spain, the S.L. and S.A. are also the most popular forms. Another popular option for foreign companies intending to operate in Spain is the opening of a branch office (Sucursal). Self-employed individuals can work as trabajadores autónomos in Spain, the legal form of sole proprietorship. Two types of partnerships, the general partnership, Sociedad Colectiva (S.C.), and the limited liability partnership, Sociedad Comanditaria (S.Com.), are occasionally chosen as a legal form to start up businesses.

A number of more rare legal forms such as the Sociedad Limitada Nueva Empresa (S.L.N.E.), the Comunidad de Bienes, the Sociedad Civil, the Sociedad Cooperativa and the Sociedad Laboral are also presented briefly.

The most relevant entitles of the legal forms mentioned above are subsequently analysed using the following 12 criteria:

- Legal capacity and right of disposition
- Process and requirements of incorporation/formulation

- Requirements for associates/shareholders and regulations concerning shareholders' meetings
- Articles/memorandum of association
- Minimum contribution/initial capital
- Commercial register
- Regulations concerning corporate name
- Transfer of shares/regulations in the case of shareholder death
- Liability of shareholders and directors
- Applicable accounting standards
- Disclosure requirements
- Employee participation.

The corresponding features of each of the relevant legal forms are then summarized. However, it has to be mentioned at this point that in many instances – especially in case of non-incorporated companies – the law provides only minimum standards or general rules. The founders of a company have a great deal of flexibility in tailoring the structure of the company to their specific needs through inclusion of certain clauses in the bylaws, for which purpose they should seek proper legal advice.

10.2.1 Stock Corporation (Sociedad Anónima, S.A.)

A Sociedad Anónima (abbreviated as S.A.) is a joint stock company, which is a type of business entity, i.e. a type of corporation or partnership. Thus, an S.A. represents the counterpart to the German Aktiengesellschaft (AG). Stock corporations issue certificates of ownership or stocks in return for each contribution. In most countries there are two different categories: private (i.e. unlisted) and public (i.e. listed) stock companies.

Traditionally, the Spanish corporation, S.A. has been the most commonly used form by far. However, the limited liability company (Sociedad Limitada, abbreviated as S.L.), which is analysed in detail in Sect. 10.2.2, has gained more and more popularity in recent years. The Spanish S.A. is regulated by the "Ley de Sociedades Anónimas (1989)" Law.

10.2.1.1 Legal Capacity and Power of Disposition

A Sociedad Anónima has the capacity to act as a legal entity. The S.A. is not incorporated and thereby, also has legal legitimacy before it is registered in the commercial register.

The S.A. can be represented by following bodies:

- Through a sole administrator
- Through two or more solely authorized administrators
- Through two or more jointly authorized administrators
- Through an administrative board.

Furthermore, it is possible to empower the chief executive officers, the department heads, other associates or third parties with or without restrictions.

10.2.1.2 Process and Requirements for Incorporation

According to Spanish law, only one shareholder is required to incorporate an S.A. The shareholders or their representatives must appear before a notary in order to execute the public deed of incorporation. It is also possible for the corporation to be incorporated by a third person through a certificate of authority. Thereafter, the public deed of incorporation has to be registered in the commercial register. The company ultimately acquires legal status and capacity after the completion of the registration.

In addition, there is an alternative way of incorporation named "successive formation". Basically, this procedure involves an offering to the public as a whole by the promoters to subscribe shares before the execution of the public deed of incorporation. For this purpose, means such as financial brokers or publicity may be used. However, this system is rarely used in practice.

Before the incorporation can take place, a certificate from the commercial register stating that another Spanish entity does not already use the company's favoured name is needed. This certificate must be verified and approved (certificación negativa) by the commercial register in Madrid. The application for this certificate from the Central Commercial Registry costs approximately EUR 13 and generally takes about 10 days. The notary's preparation of the deeds of incorporation and for all shareholders to sign it may take anywhere from 5 days to 1 week. This operation accrues the tax "Impuesto de Operaciones Societarias" with a tax rate equal to one percent of the company's capital. The incorporation tax (impuesto sobre Operaciones Societarias) must be paid within 30 working days. The registrar responsible for the registration of the deed in the commercial registry, which is due after the tax has been paid, has to qualify the deed and register it within a month. The corporation can transact business immediately after the memorandum of association has been granted.

As a general rule, it can be assumed that the whole process of incorporation takes between 6 and 8 weeks, although this period may be considerably longer if a Foreigners' Identity Number (NIE) needs be obtained for any of the foreign directors.

The following costs accrue before and during the incorporation:

- Incorporation tax amounting to one percent of the share capital.
- Fees of the notary public handling the incorporation. These fees vary from EUR 300 for a small company to EUR 2,000 for a large company.
- Fees for the registration of the company in the local commercial register and its incorporation in the presence of the notary. These fees vary from EUR 300 to EUR 1000.
- Opening licence tax; a one-time municipal levy, which constitutes a relatively small amount and which is not due in all cases.

10.2.1.3   Requirements for Associates/Shareholders and Regulations Concerning Shareholders' Meetings

As mentioned above, no minimum number of shareholders is required by Spanish law to incorporate an S.A., even though sole shareholder companies are subject to a special system of reporting, which is separately discussed at the end of this section. In general, shareholders can be individuals or companies of any nationality and residence.

The shareholders' meeting is one of the two governing bodies of an S.A. (the second are the directors who may or may not be organized as a board of directors). It is generally stated that the shareholders' meeting is the S.A.'s supreme governing body. The law distinguishes between two types of meetings: ordinary and extraordinary. Additionally, both ordinary and extraordinary meetings can be held as universal meetings, as discussed below.

An extraordinary shareholders' meeting may be held as such and when stipulated by the bylaws. An ordinary meeting, on the other hand, must be held within the first 6 months of the financial year to review management's conduct of the business and to approve or reject the financial statements of the prior year and the proposed distribution of the prior year's earnings.

Any meeting of the shareholders other than as described above is an extraordinary shareholders' meeting. An extraordinary shareholders' meeting can be either called by the company's directors if and when they consider it in the company's interests to do so or when they are requested to do so by shareholders representing at least five percent of shares. In addition, a court may call an extraordinary shareholders' meeting if the directors disregard the notification referred to above.

The formal requirements for calling a meeting, which relate to advance notice and public notification, are the same for ordinary and extraordinary meetings. Meetings must be called by a notice published in the Official Gazette of the Mercantile Register at least 15 days in advance of the meeting and in a high-circulation newspaper of the province in which the company has its registered offices.

Regardless of the type of shareholders' meeting (ordinary or extraordinary), the formal call requirements need not be followed if shareholders representing 100 percent of the capital stock are present and unanimously agree to hold a shareholders' meeting. These kinds of meetings are called "universal" shareholders' meetings.

Shareholder meetings may usually adopt resolutions by simple majority given the following quorum requirements are met:

At the first call, the quorum for a shareholders' meeting exists when the shareholders at the meeting own at least 25 percent of the voting capital stock. In case a second call needs to be made because there was no quorum at the first call, the meeting is considered to be legally convened regardless of the percentage of capital stock present at the meeting. In addition, bylaws may set special call and quorum requirements for shareholders' meetings. These special quorum requirements may, however, not be lower than the legal requirements outlined above.

By law, special quorums are required for the adoption of resolutions on certain matters such as a merger or dissolution of the company, capital increase or reduction, debenture issuance, any transformation and, in general, for the adoption of resolutions amending the bylaws. In such cases, the quorum requires different majorities that are not discussed further.

As mentioned earlier, sole shareholder companies are subject to a specific regime involving special reporting and registration requirements. For example, the fact that a company has a single owner needs to be acknowledged on all company correspondence and commercial documentation by adding an analogous name affix ("Sociedad Unipersonal"). Similarly, contracts between the company and its sole owner have to be recorded in a special commercial register. Overall, such requirements can be considered merely administrative and reporting requirements, but adherence to the specific rules is of high importance, because otherwise and/or under certain circumstances, the company can lose its limited liability status, making the shareholder personal and unlimited liable. Moreover, there are specific regulations for sole shareholder companies regarding shareholder meetings and legal transactions between the sole shareholder and the company. However, those peculiarities will not be discussed further.

10.2.1.4 Articles of Association

An S.A. is basically governed by its own bylaws and by corporate law. Therefore, the bylaws of an S.A. should be drafted in accordance with corporate law requirements, have to be notarized and must at least include reference to the following items:

- Name of the company.
- Business purpose. The purpose should be stated in a concrete and precise manner because:

  - it serves to establish the general framework for the activities of the company.
  - the completion of the stated business purpose automatically leads to dissolution of the company, unless an indefinite duration is defined in the bylaws.
  - in case the business purpose is modified in such a way as to be replaced, the dissenting shareholders and non-voting shareholders, if any, have the option to withdraw from the company and are eligible to be reimbursed for their shares.

- Duration of the company. The bylaws will generally determine that the duration is indefinite in order to avoid triggering an automatic dissolution.
- The date on which activities commence, which usually cannot be earlier than the date completing the public deed of incorporation.
- The location of the company's registered office, which must be in Spain, and the body competent to establish, transfer or close branches.
- Capital stock and shares.
- Managing body. The bylaws have to determine whether the administration is entrusted to a board of directors or to some other body or person. In the case of

collective management bodies, the manner of debate and of adopting resolutions must be specified, as also the system for directors' remuneration.

- Restrictions, if any, on the free transferability of shares.
- Ancillary obligations, if any. If ancillary obligations are created, the bylaws must state the content of such obligations, whether or not they are remunerated, and the penalties, if any, for breach thereof. Ancillary obligations are explained in further detail below.
- The accounting year-end. If not stated expressly, the company will be deemed to end its accounting year on December 31st. The business year may not exceed 12 months.
- Special rights reserved to founders or promoters, if any.

In conclusion, the subject of the corporation must be defined very precisely. Definitions that are too general in nature are not allowed. In addition, the public deed of incorporation, which includes the bylaws, may contain whatever agreements and covenants the founders consider to fit, given that they do not violate any law or the fundamental principles that govern S.A.s.

In the articles of association, the personal data from the shareholders must be recorded. These contain the following:

- First name, surname, date of birth, nationality, domicile,
- ID card or pass number, place of issue, date of issue,
- NIE number.

Mostly, the memorandum of associations is included into the incorporation deed because it is assumed that the constituent meeting of the founder members is held at the same time that the deed is signed.

10.2.1.5 Minimum Contribution/Initial Capital

According to corporate law, the minimum amount of capital stock required for an S.A. is EUR 60,102.21 (this amount refers to the Euro conversion). The capital must be fully subscribed and at least 25 percent of the par value of the shares must be paid in (EUR 15,025.30). The remaining 75 percent (EUR 45,075.91) needs to be paid within a maximum term of 5 years.

If the capital stock is not fully paid in, the bylaws must state the manner and time period for paying the remaining portion of subscribed capital. No maximum time period for payment of calls on capital by contributions in cash is stated in the law, but 5 years is the maximum time available for full payment of contributions in kind. The capital must be deposited before the incorporation. The Spanish bank will issue a certificate that forms part of the articles of association.

It is generally recommended that the company is sufficiently capitalized with respect to the potentially accruing costs because insufficient capitalization puts the shareholders at risk. They are made personally liable and may also lead to them being criminal liable.

In addition, specific regulations may provide that the capital stock of corporations active in certain fields of business (e.g. banking, insurance, etc.) must, at the time of incorporation, provide more capital than requested by the minimum amount stated in the corporate law.

10.2.1.6 Commercial Register

The stock company is registered in the commercial register in the province where its domicile is situated. The registration in the commercial register is one of the two steps necessary to incorporate an S.A., eventually enabling the company to obtain legal capacity and become a legal entity.

10.2.1.7 Regulations Concerning Corporate Name

The applicable law is the regulation of the commercial register. The name of the Spanish stock company is basically arbitrary, as long as it consists of Latin and Arabic letters or Roman numbers, followed by the abbreviation S.A. However, the registrar will refuse registration for similar or equal names.

In Spain, every company is not only registered in the appropriate local commercial register, but also in a central commercial register in Madrid. The availability of the desired company name has to be, as a result, verified at this register.

10.2.1.8 Transfer of Shares/Regulations in the Case of Shareholder Death

The shares of a stock company are considered to be securities. The requirements of the transmissibility depend on the type of shares the company has. Basically, the shares are transmissible and thus, also inheritable.

The following categories of shares may be distinguished:

- Registered vs. bearer shares,
- Common vs. preferred stock,
- Shares issued with a premium,
- Non-voting stock,
- Redeemable shares,
- Shares with ancillary obligations,
- Basic shareholder rights,
- Share certificates.

The particularities of the individual stock types are not further discussed since the distinction is not relevant for the purpose of this analysis.

10.2.1.9 Liability of Shareholders and Directors

An S.A. is a company with capital in which the liability of the shareholders is generally limited to the amount of capital contributed by each shareholder.

The capital of an S.A. is divided into shares. The general rule is one of limited liability. However, the corporate veil may be breached under very exceptional circumstances in order to protect the interest of third parties. In these exceptional cases, the courts follow the criteria of "piercing the corporate veil" as a reaction to the situation when the shareholders or partners take advantage of the company's legal status for fraudulent purposes. As a consequence, the courts may breach the corporate veil by splitting the equity of each of the partners to establish liabilities.

The S.A.'s directors are generally held to a standard of faithful defence of the corporate interests, loyalty and secrecy. They are liable to the company, its shareholders and its creditors for damages caused by acts that are illegal, contrary to the bylaws or done in breach of duties pertaining to their office. In all cases mentioned above, all the directors are jointly and separately liable. The directors are also liable if the annual financial statements are not presented to the commercial register.

Persons who enter into contracts on behalf of the corporation prior to its registration are generally jointly and severally liable for their performance. A potential exception to this general rule is a case in which the performance was made conditional on the corporation's registration and, if applicable, the corporation's later assumption of liability.

Prior to its registration in the commercial register, the corporation may accept contracts made in the corporation's name and on its behalf within 3 months from date of registration. However, a corporation in the process of formation and its shareholders are liable for certain special types of contracts prior to registration up to the limit of the amount they have committed to contribute.

Before registration, the corporation becomes bound by the foregoing acts and contracts. In these cases, and if the corporation accepts acts performed prior to its registration within 3 months from the date of registration, the joint and several liability of directors, shareholders or representatives lapses.

10.2.1.10 Applicable Accounting Standards

The Commercial Code and the companies' law both define the annual financial statements as consisting of the balance sheet, the income statement and the notes to financial statements. These three items jointly form a single body of information. In addition, a management report is required even though it is not an integral part of the financial statements.

The Commercial Code and the companies' law both provide the relevant accounting principles and valuation standards. Moreover, the law assesses the balance sheet and the income statement formats that are in line with the specimens set forth in Articles 9 and 24, respectively, of the EU Fourth Directive, and defines the necessary disclosures, which must be included in the notes to financial statements.

The Spanish National Chart of Accounts has been approved by Royal Decree 1643/1990 and applies to all enterprises, whatever their legal form, for all fiscal years beginning after December 31, 1990. The Charter further implements the accounting aspects of Spanish companies' law. The contents of the Spanish National Charter of Accounts are as follows:

- Part I: Accounting principles
- Part II: Chart of Accounts
- Part III: Accounting definitions and relationships
- Part IV: Financial statements
- Part V: Valuation standards.

10.2.1.11 Disclosure Requirements

The Spanish companies law requires all Spanish enterprises to file their financial statements (i.e. balance sheet, income statement, notes) at the commercial register at the location of their registered office within 1 month of their approval. Documents that have to be additionally filed are a certificate of the resolutions adopted at the shareholders' meeting approving the financial statements, copies of the financial statements, the proposed distribution of income, the management report and the auditors' report – in those cases where the enterprise is required to have its financial statements audited or had them audited at the request of minority shareholders.

The commercial registry is a public agency that keeps a file of the corporate documents and issues a certificate for each entry. Moreover, Securities Market Law 24/1988 requires all listed enterprises (e.g. a listed S.A.) to file copies of their financial statements and related auditors' report with the Spanish National Securities Market Commission (CNMV). These official files and other relevant documents filed at the commercial register and the CNMV are available to the public.

10.2.1.12 Employee Participation

No general statutory right exists for employee board-level representation in Spain. However, there are a small number of employees on the boards of some public as well as recently privatized companies and savings banks.

Elected works councils are the main channels for workplace representation for employees in Spain, although the law gives a specific role to the unions at the workplace. Workplace representation in Spain has a clear legal framework, provided mainly by the 1980 workers statute and the 1985 law on trade union freedom. The law provides for elected representatives (employee delegates or works council) of the whole workforce in all companies except small companies. There are also separate union delegates in bigger companies.

In stock companies, workers may participate financially only if they actually own shares in the company or if they belong to company management. In order to promote employee financial participation, the company has the option to implement stock option programs to their employees. However, the current level of employee financial participation in Spain is one of the lowest in the EU-27. In particular, Spain shows a significantly low incidence of share ownership schemes.

10.2.2 Limited Company (Sociedad Limitada – S.L.)

The Sociedad Limitada (abbreviated as S.L.), which is alternatively referred to as Sociedad de Responsabilidad Limitada (S.R.L.), is similar to a limited liability company in the United Kingdom, which is a corporation whose liability is limited by law. The German equivalent is the Gesellschaft mit beschränkter Haftung (GmbH). The Spanish S.L. is regulated by the "Ley de sociedades de responsabilidad limitada (L.S.R.L.)" Law.

Law 2/1995 on Sociedades de Responsabilidad Limitada came into effect on 1st June, 1995, and made certain important changes to the legal framework governing the limited liability company (S.L.). The limited liability company S.L. has recently gained more and more popularity in Spain as a result – among other reasons – of its comprehensive regulation under Law 2/1995, thereby making S.L. a popular alternative form of business entity in comparison to the S.A.

10.2.2.1 Legal Capacity and Power of Disposition

A Sociedad Limitada has legal capacity and capacity to act as a legal entity. The S.L. is not incorporated and thereby, also legally capable before it is registered in the commercial register.

The S.L. can be represented by following bodies:

- Through a sole administrator
- Through two or more solely authorized administrators
- Through two or more jointly authorized administrators
- Through an administrative board.

Furthermore, it is possible to authorize, with or without restrictions, the chief executive officers, the department heads, other associates or third parties.

10.2.2.2 Process and Requirements for Incorporation

The formation of an S.L. is a two-step process (similar to the incorporation process for an S.A. described in Sect. 10.2.1) involving the execution of the public deed before a notary public and registration in the commercial register. It is only upon registration of the public deed of incorporation that the corporation acquires legal capacity and becomes a legal entity.

The steps and expenses involved for incorporating an S.A. and an S.L. are similar. Consequently, the process and requirements of incorporation for an S.L. are not discussed separately because those of an S.A. have already been discussed in detail in Sect. 10.2.1.

10.2.2.3 Requirements for Associates/Shareholders and Regulations Concerning Shareholders' Meetings

The requirements for a limited liability company (S.L.) associates are very similar to those of a stock company (S.A); That is, no minimum number of associates/shareholders is required by Spanish law. The special system of reporting for sole shareholders also applies to S.L.s. Associates/shareholders can also be individuals or companies of any nationality and residence.

Regulations concerning shareholders' meetings (ordinary and extraordinary) are also similar and therefore, are not discussed separately.

10.2.2.4 Articles of Association

The bylaws of an S.L. must be notarized and include reference to the business purpose of the company, which should be stated in a concrete and precise manner. Altogether, the less restrictive requirements for bylaws of an S.L. (compared to those of an S.A.) allow the participation unitholders (members) of an S.L. great flexibility in setting up, in the bylaws and in the rules concerning the internal governance of an S.L. The premises for the necessary shareholder personal data for the memorandum of association are the same as in the case of the S.A.

10.2.2.5 Minimum Contribution/Initial Capital

An S.L. must have at least EUR 3,006.06 as initial capital, which must be fully paid in at its organization. The capital must be deposited before incorporation. The Spanish bank will issue a certificate that is part of the memorandum of association. The capital stock must be divided into participation units, which do not need to be all the same amount and can be contributed either as payment inkind or as cash.

An independent appraiser's report on non-monetary contributions is not required, although the founders and shareholders are jointly and severally liable for the credibility of the non-monetary contributions made.

10.2.2.6 Commercial Register

The limited liability company is registered in the commercial register in the province its domicile is situated. The registration in the commercial register is one of the two steps necessary to incorporate an S.L., eventually enabling the company to obtain legal capacity and to become a legal entity.

10.2.2.7 Regulations Concerning Corporate Name

The applicable law is the regulation of the commercial register. The name of the Spanish limited is basically arbitrary, as long as it consists of Latin and Arabic letters or Roman numbers, followed by the abbreviation S.L. or S.R.L. However, similar or equal names will be denied by the registrar.

10.2.2.8 Transfer of Shares/Regulations in the Case of Shareholder Death

In principle, an S.L. is intended to be a more closely held entity (compared to an S.A.), as evidenced by the fact that participation units are generally not freely transferable unless acquired by other participation unit holders, descendants, ascendants or companies within the same group. In fact, unless otherwise provided in the bylaws, the law establishes a pre-emptive acquisition right in favour of the other partners or the company itself in the event of transfer of the participation units to persons different than those mentioned above. The participation units are therefore basically inheritable. However, this inheritability can be excluded by regulations in the bylaws.

10.2.2.9 Liability of Shareholders and Directors

Just like the S.A., the S.L. is a company with capital in which shareholder liability is generally limited to the amount of capital contributed by each shareholder.

An S.L.'s capital is divided into participation units. The general rule is clearly one of limited liability. However, as discussed in Sect. 10.2.1, the corporate veil can be pierced to protect the interest of third parties similar to regulations for an S.A.

The liability of the associates prior to and after company incorporation/registration is also similar to that of the S.A. shareholders.

10.2.2.10 Applicable Accounting Standards

The requirements in the companies law regarding annual financial statements discussed for stock companies in Sect. 3.1.10 also apply to limited liability companies.

The Commercial Code and the companies' law both define the annual financial statements as consisting of the balance sheet, the income statement and the notes to financial statements. These three items jointly form a single body of information. In addition, a management report is required even though it is not an integral part of the financial statements.

The Spanish National Chart of Accounts is also applicable for limited liability companies (see Sect. 10.2.1).

10.2.2.11 Disclosure Requirements

The Spanish companies law requires all Spanish enterprises to file their financial statements (i.e. balance sheet, income statement, notes) at the commercial registry at the location of their registered office within 1 month of their approval.

10.2.2.12 Employee Participation

No general statutory right exists for employee board-level representation in Spain.

10.2.3 Sole Proprietorship (Trabajador Autónomo)

The simplest and most common form of doing business in Spain is to work as a self-employed freelancer (Autónomo or Empresario Individual). Comparable to the "Einzelunternehmen" in Germany, this legal form of proprietorship encompasses any self-employed activity of individuals. Trabajadores Autónomos represent business entities that legally have no separate existence from their owners. Hence, the limitations of liability enjoyed by a corporation and limited liability partnerships do not apply to self-employed freelancers. Furthermore, they pay income taxes rather than corporate taxes on their profits, enjoy less restrictive accounting requirements and work individually, whereas self-employed freelancers are not able to hire employees unless they are also self-employed. Overall, this legal form tends to involve less paperwork during the process of starting the venture as well as while running the business and there may be certain fiscal advantages.

10.2.3.1 Legal Capacity and Power of Disposition

A foreign single person can start a business in Spain; he must have legal capacity, in accordance with the law of his home country, to carry on businesses activities. The legal capacity of the sole shareholder company is identical with the legal capacity of the natural person (and owner).

10.2.3.2 Process and Requirements for Incorporation

Before setting up as an Empresario Individual, it is necessary to obtain a Foreigner's Identification Number (NIE). Furthermore, anybody who wishes to be self-employed, regardless of their nationality, will then need to carry out the following steps:

- Register to pay IAE (Impuesto de Actividades Económicas)
- Register a declaration for starting a business (Declaración Censal de Inicio de Actividad) – this can be done at the tax office (Delegación de Hacienda)
- Register for social security within 30 days of registering to pay IAE.

10.2.3.3 Requirements for Associates/Shareholders and Regulations Concerning Shareholders' Meetings

The number of owners of Empresarios Individuales is limited. The soleproprietor acts as sole shareholder.

10.2.3.4 Articles of Association

In the case of Empresarios Individuales, no articles of association are needed as no association is established.

10.2.3.5 Minimum Contribution/Initial Capital

Due to the fact that the owner is personally liable, no minimum capital contribution is required.

10.2.3.6 Commercial Register

Beyond the above-mentioned registrations, especially with the tax and social security offices, no registration in the commercial register is needed for trabajadores autónomos.

10.2.3.7 Regulations Concerning Corporate Name

A sole proprietor may do business with a trade name other than his legal name.

10.2.3.8 Transfer of Shares/Regulations in the Case of Shareholder Death

Generally, transfer of stakes in the business is possible; in the case of death of the sole proprietor, the business is handed down to the inheritor.

10.2.3.9 Liability of Shareholders and Directors

The sole proprietor will be personally and unlimitedly liable for his debts and all the services provided; his or her personal belongings can be held by the creditors.

10.2.3.10 Applicable Accounting Standards

The Spanish National Charter of Accounts (see Sect. 10.2.1) is also applicable for sole proprietors.

10.2.3.11 Disclosure Requirements

De facto, sole proprietors are not liable to any disclosure requirements.

10.2.3.12 Employee Participation

Sole traders are not allowed to hire employees unless they are also self-employed. Given the fact that autónomos are self-employed individuals, the issue of employee participation is not relevant for this legal form.

10.2.4 General Partnership (Sociedad Colectiva – S.C.)

The legal form Sociedad Colectiva (S.C.) or Sociedad Regular Colectiva (S.R.C.) is one of the partnerships used in Spain. In this type of partnership, the partners have joint, several and unlimited liability for the debts and actions of the partnership. The S.C. must be incorporated before a public notary and registered in the commercial register. Once registered, it becomes an independent legal entity. To a certain extent, the Sociedad Colectiva parallels the German Offene Handelsgesellschaft (OHG).

10.2.4.1 Legal Capacity and Power of Disposition

The Spanish S.C. has a legal status and thereby, capacity to act in the legal system.

10.2.4.2 Process and Requirements for Incorporation

Unlike the establishment of a German OHG or a German general partnership, the formation of a Spanish S.C. requires a notary certification. During the formation process, costs have to be incurred for the notary act, the registration with the commercial register, and further transaction costs – all of which depend on the associates' capital contribution. It is generally recommended to contract a lawyer to formulate the articles of association.

10.2.4.3 Requirements for Associates/Shareholders and Regulations Concerning Shareholders' Meetings

The S.C. is composed of at least two associates. All associates serve as company representatives, unless other rules have been defined in the articles of association. Both legal bodies and natural persons may act in the role of associates.

10.2.4.4 Articles of Association

An S.C.'s articles must be notarized and have to include reference to the company's business purpose, which should be formulated in a precise manner.

Provisions governing capital contributions, management of the partnership, changes in its members, and liquidation of the partnership are usually recorded in a partnership agreement. The Commercial companies law establishes standard rules governing partnerships that fail to provide for such matters in an agreement.

In the absence of a provision in the agreement specifying arrangements for management responsibilities, any partner can conduct business on behalf of the entire partnership. If an agreement designates several partners as managers without specifically enumerating their duties, they can similarly take any action for purposes of administering the partnership's business. The Commercial companies law provides for the removal of any manager or partner at any time for any reason by a unanimous vote of the partners, but general partnership agreements require more than a simple majority to unseat a partner. The Commercial companies law also provides that modifications to a partnership agreement require the unanimous approval of the partners. The approval of the shareholders who have majority of the partnership's capital is required for other resolutions if it is stipulated in the partnership agreement. A partner cannot take any action that involves competition with the partnership without the expressed unanimous consent of the remaining partners.

10.2.4.5 Minimum Contribution/Initial Capital

The Spanish Sociedad Colectiva is not liable for any minimum contribution/initial capital requirements. Reason is that – comparable to the German OHG – all associates of a Spanish S.C. are jointly and severally liable for the debts. In this form of companies, not all of the partners need to contribute capital. There are also the industrial partners (socio industrial), who do not contribute capital, but bring their knowledge and labour to the partnership. In return, these partners receive some interests in the partnership. Unless otherwise provided in the partnership agreement, partnership profits and losses are attributed to the partners in proportion to their interest in the partnership.

10.2.4.6 Commercial Register

The S.C. has to be entered in the Spanish commercial registry.

10.2.4.7 Regulations Concerning Corporate Name

The name of the S.C. has to consist of either the names of all existing associates or alternatively of the names of one or more associates supplemented by the term "y Compañía". General partnerships are not allowed to choose made-up names.

10.2.4.8 Transfer of Shares/Regulations in the Case of Shareholder Death

A partnership may not be offered to third parties without the agreement of all partners. If an associate dies, Spanish law suggests the liquidation of the S.C. If so, the value of the stake in the general partnership is added to the inheritance of the deceased associate. However, different proceedings are possible if explicitly expressed in the articles of association. Prevalent approaches would be to agree upon continuing operations with the remaining associates or alternatively to replace the deceased associate with his or her inheritor as partner in the firm.

10.2.4.9 Liability of Shareholders and Directors

All owners of Spanish Sociedades Colectivas are personally, jointly and severally, and absolutely liable for any legal actions and debts the company may face. The creditor of the partnership has to execute the assets of the company first and later, the private assets of the partners.

10.2.4.10 Applicable Accounting Standards

The Spanish National Charter of Accounts (see Sect. 10.2.1) is also applicable for Sociedades Colectivas.

10.2.4.11 Disclosure Requirements

The Spanish companies law requires the S.C. and all other Spanish enterprises to file their financial statements (i.e. balance sheet, income statement, notes) at the commercial register in the location of their registered office within 1 month of their approval.

10.2.4.12 Employee Participation

A general statutory right for employee board-level representation does not exist in Spain.

10.2.5 Limited Liability Partnership (Sociedad comanditaria – S. Com.)

The Sociedad Comanditaria – similar to the German KG – is another type of partnership used in Spain. The peculiarity of this partnership is that it has two categories of partners, those with unlimited liability (general partners or Socios Colectivos) and those with limited liability (limited liability partners or Socios Comanditarios). The participation of limited liability partners may or may not be represented by shares. However, if there are no general partners, then at least one of the limited liability partners will be held personally responsible for the company's debts. The general partners' obligations are the same as for the general partnership (Sociedad Colectiva), which includes personal management of the company, unless it is agreed to be delegated to someone else; though not with a competing company.

10.2.5.1 Legal Capacity and Power of Disposition

Similar to the Spanish general partnership S.C., the Spanish limited partnership S. Com. has legal status and thereby, capacity to act in the legal system.

10.2.5.2 Process and Requirements for Incorporation

A limited liability partnership (S. Com.) is established through the formulation of the articles of association between at least one general partner and one limited liability partner. The restriction of liability for limited liability partners is effective as soon as the S. Com. is incorporated before a public notary and registered in the mercantile register.

10.2.5.3 Requirements for Associates/Shareholders and Regulations Concerning Shareholders' Meetings

There must be at least one general partner who participates in management of the partnership and one limited partner who only contributes capital.

10.2.5.4 Articles of Association

The partnership agreement – recorded in a partnership deed – stipulates the amounts of capital to which limited and active partners subscribe.

As in all partnerships, provisions for management should be set forth in the partnership agreement. Generally, only the active or general partners handle the administration of the partnership's affairs, although the agreement may call for a third-party manager. Limited partners cannot play any active role in management without losing their silent partner status and thus, their shield from liability. However, they are allowed to inspect partnership records and to voice opinions on partnership business at partner meetings.

The partnership agreement governs procedures for partners' meetings and voting rights. Meetings are held annually to consider financial statements, distribution of profits, management performance and other business. Both active and limited partners are entitled to vote in meetings. For purposes of establishing a quorum and voting rights, active partners are considered to have designated amounts of capital divided into shares similar to those held by the limited partners.

Furthermore, the partnership agreement should provide a mechanism that allows the partnership to survive the loss of a partner, whether through death, insolvency or voluntary departure. The agreement usually also sets forth conditions under which liquidation is mandatory, such as when a partnership's losses equal its capital, as well as processes for voluntary liquidation. In the absence of a specific provision in the agreement, liquidation can be achieved only through the unanimous approval of the partners.

10.2.5.5 Minimum Contribution/Initial Capital

The Spanish S. Com. is not liable to any minimum contribution/initial capital requirements.

10.2.5.6 Commercial Register

This limited partnership must be incorporated before a public notary and registered in the mercantile register. Once it is registered, it becomes an independent legal entity with the two types of partners. The difference between the two types of partners and thus, capital must be clearly stated in both the deed of incorporation and in the balance sheet of the partnership.

10.2.5.7 Regulations Concerning Corporate Name

The creation of a limited partnership (Sociedad Comanditaria) is similar to that of a public limited company (Sociedad Anónima), but the S. Com. also has specific naming conventions regarding the use of y Compañía and (or S. Com por A.), further stipulating that limited liability partners' names may not appear in the company name. The S. Com. must always be identified by the words "y Compañía" after the names of the partners.

10.2.5.8 Transfer of Shares/Regulations in the Case of Shareholder Death

Transfer of shares is possible provided that all existing partners agree upon the transfer. However, different rules can be defined in the articles of association. Company law suggests that if a general partner dies, the stake in the partnership is not bequeathed. In the case of death of a limited liability partner, the stake is bequeathed.

10.2.5.9 Liability of Shareholders and Directors

The general partners are jointly and severally liable for the debts of the partnership, and the limited partners are only liable to the extent of the capital they contribute.

10.2.5.10 Applicable Accounting Standards

The Spanish National Chart of Accounts (compare Sect. 10.2.1) is also applicable for Sociedades Comanditarias.

10.2.5.11 Disclosure Requirements

The Spanish companies law requires the S. Com. and all other Spanish enterprises to file their financial statements (i.e. balance sheet, income statement, notes) at the commercial register at the location of their registered office within 1 month of their approval.

10.2.5.12 Employee Participation

A general statutory right for employee board-level representation does not exist in Spain.

10.2.6 Branch Office (Sucursal)

The Sucursal describes a secondary establishment or branch office with a permanent representation and certain managing independence, by means of which the activities of the head office are totally or partially developed. It has no legal personality independent of that of the head office.

Setting up a branch is normally faster than establishing a new company, but it still has to be done through a public deed and the branch needs to be entered in the commercial register. Prerequisite for the establishment of a Sucursal would be, for example, to have a permanent address and a fiscal representative in Spain. With regard to the yearly accounting and obligations, they are very similar to those for a limited company.

The following laws regulate the rights and responsibilities of Spanish Sucursales: Ley de Sociedades Anónimas, Ley de Sociedades de Responsabilidad Limitada y Reglamento del Registro Mercantil.

10.2.6.1 Legal Capacity and Power of Disposition

A branch is not a legal entity of its own, but rather an organization depending on its head office: Sucurcales are branches incorporated by Spanish or foreign companies or corporations.

10.2.6.2 Process and Requirements for Incorporation

The establishment of a branch in Spain requires registration with the Spanish commercial registry (registro mercantil). The following documentation is required for registration:

- A certificate issued by the Spanish consul or by the authorities of the commercial registry or a public notary that the parent company is incorporated and authorized pursuant to the law of country concerned
- A certificate from the commercial registry or public notary or Spanish consul in the country of residence, which must bear the Apostille of the 1961 Hague Convention, stating that the articles of association and the appointment of the directors of the parent company are in force
- Certified minutes of the shareholders' general meeting or certificates issued by the board (depending upon the body in charge of deciding upon the branch incorporation) to the effect that the company has resolved to set up a branch in Spain with the details of the working capital allocated (for foreign investment registration and transfer tax purpose only). Additionally the objects of the branch, the registered office of the branch and the authorized representatives, with their authorities duly specified, appear before a Spanish public notary for the establishment of the branch and the director of the branch must be included. This certificate must be signed and legalized by the notary public and must bear the Apostille of the 1961 Hague Convention.

10.2.6.3 Requirements for Associates/Shareholders and Regulations Concerning Shareholders' Meetings

The branch has a permanent representative. The management body of the mother company also provides the branch with its facilities.

10.2.6.4 Articles of Association

Branches legally belong to their mother companies and therefore, no separate articles of association are needed. Having the consideration of permanent establishments for tax purposes, branches shall have their own accounting based on the transactions they enter into and the assets assigned to them. Additionally, the branch is to register the head office's annual accounts, a certification of their deposit in its commercial register, or in certain cases, the accounts corresponding to the branch activity with its corresponding commercial register.

10.2.6.5 Minimum Contribution/Initial Capital

No capital is required for the incorporation of a branch, although for practical reasons, it is advisable to provide the branch with such capital.

10.2.6.6 Commercial Register

Together with the public deed creating the branch, the documents attesting the existence of the head office, its enforced bylaws, its directors and its decision of opening the branch, duly legalized, shall be filed with the commercial registry for registration.

10.2.6.7 Regulations Concerning Corporate Name

Generally, applicable laws for companies include the registration with the commercial register. However, for branches, it is not necessary to apply for a name. It would be necessary though, if the mother company wanted to make sure that its name is not used by any other company.

10.2.6.8 Transfer of Shares/Regulations in the Case of Shareholder Death

The issue of transferring shares and regulations in the case of shareholder death is not relevant for foreign branches, since the owner structure of companies is not affected by the establishment of branches abroad.

10.2.6.9 Liability of Shareholders and Directors

Generally, the mother company assumes liability. The permanent representative is liable for his acts on behalf of the branch.

10.2.6.10 Applicable Accounting Standards

The Spanish National Chart of Accounts (see Sect. 10.2.1) is also applicable for Sucursales.

10.2.6.11 Disclosure Requirements

Disclosure of branches is part of the disclosure procedures of the parent company.

10.2.6.12 Employee Participation

Similarly, the employee participation is organized at the parent company level.

10.2.7 Further Legal Forms

In addition to the above-mentioned legal forms, Spain offers several more business entity options for companies. In order to give a nearly complete overview of the existing forms of organization, some more legal business structures are briefly introduced.

10.2.7.1 Sociedad Civil

The partnership, or Sociedad Civil, in Spain – similar to the German GbR ("Gesellschaft bürgerlichen Rechts") – is a business relationship formed by two or more people who contribute money, equipment and/or labour and divide the profits amongst themselves as agreed upon. Accordingly, any debts or financial obligations will also be divided amongst the parties.

In Spain, anything not expressly agreed upon, either publicly or privately, will be governed by the Spanish Civil Code. The Sociedad Civil does not actually need to become an "official" business except in certain cases, if one of the parties should contribute real estate, for example. For that reason, no minimum financial investment is required. However, if you do make the business "official", the business name should include the words Sociedad Civil. An "official" Sociedad Civil in Spain must create a partnership agreement for the business (contrato de constitución) that is then signed before a notary and has to be registered to pay IAE tax (Impuesto de Actividades Económicas).

10.2.7.2 Sociedad Limitada Nueva Empresa (S.L.N.E.)

As mentioned in Section 10.2.2., the limited liability company has gained popularity as a result – among other reasons – of its comprehensive regulation under Law 2/1995 and a lower minimum capital requirement than that for S.A.'s. The recently created new enterprise limited company, or Sociedad Limitada Nueva Empresa, is considered to be a simplified form of the limited liability company (Sociedad de

Responsabilidad Limitada) in Spain and as such, is an autonomous legal entity. The S.L.N.E. has its own set of requirements, including a set of specific naming requirements. The company name must include a registration number, one of the founders' names and the words Sociedad Limitada Nueva Empresa or S.L.N.E. To start with, there may only be one to five founders or shareholders; yet by transfer, the company may incorporate new shareholders as long as they are actual, physical people and not legal persons, i.e. they are not other companies or corporations.

In addition, a Sociedad Limitada Nueva Empresa requires an available investment of between EUR 3,012 and EUR 120,202 and must pay company Tax (Impuesto sobre Sociedades), currently at 25–32.5 percent for this type of sociedad. Nevertheless, this kind of company has some special fiscal benefits, for example, the extension of tax benefits in the first 2 years of the company.

10.2.7.3 Sociedad Laboral

The worker-owned company, or Sociedad Laboral, in Spain is a special type of public limited company (Sociedad Anónima) or limited liability company (Sociedad de Responsabilidad Limitada). The shares are held by workers (clase laboral) and shareholders, who do not work for the business (clase general). Workers who directly contribute their labour to the business must own at least 51 percent of the shares. Workers who do not own shares must not work more than 15 percent of the total hours worked each year or not more than 25 percent if the company has less than 25 workers with shares.

The Sociedad Laboral is created and governed as either a Sociedad Anónima or a Sociedad de Responsabilidad Limitada, but with a few exceptions. Before registering with the commercial register in Spain, the company must be registered at the Registro de Sociedades Laborales del Ministerio de Trabajo y Asuntos Sociales. According to its base entity type, the company's name must also include Sociedad Anónima Laboral (or S.A.L.) or Sociedad de Responsabilidad Limitada Laboral (or S.L.L.). The Sociedad Laboral requires a minimum capital of EUR 25,000 and three workers as partners.

10.2.7.4 Sociedad Cooperativa

The cooperative, or Sociedad Cooperativa, is designed for groups of people or companies in Spain to work together as a democratic block for common economic or social reasons, while operating with a profit motive. Some examples include producer cooperatives, trade cooperatives, consumer cooperatives and financial cooperatives. Unless stipulated otherwise, all cooperative members have the same rights.

The minimum required investment is EUR 1,804, with the exception of student cooperatives. As a sociedad, the Sociedad Cooperativa must pay company tax (Impuesto sobre Sociedades), yet it has certain tax advantages other sociedades do not have.

To create a Sociedad Cooperativa, a Certificado de Denominación de la Sección Central del Registro de Cooperativas must be requested from the cooperatives registry (Registro de Cooperativas). Like the CNN for public limited companies (Sociedades Anónimas), this is designed to prove that another company is not already using the proposed name. Secondly, the articles of incorporation have to be drafted and notarized. Furthermore, a public deed for the cooperative's incorporation (Escritura Pública de Constitución), the registration with the Cooperatives Registry (Registro de Cooperativas) as well as a request for a CIF (Código de Identificación Fiscal, Tax Identification Code) are needed.

The cooperative will also be required to keep at least three types of official "accounting books": the Libro Registro de Socios (a record of the cooperative's members), the Libro Registro de Aportaciones al Capital Social (a record of the financial contributions of each member) and the Libro de Actas de la Asamblea General (a record of the general assembly's minutes).

10.3 Summary

In order summarize the main findings of the conducted analysis in an efficient and comprehensive way, the main advantages and disadvantages of the two most popular and relevant legal forms, namely the Sociedad Anónima (S.A.) and the Sociedad Limitada (S.L.), are listed in the following. From a foreigner's perspective, who intends to start a company in Spain, these two legal forms are the most frequently chosen and they also seem to be suitable from an objective perspective of the majority of business types.

The main advantages of a Spanish stock company S.A. are

- Limited liability
- Shares can be freely transferred
- Debentures and other securities can be issued (in contrast to an S.L.)
- No maximum number of directors (S.L.: max. 12 directors).

The main disadvantages of a Spanish stock company S.A. are

- The organization is more complex
- Relatively high operating costs (compared to an S.L.)
- Numerous disclosure and publicity requirements.

The main advantages of a Spanish limited liability company S.L. are

- Limited liability
- Legislation is less strict than for S.A.'s
- Less disclosure and publicity requirements (compared to an S.A.)

- Less initial capital required
- Less operating costs.

The main disadvantages of a Spanish limited liability company S.L. are

- Restrictions in involving certain businesses (e.g. banks and insurance companies)
- Shares cannot be freely transferred or traded in a convenient way.

Altogether, the S.L. seems to be the most appropriate legal form for most kinds of businesses. However, S.A.'s can still be recommended for high-volume companies and companies active in certain industries, such as the financial institution industry.

The question that still remains unanswered for a foreigner who plans to start-up a business in Spain is, whether it is preferable to open a branch or a subsidiary (as either S.A. or S.L.). The upcoming presentation deals with this issue and attempts to provide some suggestions and relevant decision criteria in order to provide a basis for the final legal form selection.

Chapter 11
Switzerland

Anton Blatter and Michael J. Munkert

Abstract In the chapter on Switzerland, the authors Anton Blatter and Michael J. Munkert start with an introduction into the general laws and regulations with regard to setting up and running a business and provide an overview of possible legal forms. They use the general analysis framework for the handbook on legal forms in Europe to analyse seven relevant legal forms: the sole proprietorship (Einzelfirma), the ordinary partnership (Einfache Gesellschaft), the general partnership (Kollektivgesellschaft), the partnership limited by shares (Kommanditgesellschaft), the silent partnership (Stille Gesellschaft), the corporation (Aktiengesellschaft) and the limited liability company (GmbH).

The authors conclude their discussions with an evaluation of the advantages and disadvantages of the different legal forms and provide exemplary recommendations depending on the individual case of the founders.

Contents

M.J. Munkert (✉)
MUNKERT ● KUGLER + PARTNER GbR, Äußere Sulzbacher Straße 29, 90491, Nürnberg, Germany
e-mail: m.munkert@munkert-kugler.de

Anton Blatter: Deceased

M.J. Munkert et al. (eds.), *Founding a Company*,
DOI 10.1007/978-3-642-11259-1_11, © Springer-Verlag Berlin Heidelberg 2010

11.1 Introduction

In terms of legal constitution, legal forms in Switzerland can be distinguished by its capacity to act. Legal persons are the corporation (Aktiengesellschaft), the limited liability company (Gesellschaft mit beschränkter Haftung), the partnership limited by shares (Kommanditaktiengesellschaft), cooperatives (Genossenschaften), membership corporations and foundations. The ordinary partnership (Einfache Gesellschaft) is not a legal person, whereas the general partnership (Kollektivgesellschaft) and the limited partnership (Kommanditgesellschaft) take medial positions. The sole proprietor (Einzelfirma) is not a corporation, but nonetheless of high significance.

Depending on how they are earmarked, membership corporations and foundations do not pursue business goals. The same is true for the "Genossenschaft" (cooperative), which typically serves the self-help of its members. Because of its low significance for business purposes, the paper does not cover these legal forms. The same is true for the "Kommanditaktiengesellschaft" (partnership limited by shares), as it has no practical relevance in Switzerland. In 1999, there were only nine such entities in Switzerland, with no recent changes.

The capital stock and the management as well as personal liability are the main differences that private companies (Einfache Gesellschaft, Kollektivgesellschaft and Kommanditgesellschaft) have compared to other legal forms. Corporate enterprises are only liable with the company's assets.

The Einfache Gesellschaft normally serves only for a certain time and purpose. All other legal forms are normally founded sine die.

The in-house relations that deal with the connection of the partners among themselves can be freely regulated for private companies. However, for corporate enterprises, this only holds partly true. The relations to the environment are basically based on obligatory regulations. This is especially true concerning liability matters.

In Swiss law, only legal forms that are described in the law can be applied. That means that there are no hybrid forms, hence, it is not possible to incorporate, for example, a GmbH & Co. KG as it is possible in Germany.

The sole proprietorship has no exclusive rights compared to other corporations. Persons or companies that have annual revenues in excess of CHF 100,000 must register in the commercial register. In 2006, there were about 150,000 sole proprietorships registered. In the same year, there were 175,000 corporations, about 92,500 limited liability companies, 14,500 general partnerships, and 2,600 limited partnerships registered. In case of the ordinary partnerships, there are no numbers available, as registration in the commercial register is not obligatory. However, it can be presumed that there is a high significance of the Einfache Gesellschaft, because ordinary partnerships can be incorporated, even without the knowledge of the partners.

Another legal form, the silent partnership (Stille Gesellschaft), is not mentioned in the law, but legally accepted. The same regulations as in Germany can be applied. Because the silent partnership is only an in-house relation, there are no numbers available concerning the overall relevance.

When comparing the importance of private companies and corporate enterprises, it is obvious that the Swiss economy is principally based on corporate enterprises, as the number of private companies is significantly lower.

In the following, we discuss the details of the most important legal forms in Switzerland. For corporate enterprises, the focus is on the Aktiengesellschaft and the GmbH. For private companies, the relevant and discussed forms are the Einfache Gesellschaft, the Kollektivgesellschaft and the Kommanditgesellschaft. In addition, the Stille Gesellschaft will be discussed.

Swiss corporate law is centralized in the "Obligationsrecht (OR)" or Law of Obligations. At the beginning of 2008, this law was partly changed. Relevant changes are discussed. Declared references of articles are from the revised Law of Obligations.

11.2 Description of Relevant Legal Forms

11.2.1 Sole Proprietorship (Einzelfirma)

The sole proprietorship is still the most popular legal form. Legally, it means that a sole proprietor performs a commercial activity. Thereby, a commercial activity is understood as undertaking a business. In Swiss legislation, the one-man business is not subject to privileges.

11.2.1.1 Legal Capacity and Power of Disposition

The capacity to act as a sole proprietor is similar to that of a sole proprietor running a one-man business. The sole proprietor fully decides on the corporate policy.

11.2.1.2 Process and Requirements for Incorporation

For incorporating a sole proprietorship, a specific act of foundation is not necessary. The operations can be commenced at the same time as the sole proprietorship is incorporated. In addition, a registration in the commercial register is possible.

Accordingly, the formalities to incorporate an Einzelfirma are quite simple. The costs for consulting and registration in the commercial register are under CHF

1,200 – depending on the need for consultancy and the possible registration in the commercial register.

11.2.1.3 Requirements for Associates/Shareholders and Regulations Concerning Shareholders' Meetings

A natural person must be the owner. The sole proprietor as the owner of the Einzelfirma is entitled to execute all corporate transactions.

11.2.1.4 Articles of Association

For the incorporation of a sole proprietorship, a partnership agreement is impossible, as it is not a corporation.

11.2.1.5 Minimum Contribution/Initial Capital

There are no regulations concerning equity. The amount of equity is only limited by the owner's assets. Therefore, there are no minimum capital requirements as the sole proprietor is liable to the full extent.

11.2.1.6 Commercial Register

It is not necessary for the sole proprietor to register in the commercial register. However, if the annual revenue exceeds CHF 100,000, the proprietorship is obligated to register. If the annual revenue is below that sum, the registration can be done voluntarily. With the registration, the company's name is protected/trademarked.

11.2.1.7 Regulations Concerning Corporate Name

The name of the company must contain the name of the founder (with or without first name) (OR 945). Any other names are only permitted as a supplement.

11.2.1.8 Transfer of Shares/Regulations in the Case of Shareholder Death

The sole proprietorship cannot be sold or transferred. Only the assets and liabilities of the company can be transferred.

11.2.1.9 Liability of Shareholders and Directors

The proprietor of the Einzelfirma bears all risks associated with running the business. The liability extends to both the assets of the company and the private assets. As a result, there is no concept of limited liability.

11.2.1.10 Applicable Accounting Standards

If registered in the commercial register, the proprietor is obliged to maintain double-entry bookkeeping (OR 957).

In general, the regulations of the Swiss bookkeeping standards apply. The accounting bookkeeping is regulated in Arts. 957–964. The person who is obliged to keep the books needs to do that in a manner that the financial situation of the company as well as all liabilities connected to the business (including, e.g. receivables) and the income statement can be determined (OR 957). OR 960 II regulates the principle of valuation by stating to keep books carefully.

All business activities are subject to a valuation that is, at a maximum, the value for the business at the time the balance sheet is made. Therefore, in case of doubt, assets are assessed below market values and liabilities above market values.

However, if the company is registered in the commercial register, there is a responsibility to record business activities. This means, for the tax authority, all incomes and expenditures must be kept in written form. Additionally, all receipts must be stored structurally.

11.2.1.11 Disclosure Requirements

No disclosure requirements are applicable.

11.2.1.12 Employee Participation

No supervisory board with employee representation is required.

11.2.2 Ordinary Partnership (Einfache Gesellschaft)

The ordinary partnership is regulated in OR 530–551. It is an association made by contract of two or more persons to reach a common (economic) goal. The main difference to the later described Kollektivgesellschaft is that the Einfache Gesellschaft is not entitled to have enduring commerce purpose. The ordinary partnership is appropriate for a multiplicity of purposes. It is considered as being the standard of Swiss corporate law. In addition, it is a subsidiary, which means that whenever no other form of company is applicable, the ordinary partnership is used. To ensure that this type of company can be broadly used, the legal framework is as easy as possible.

11.2.2.1 Legal Capacity and Power of Disposition

The ordinary partnership is not an entity. To the external world, the Einfache Gesellschaft is only perceived as a combination of interests. It is not only the entity that is missing, but also the capacity to act, the capacity for processes, and the capacity to operate. Active and passive legitimization can only be made by the partners.

In case of lawsuits, every partner needs to file the lawsuit, as long as the rights to do so are available for all of the partners. In case of lawsuit against the company, all partners can be held liable.

In case of doubt, the ordinary partnership is an association of people, who are entitled to certain assets.

Every partner is entitled to the position of the chief executive officer. However, if a contract has been made between the partners, naming one or more of the partners or a third party as the chief executive officer, this can be changed (OR 531I). In case of several chief executive officers, every one of them is entitled to act in the name of the company. However, every other partner who is entitled to act as a chief executive officer can lodge a protest before the act is completed (OR 535 II).

11.2.2.2 Process and Requirements for Incorporation

The formation is implemented by a partnership agreement of at least two partners. There are no regulations concerning the partnership agreement. In order to incorporate an ordinary partnership, the agreement of several persons to pursue a certain purpose/goal is sufficient. For the rest, the accepted law is applied. Nonetheless, every point that is brought up by at least one partner needs to be discussed and an agreement reached.

The formation of an ordinary partnership can also be carried out by implied actions. In practice, this is the reason why an unintended Einfache Gesellschaft is often incorporated without the knowledge of the parties involved in the process. In case of lawsuits, this can be a dangerous situation. If the partners commit themselves to business actions that require a certain form to become legitimate, these forms must be considered.

According to OR 530 II, if a company does not meet requirements for any other legal form, the company is automatically considered as an ordinary partnership. Therefore, the law of the Einfache Gesellschaft is also the basis for other legal regulations, even for statutory companies (see OR 557 II, 598 II, ZGB 62). The ordinary partnership is thereby a subsidiary in case no other legal form is suitable.

The costs of founding are very low, partly because there is no possibility for registration in the commercial register. Additionally, the time for the incorporation is minimal.

11.2.2.3 Requirements for Associates/Shareholders and Regulations Concerning Shareholders' Meetings

The basic prerequisite is that there must be at least two partners. These partners can be individual persons or a legal entity. However, the ordinary partnership does not have the right to run a commercial business. Corporate decisions must be made in agreement with all partners. However, if the articles of incorporation determine that a voting majority is sufficient, the majority needs to be calculated by these contractual regulations (OR 534).

For the inner organization, the rules are set up in an open form, so that they can be individually designated (optional law or "dispostives Recht").

11.2.2.4 Articles of Association

For the partnership agreement, there are no formal requirements that need to be taken into account. Both verbal and written forms are possible. A partnership agreement can be made by implied behaviour.

11.2.2.5 Minimum Contribution/Initial Capital

In an ordinary partnership, there are no minimum capital requirements.

11.2.2.6 Commercial Register

There is no possibility for an ordinary partnership to register for the commercial register.

11.2.2.7 Regulation Concerning Corporate Name

The ordinary partnership cannot have a company name. However, the usage of a brief description can be applied. However, in this case also, the partners have direct liability.

Additionally, there is no registered office, because there is no location where the legal relationships of the company can be thought of as being concentrated.

11.2.2.8 Transfer of Shares/Regulations in the Case of Shareholder Death

Partner rights cannot be transferred. The transformation of memberships and the entry of additional partners are only possible if all other partners agree (OR 542 I).

The ordinary partnership is dissolved as soon as at least one partner retires. However, the contract can allow a continuation of the company despite the retirement of one member. The membership of the partnership is not transferable.

11.2.2.9 Liability of Shareholders and Directors

The partner's liability is personal and solidary. This means that one partner can also be held liable for other partners' accrued liabilities. However, internally, there can be "regression claims". According to this, every individual partner is jointly and separately liable. This is in the interest of the trustees. They should not be forced to consider the entity of partners in order to obtain their claims.

If a partner retires from the company, he is still liable for those liabilities that accrued before his retirement from the company.

11.2.2.10 Applicable Accounting Standards

Because the ordinary partnership cannot be registered in the commercial register, there are no extensive bookkeeping standards that need to be applied.

11.2.2.11 Disclosure Requirements

No disclosure requirements are applicable.

11.2.2.12 Employee Participation

No supervisory board with employee representation is required.

11.2.3 General Partnership (Kollektivgesellschaft)

The Kollektivgesellschaft is regulated in the Arts. 552–593. It is a company that is independent of the external environment and pursues business purposes (commerce, fabrication, see OR 552) as a general rule. The liability of the partners can be absolute and solidary for total liabilities (as well as total assets).

11.2.3.1 Legal Capacity and Power of Disposition

In legal terms, the general partnership is not a legal entity. However, it can appear to the external world under its own name (552), acquire property rights, have liabilities or serve as a party in a lawsuit (562).

According to OR 552, the general partnership appears internally as well as externally under its own name. If not mentioned differently in the commercial register, a third party can assume that every partner is entitled to the power of representation (for all legal acts that come along with the business purpose, see OR 563). Other regulations need to be registered in the commercial register. The principle of the power of representation for every single partner can be modified in several ways (OR 555), with the restriction that at least one partner needs to have the power of representation.

The general partnership is based on the principle that the partners are chief executive officers at the same time. In general, every partner is entitled to transact business. Individual partners can be barred from being authorized to represent the company. However, that does not mean that the company might be run completely by external chief executive officers. For representation as well as by definition of the articles of incorporation, the freedom of contract prevails.

11.2.3.2 Process and Requirements for Incorporation

A general partnership is formed by at least two parties (552 I). The articles of association incorporate it. Despite the fact that the general partnership must be registered in the commercial register, registration is not constitutive. The Kollektivgesellschaft is incorporated by a purpose agreement of the partners to pursue a joint partnership in the form of a commercial company.

If the company is not pursuing commercial activities, the company is not incorporated until the registration in the commercial register (Art. 533).

A general partnership is also incorporated if a partnership limited by shares, consisting of at least two general partners and one limited partner, is faced with the retirement of the limited partner and the remaining partners continue operations.

The expected costs of incorporation are between CHF 2,400 and 4,400, depending on the level of consultancy that is needed.

11.2.3.3 Requirements for Associates/Shareholders and Regulations Concerning Shareholders' Meetings

At least two parties are necessary to found a Kollektivgesellschaft. Members can only be natural persons. The only "body" of the company is the company's general meeting (in order to pass resolutions).

11.2.3.4 Articles of Association

The company is incorporated by a joint purpose contractual agreement. This does not have to be done in a written form. Therefore, there are no formal requirements that need to be taken into account. In the articles of the association, legal requirements can be changed. These changes must be in accordance with the legal regulations that set limits and constraints.

11.2.3.5 Minimum Contribution/Initial Capital

There are no minimum requirements needed in order to incorporate a general partnership.

11.2.3.6 Commercial Register

Despite the fact that the Kollektivgesellschaft must be registered in the commercial' register (552 II), this registration is not constitutive. However, if the general partnership is not pursuing a commercial business, the general partnership is not incorporated until it is registered (553).

The registration generally has to be executed by all partners in person and must be signed at the commercial register office. A notarized signature is also possible (556 I).

11.2.3.7 Regulations Concerning Corporate Name

The name of the general partnership must bear either the names of all partners or the name of just one partner combined with an amendment that indicates the corporate relationship (OR 947 I). With the addition of other/new partners, the name can be continued.

The general partnership needs a place of business that is the centre of business operations.

11.2.3.8 Transfer of Shares/Regulations in the Case of Shareholder Death

Similar to the ordinary partnership, the general partnership is dissolved with the retirement of one of its partners. In addition, there are legal exceptions:

- The general partnership should be maintained with the retirement of one of its partners (OR 576).
- In contrast to the ordinary partnership, a partner can be excluded from the company by a judge (OR 577).
- A partner can be excluded by the other partners in case of his insolvency or by refunding his part of cash contributed to the company (OR 578).

The excluded partners or his/her heirs have the right of compensation. The value of this compensation is not determined by the liquidation value of the company, but rather with the going face value. Entry or transfers of membership are regulated by the regulations of the ordinary partnership (OR 542 I). For third parties, these changes take effect with the associated announcement.

For private companies, it is often the case that articles of convention are arranged. A general partnership is to be continued if one partner dies, but in the modified form of a partnership limited by shares, so that the heirs are restricted to being only limited partners.

11.2.3.9 Liability of Shareholders and Directors

For the liabilities of the company, the partner's assets are decisive. These separate assets are exclusively for the creditors of the company. In addition to this, all partners are personally unrestricted and severally liable (OR 568 I). This liability is only relevant if one of the following requirements (Belangbarkeitsvoraussetzungen) is met:

- Closure of the company
- Ineffective business or beginning the bankruptcy process
- Insolvency of the prosecuted partner.

A new partner is also liable for those liabilities that have been accrued before his entry into the company (OR 569 I). However, the retired partner is liable for 5 years after his departure (OR 591), which means that limitation of time regulations could be applied. The partner accounting for the liabilities has the right of recourse; first of all, to its full extent against the company itself. Secondly, there are rights of recourse against the other partners (in equity proportion).

11.2.3.10 Applicable Accounting Standards

For the bookkeeping regulations of the general partnership, see the corresponding chapter of the sole proprietorship (see Sect. 11.2.1.10).

In addition, the company is also has to provide an income statement as well as a balance sheet in order to determine the individual profit or loss for each of the partners.

11.2.3.11 Disclosure Requirements

No disclosure requirements are applicable.

11.2.3.12 Employee Participation

No supervisory board with employee representation is required.

11.2.4 Partnership Limited by Shares (Kommanditgesellschaft)

The partnership limited by shares is regulated in the Law of Obligations with the Arts. 594–619. It is a company related to natural persons and externally a discrete entity that pursues economic purposes. One or more partners (complements must be natural persons) are liable (besides existing assets of the company) with their own personal assets. One or more partners (limited partner, not necessarily a natural person) have only limited liability (594 II).

Often, the partnership limited by shares is chosen if a sole proprietorship or a general partnership needs additional funds without being obligated to the extent of the shareholder's base.

Nonetheless, the partnership limited by shares plays an unimportant role in Switzerland.

11.2.4.1 Legal Capacity and Power of Disposition

From a legal perspective, the Kommanditgesellschaft has no own legal personality and is therefore, not a legal entity. However, the company can, in the name of the company, acquire property rights, incur liabilities and take judicial actions (602). The regulations are the same as for a general partnership.

The legal position of the counterpart is similar to those of a partner in a general partnership. It is highlighted in the regulations that the counterpart has the right and the obligation to take over the management of the company (OR 599). However, limited partners can have, based on OR 600 (Abdingbarkeit), significant influence within the company.

11.2.4.2 Process and Requirements for Incorporation

The incorporation of the company requires at least one counterpart and one limited partner (594 II). It is constituted with its contract of association. Despite the fact that the partnership limited by shares must be registered in the commercial register, the registration is not constitutive.

If the company is not running a commercial company, the company is incorporated by registration in the commercial register (595).

The associated costs with incorporation are between CHF 3,400 and 5,400, depending on the level of consultancy.

11.2.4.3 Requirements for Associates/Shareholders and Regulations Concerning Shareholders' Meetings

At least two partners are necessary to incorporate the company. On the one hand, counterparts with unlimited liability must be natural persons. On the other hand, limited partners can also be legal persons (594 II).

The legal relationship among the partners is determined by the articles of the company (598 I). With no other agreements, the regulations of the general partnership are applied (598 II).

11.2.4.4 Articles of Association

The partnership limited by shares is constituted with the articles of association. Therefore, there are no formal requirements that need to be taken into account. In the articles of the association, legal requirements can be changed. These changes must be in accordance with the legal regulations, setting limits and constraints.

11.2.4.5 Minimum Contribution/Initial Capital

For a Kommanditgesellschaft, there are no regulations concerning minimal capital requirements. However, there are fixed deposits for the counterpart and the limited partner. The amount of these deposits is not legally fixed and may be regulated privately. The exact amount of the limited partner has to be disclosed to the commercial register agency.

11.2.4.6 Commercial Register

For the general partnership, registration in the commercial register is obligatory (594 III). The registration is obligatory, but not constitutive. However, if the partnership limited by shares is not pursuing a commercial business, the general partnership is not incorporated until it is registered (595). The registration of required information and changes to them must be signed by all counterparts and need to be delivered to the commercial register office (597).

11.2.4.7 Regulations Concerning Corporate Name

The name of the partnership limited by shares must contain at least one of the partners' names (947 III). The names of the limited partners cannot be part of the company's name (947 IV). This is the reason for the rule of exception, which states that the limited partner, despite his limited liability, is totally liable if his name appears in the company's name.

11.2.4.8 Transfer of Shares/Regulations in the Case of Shareholder Death

In the case of death, changes in partners or the death of the limited partner, the same rules as for the general partnership will be applied. In contrast, the death or the incapacitation of the limited partner does not lead to the closure of the company (619 II).

11.2.4.9 Liability of Shareholders and Directors

Counterparts are liable for the liabilities of the company, similar to the partners of the general partnership. In contrast, limited partners are liable at most, to the extent of their deposit, even if they have factual power over the company (according to the articles of association). To this extent, their liability, with their total assets, is subsidiary and solidary. However, this constraint of liability is abrogated in the interest of the creditors in the following exceptional cases:

- The limited partner is totally liable if he is doing business in the name of the company without clearly stating that he is taking these actions as an authorized officer or agent and not as a partner (OR 606).
- Liabilities that accrued before the time of registration in the commercial register. An exception is the case where the third party knew that he would just have limited liability (OR 606).
- If the name is part of the company's name.

11.2.4.10 Applicable Accounting Standards

The regulations of companies registered in the commercial register are applied.

11.2.4.11 Disclosure Requirements

No disclosure requirements are applicable.

11.2.4.12 Employee Participation

No supervisory board with employee representation is required.

11.2.5 Silent Partnership (Stille Gesellschaft)

There are no regulations governing the silent partnership in Law of Obligations. However, the Stille Gesellschaft is legally accepted. Basically, the regulations for the silent partnership are similar to those of the ordinary partnership. A natural person (silent partner) takes a share of a company that is run by another (main partner) and therefore, a corresponding share of profits. The silent partnership is purely an internal relationship. The only partner who represents the company to external entities is the "main partner". At the same time, he is the only one who can become contractually capable and bear all the risks associated with the operations.

11.2.5.1 Legal Capacity and Power of Disposition

The silent partnership has no own legal personality. The silent partnership is not perceived by the external environment. The main partner becomes contractually active in his own name and not as a representative. From a legal perspective, the internally jointly run company is a sole proprietorship. The main partner has the power of control over the company's assets. The deposits made by the silent partner become part of the main partner's assets. The silent partner takes part in the internal management of the company. The extent to which the silent partner can become active in the company is debatable. However, what remains undisputed is that the silent partner needs to have rights to take part in decision making; otherwise, the money contributed by him would only be a credit.

11.2.5.2 Process and Requirements for Incorporation

There are no specific formal requirements to incorporate a silent partnership. The incorporation has no external presence.

11.2.5.3 Requirements for Associates/Shareholders and Regulations Concerning Shareholders' Meetings

The same regulations as for the ordinary partnership apply.

11.2.5.4 Articles of Association

The same regulations as for the ordinary partnership apply and there are no specific formal requirements. There is also the possibility for implied power ("konkludent").

11.2.5.5 Minimum Contribution/Initial Capital

There are no minimal capital requirements, but nominal determinations about the deposit of the silent partner apply.

11.2.5.6 Commercial Register

The same regulations as for the ordinary partnership can be applied.

11.2.5.7 Regulations Concerning Corporate Name

The same regulations as for the ordinary partnership apply.

11.2.5.8 Transfer of Shares/Regulations in the Case of Shareholder Death

Basically, the same regulations as for the ordinary partnership are applied. However, there is no need to liquidate the silent partnership, as a so-called clearing relationship applies.

11.2.5.9 Liability of Shareholders and Directors

The main partner bears total liability. For creditors, the only funds that are available from the silent partner are the deposits made in the company.

11.2.5.10 Applicable Accounting Standards

The same regulations as for the ordinary partnership apply.

11.2.5.11 Disclosure Requirements

The same regulations as for the ordinary partnership apply.

11.2.5.12 Employee Participation

The same regulations as for the ordinary partnership apply.

11.2.6 Corporation (Aktiengesellschaft – AG)

The Aktiengesellschaft (AG) is regulated in the Arts. 620–763 within the Law of Obligations. The corporation is a capital-based corporation that pursues business purposes. With regard to the liabilities of this corporation, the liability is limited by its own assets. The authorized capital is determined and divided in partial sums (shares).

The corporation pursues business purposes in a such way that it tries to create economic benefits for its shareholders. However, as an exception, the corporation can also be used for non-economic reasons (see OR 620 III). The ultimate goal of the AG is to maximize profits for its shareholders and distribute them via dividends.

11.2.6.1 Legal Capacity and Power of Disposition

The Aktiengesellschaft has its own legal status, own rights and responsibilities, can take action on its own behalf, close contracts and can only be held accountable for illegal activities carried out by its "organs" (OR 722). The corporation is founded with the registration in the commercial register. At the same time, the corporation is also internally independent. It holds all rights on the corporation's assets and is independent from its shareholders in the sense that it is not affected by a change in shareholder structure. The principle of the "Drittorganschaft" or third-party affiliation can be applied here.

Additionally, it is a legal entity with shareholders who have certain rights and responsibilities. Also, the members of the corporation decide on the company's activities.

The membership of a shareholder is only capital-based. The responsibilities resulting from this "limited" membership are also based on asset liabilities.

The management board or board of directors is responsible for the management of the Aktiengesellschaft (OR 716 II). At the same time, it is also authorized to represent the corporation externally, whereas the possibility of every member of the management board to represent the corporation externally can be changed (OR 718 I). The extent of the power of representation is regulated in OR 718a I. The management board can make decisions on every aspect of business that is not assigned as per the bylaws of the company or laws from the general assembly.

11.2.6.2 Process and Requirements for Incorporation

A corporation can be incorporated by one or more natural or legal persons or other companies (625).

The incorporation is strictly limited by necessary formalities (Art. 631). It is required to create bylaws that must contain a certain legal standard. Nonetheless, they give a bit of flexibility. In addition, the required capital needs to be available. Until the registration in the commercial register, the required founding capital is restricted (633 II). Between the act of founding the company and the registration in the commercial register, the company is perceived as an ordinary partnership (530 II). A general meeting needs to accredit the bylaws of the corporation and elect the necessary organs. During this act of founding, the founders apply for shares and determine that all the shares have been distributed successfully. In addition, they determine that the bylaws and legal requirements concerning the deposits have been met. The resolutions of the assembly have to be made available to the public by a notary. By meeting the former requirements, the corporation is created, but has not yet reached its final status. The final status is reached only on successful registration in the commercial register.

The act of incorporation is more complex and the associated costs are, in general, higher than those of private companies. The traditional way of founding a corporation costs approximately CHF 7,000–9,000. If consultancy and information are only received by electronic means, the costs are CHF 1,900–2,450.

11.2.6.3 Requirements for Associates/Shareholders and Regulations Concerning Shareholders' Meetings

Every natural or legal person can become a shareholder (from the home country or abroad). To incorporate an Aktiengesellschaft, at least one shareholder is required.

The annual general meeting of the shareholders is the highest body of a corporation. The general meeting defines the bylaws, elects the board of management, the auditing agency, accepts or rejects the annual report and decides how the annual net profit will be used. An annual general meeting must be organized every year, 6 months after the end of the fiscal year. In addition, it is also possible to organize extraordinary general meetings (OR 699 II); these have no legal differences compared to the annual general meetings.

The division of votes is based on the majority of the shareholders who attend the general meeting. Abstention from voting, as per regulations, is automatically counted as a negative vote. Therefore, the attendance in the general meeting is always accompanied with voting (in contrast to the German system).

11.2.6.4 Articles of Association

The articles of association of an Aktiengesellschaft are determined by its bylaws. A public authentication is needed for the bylaws (629 I). In general, the written bylaws contain not only the regulated minimum standards that are required by law, but also detailed arrangements. The regulations about the board of management are fundamental for the articles, as are the division of shares, the registered office, the purpose, name and minimum capital of the corporation. In order to change the bylaws, a majority of two-thirds of the voting rights and the absolute majority of the value of the shares (present and voting at the general meeting) are needed (704 I).

11.2.6.5 Minimum Contribution/Initial Capital

The capital stock must be at least CHF 100,000 (621). Upon incorporation, a minimum of 20 percent of the face amount of every share must have been submitted. In all cases, the deposits must be at least CHF 50,000. Contribution, under certain prerequisites, can also be made in kind (634).

11.2.6.6 Commercial Register

The registration in the commercial register is obligatory (643). The corporation is established with the constitution of the articles of associations and the act of incorporation. However, only with the registration in the commercial register is the company finally incorporated. Not till then can decisions be made about the use of the deposits. Every decision made by the general meeting or of the board of directors must be publicly certified and registered in the commercial register.

11.2.6.7 Regulations Concerning Corporate Name

The corporation can freely choose the name of the company (OR 950 I). The registered office can be chosen freely within the borders of the Switzerland. The name of the corporation must be distinguishable from every other company that is registered in Switzerland (951).

11.2.6.8 Transfer of Shares/Regulations in the Case of Shareholder Death

The transmission and inheritance is basically possible.

As for other instruments payable to bearer, the sale of shares is based on the regulations of the property law. The corporation must treat the shareholders as beneficial owners (OR 978 I).

For the transmission of registered securities (that is associated with the membership in the corporation), the same conditions hold as for the transmission of bearer stock in combination with an endorsement (OR 684).

Another possibility is the cession of shares. The corporation needs to accept the new shareholder and register him in the register of shareholders (OR 686 IV).

The conditions to transmit registered shares with restricted transferability are basically the same as for registered shares. However, the main difference is that the bylaws make the registration into the register of shareholders dependent on certain conditions, so that a legal claim of the buyer on acceptance as shareholder can be limited and subject to certain conditions. For corporations whose shares are traded on a stock exchange, OR 685b is important. Percentage articles are also accepted (OR 685d). For corporations whose shares are not traded on a stock exchange, there is more flexibility (OR 985b): Restrictions based on important reasons are accepted, as well as the denial without any indication of reasons, if the shares are transferred on the date of the request ("Escape Clause").

11.2.6.9 Liability of Shareholder and Directors

As the Aktiengesellschaft is a public limited company, the liability of the shareholders is limited to the assets of the corporation (620 II).

The corporation is liable for damages based on illegal activities that are executed by the management board or by a person who is authorized to represent the company to execute business responsibilities (722).

The board of directors is personally liable for damages that they cause consciously and carelessly.

11.2.6.10 Applicable Accounting Standards

The regulations for companies that are registered in the commercial register are applied. Advanced legal regulations can be found in OR 662–670. These regulations are special regulations for accounting principles of certain parts of the corporation, for example, regulations about depreciation, cumulative value adjustments, accruals and unrealized gains. Additionally, accounting regulations on investments, authorizations, patents and licences can also be found.

11.2.6.11 Disclosure Requirements

First of all, the annual report or the consolidated annual report must be accepted by the general shareholders' meeting. The consolidated annual report and the audit report should then be made public through the Swiss "Handelsamtsblatt" (Swiss Official Gazette of Commerce) and, at the company's cost, to any person who requests a copy, if

- the corporation has outstanding bonds,
- the shares of the corporation are traded on the stock exchange.

All other corporations must make their income statement, balance sheet and the audit reports available for creditors. In case of conflict, a judge is to make the decision (697 h).

11.2.6.12 Employee Participation

In Swiss law, there is no institution to supervise the managing board. As a consequence, a supervisory board with employee representation is not required.

11.2.7 Limited Liability Company (GmbH)

The regulations of the GmbH can be found in the Arts. 772–827 within the Obligation Law. The limited liability company is a partly capital-based, partly person-based corporation that pursues business purposes and has a certain amount of capital stock.

11.2.7.1 Legal Capacity and Power of Disposition

The limited liability company is a corporate entity in its own right and acts as a legal person (772). The corporation becomes a legal person by registration in the commercial register (779).

The management board of the GmbH is equal to the board of directors of the corporation. In principle, all members are entitled and obliged to manage the company. However, the bylaws of the corporation can change this (809 I). The management of the GmbH can only be held by natural persons. Art. 811 states that only members of the corporation can manage the company (Selbstorganschaft or personal directors), but makes it possible to transfer the management to persons who are not partners (812 I).

If a member of the corporation is a legal person or a trading company, it can name a natural person who assumes the function instead of this legal entity. The bylaws can demand the approval of the company's general meeting (809 II). If the corporation has several chief executive officers, the general meeting must decide about the chairmanship (809 III). If the votes are equally distributed, the vote of the chairman of the general meeting has ultimate say (809 IV).

11.2.7.2 Process and Requirements for Incorporation

In order to incorporate a GmbH, one or several natural and/or legal persons are needed (775). A limited liability company's process for incorporation is basically the same as for the corporation. The associated costs are slightly lower than for a corporation. The traditional incorporation costs between CHF 6,000 and 8,000. If the founders decide to have only electronic information and consultancy, costs are about CHF 1,800–2,150.

11.2.7.3 Requirements for Associates/Shareholders and Regulations Concerning Shareholders' Meetings

The GmbH can be incorporated by one or more natural or legal persons (775). A one-person-based GmbH can also be incorporated. The company's general meeting is called by the chief executive officer (805 I). The ordinary meeting is held every year, 6 months after the end of the last fiscal year. Extraordinary meetings can be held according to the bylaws and if necessary (805 II). The majority of the regulations are the same as for the corporation (808).

11.2.7.4 Articles of Association

A public certification of the articles of association is necessary (777 I). In order to change the articles, a majority of the capital stock and two-thirds of voting rights present at the meeting are needed (808b I).

11.2.7.5 Minimum Contribution/Initial Capital

The minimum capital stock is CHF 20,000 (773). In contrast to the corporation, an entire payment is not required (777c I).

11.2.7.6 Commercial Register

The corporation must be registered in the location where the company has its place of business (778). The same holds true for subsidiaries (778a). Names of all the members must be registered in the commercial register.

11.2.7.7 Regulations Concerning Corporate Name

The same regulations as for the corporation are applied.

11.2.7.8 Transfer of Shares/Regulations in the Case of Shareholder Death

The transmission and inheritance of a GmbH's shares are possible at will. During the time of incorporation, the membership to the GmbH is obtained by making a deposit on the capital stock. At a later point in time, the membership can only be obtained by transmission. For acceptance, a qualified majority is necessary (808). In addition, there can be restrictions to transferability (up to the point where the transfer can be inhibited, 786 II Ziff. 4) that complicate the transmission, but there can also be allowances up to "Devinkulierung" (786 II Ziff. 1–3). The new regulations also allow for a transmission by written contract. Therefore, a public certification is no longer necessary.

11.2.7.9 Liability of Shareholders and Directors

The limited liability company is liable with its corporate assets (794). As a matter of fact, the liability is limited and not personal. The corporation is liable for damages based on illegal activities, when these activities are executed by the management board or by a person who is authorized to represent the company to execute business responsibilities (817). The management board is personally liable for damages caused consciously and carelessly.

Persons who act in the name of the corporation before the final incorporation are personally and severally liable (779a I).

11.2.7.10 Applicable Accounting Standards

Basically, the same accounting standards as for the corporation are applied. However, the regulations are easier, and fewer administrative regulations need to be taken into account. For example, there is no need for notes to the balance sheet. This is also the reason why there is no need to disclose the dissolution of hidden assets.

11.2.7.11 Disclosure Requirements

For the annual report, reserves and income statements, the same disclosure requirements as for the corporation are applied (801).

11.2.7.12 Employee Participation

In Swiss law, there is no institution to supervise the managing board. As a consequence, a supervisory board with employee representation is not required.

11.3 Summary

11.3.1 Advantages and Disadvantages of Different Legal Forms

The advantage of the sole proprietorship is the flexibility due to the high business liberty. That is mainly because there are no formal requirements and only low costs for the registration in the commercial register. Only if the company is registered in the company's register, enhanced bookkeeping standards need to be met. The main disadvantage is the total liability of the founder with his entire personal assets. Additionally, the name of the company cannot be chosen freely, as it is required that the name of the founder needs to be part of the company's name. A potential disadvantage is that through the company's name, the owner is publicly known.

For all private companies, there is no minimum capital requirement. The ordinary partnership is incorporated by the articles of the association, which have no formal requirements. A registration in the commercial register is not possible. The ordinary partnership is also perceived as a subsidiary corporation, as it is always the assumed form, if there is no other corporation that is fulfilling the purpose. The advantage of the silent partnership (as special form of the "Einfache Gesellschaft") is the non-public participation of the partners.

All of the private companies are easy to incorporate, as administrative requirements are relatively low. The costs of founding a private company are marginal. In the normal case, optional law is relevant, which means that the partners can formulate the organization by themselves.

Disadvantages are the interdependencies of the partners. This can be viewed especially disadvantageous when having a high number of partners. The partnership limited by shares and the general partnership must be registered in the commercial register. Additionally, the private and solidary liability is a disadvantage. The personal liability is subsidiary for the general partnership and the partnership limited by shares, which occurs only if the debtor cannot cover his liabilities with the assets of the company. The limited partner of a partnership limited by shares is only liable to the extent of his contribution is registered in the commercial register. The main disadvantage is that the counterpart can only be a natural person, but not a legal person. That might be the main reason why this legal form is not a serious option compared to corporate enterprises. The partnership limited by shares is mainly used as an enhancement of a limited partnership if the new partner has no voting rights.

The advantage of the corporation is that the shareholders are only liable for their share of equity. The management board is only fully liable if illegal or careless actions have been carried out. A corporation consisting of only one shareholder is possible, which means only one member is needed for the incorporation. Despite the fact that the Aktiengesellschaft must be registered in the commercial register, the single shareholders need not be mentioned. Accordingly, holdings need not be made public. The different forms of shares leave room for individual preferences for the founders with regard to the transmission of shares and the control of the shareholders. The name of the corporation can be freely chosen.

A disadvantage of the corporation is the high minimum capital requirement of CHF 100,000; though this does not have to be fully paid fully from inception. In addition, the formalities of the incorporation are more complex compared to private companies. The associated costs vary greatly. With the usage of electronic consultancy, the costs can be lowered, making corporate enterprises more attractive. The corporation has high bookkeeping standards, which give rise to associated administrative costs. Another disadvantage is the double taxation for the corporation's revenues and the taxation for paid dividends. A legal initiative to moderate this double taxation is likely in future.

The advantage of the GmbH compared to the Aktiengesellschaft is the relatively small capital stock with CHF 20,000. The liability is limited to the entire paid-in capital stock, right from inception. One party is sufficient for the incorporation of a limited liability company. The name of the company can be chosen freely. Due to the reform of the GmbH regulations, the paid-in capital stock can be sold without certification. Disadvantages are the higher costs for bookkeeping and administration. In addition, the limited liability company is also affected by double taxation. One disadvantage compared to the corporation is the registration of all members in the commercial register, which is, therefore, publicly available information. A silent partnership is, therefore, not possible.

11.3.2 Recommendations Depending on the Individual Case

Private companies cannot be recommended due to their unlimited liability. In addition, the strong connection to other partners can be problematic. Especially the long liability after closure of 5 years for the limited partnership and the partnership limited by shares make these legal forms unattractive.

The silent partnership allows for taking a share in a private company without making it public and with limited liability restricted to the extent of the deposit made in the internal corporation. However, there are no rights regarding external publicity.

Sole proprietors become relevant only if there are no other partners (also in the future). If there are and will be no other partners, and if the personal liability and the publicity of the financial circumstances are no criteria, the sole proprietorship can be a valid alternative.

The current numbers of chosen legal forms in Switzerland are a good indicator for the best choice. In Switzerland, corporate enterprises are the most popular. Normally, the decision is made between founding either a GmbH or an Aktiengesellschaft. The decisive point is the limited liability.

If the objective is to make the structure of the corporation not publicly available, corporation should be chosen, even if higher deposits must be paid. However, if the deposits are the main criteria, the limited liability company is a more attractive choice. The main disadvantage is that the structure of the shareholders can be looked up in the commercial register. The transmission of shares is more flexible for a corporation. Transferable shares can be transferred according to property rights. The restriction on transferability of shares is also possible, so that the structure of shareholders is controllable. Because of the latest GmbH reform, this advantage is not as relevant anymore. The normal majority of the shareholders is sufficient for transmission. Additionally, only a written form is required compared to the former requirements of certification.

Bibliography

Internet addresses (Accessed June 2009):
    http://www.beeler-treuhand.ch/firmengruendung.htm
    http://www.gruenderportal.ch/index.php?id=12
    http://www.gruenderportal.ch/index.php?id=10
    http://www.kmu.admin.ch/themen/00614/00656/index.html?lang=de
    http://www.kaerner.de/schweiz.htm
    http://www.kpmg.ch/library/publikationen_studien/11985_17698.htm
    http://www.pwc.ch/de/dyn_output.html?content.void=3317&collectionpageid=92&container void=128&comeFromOverview=true
    http://www.advokatur.ch/gruend.html
    http://www.baselland.ch/fileadmin/baselland/files/docs/jpd/handreg/formulare/allgemein_ rechtsformenvergleich.pdf
    http://www.juszh.ch/files/handlesundwirtschaftsrecht/priv_72.doc
    http://www.juszh.ch/studium.asp?topic=handlesundwirtschaftsrecht
    http://www.juszh.ch/links.asp?topic=rwfak
    http://www.wissen.de/wde/generator/wissen/ressorts/bildung/index,page=1249304.html
Wagner J (2007) Gesellschaftsrecht in der Schweiz und in Lichtenstein, 3. Auflage. Heidelberg, München, Landsberg, Berlin.

Chapter 12
United Kingdom

Andrew Lindsay and Michael J. Munkert

Abstract In the chapter on the United Kingdom, the authors Andrew Lindsay and Michael J. Munkert start with an introduction into the structure of the domestic market with regards to legal forms. They use the general analysis framework for the handbook on legal forms in Europe to analyse eight relevant legal forms: the sole trader, the ordinary partnership, the limited liability partnership, the limited partnership, the private company limited by shares (Ltd., Limited), the private company limited by guarantee, the private unlimited company and the public limited company (Plc.).

The authors conclude their discussions with an evaluation of the advantages and disadvantages of the different legal forms and provide exemplary recommendations depending on the individual case of the founders.

Contents

A. Lindsay (✉)
Denison Till, Stamford House, Piccadilly, York YO1 9PP, UK
e-mail: cal@denisontill.com

M.J. Munkert et al. (eds.), *Founding a Company*,
DOI 10.1007/978-3-642-11259-1_12, © Springer-Verlag Berlin Heidelberg 2010

12.1 Introduction

The choice of the appropriate legal structure is one of the first and most important decisions an entrepreneur has to make when starting of a company.

This chapter serves as a guideline to finding the fitting structure for the respective needs of the entrepreneur. The analysis deals with the English legal system and its legal structures. In 2007, 52.1 percent of all businesses were operated as incorporated companies (companies and public corporations), 29 percent were sole traders and 16.9 percent were partnerships.

Thus, our analysis particularly focuses on these frequently used structures and its subgroups, as indicated in the graph below (Fig. 12.1).

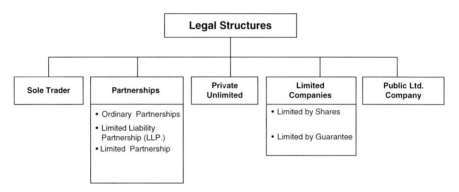

Fig. 12.1 Overview of relevant legal forms

Due to the long history of the United Kingdom, one still finds old legal structures such as the Royal Charter or the Act of Parliament, under which companies such as P&O are organized. However, these forms are not relevant for a start-up and will not be analysed further. Moreover, assuming a commercial aim of the entrepreneur, we disregard community interest companies in our analysis.

In the course of the chapter, we first analyse the different relevant legal structures with regard to unified criteria, making comparison easier. In the next step, we summarize our results showing the advantages and disadvantages of each legal structure.

12.2 Description of Relevant Legal Forms

12.2.1 Sole Trader

12.2.1.1 Legal Capacity and Power of Disposition

A sole trader (or sole proprietorship) is a type of business entity that legally has no separate existence from its owner. The individual sole trader is the only owner of the entity and has complete control. The owner is the sole agent to outside partners and makes all final decisions in the company.

12.2.1.2 Process and Requirements for Incorporation

The registration process for sole traders is simple and straightforward. The founder has to register as self-employed with the Inland Revenue within 3 months of starting-up. Within this time, the registration is free of set fees. If the deadline is not met, the owner faces a GBP 100 fine. The 3-month limit starts from the last day of the company's first month of trading. All necessary forms for the registration process are available on the website of HM Revenue and Customs. The business can start operating immediately.

12.2.1.3 Requirements for Associates/Shareholders and Regulations Concerning Shareholders' Meeting

No regulations concerning associates exist for a sole trader. Furthermore, the owner is self-employed and no shareholders exist. Consequently, no shareholder meetings need to be held.

12.2.1.4 Articles of Association

After having carried out the above-mentioned registration as self-employed, no further steps have to be taken. As a sole trader is not an incorporated enterprise, no memorandum of association is needed.

12.2.1.5 Minimum Contribution/Initial Capital

For sole traders, there is no legal minimum capital contribution.

12.2.1.6 Commercial Register

Since a sole trader is not incorporated, it does not have to be registered at the United Kingdom's Companies House.

12.2.1.7 Regulations Concerning Corporate Name

A sole trader can conduct business under the founder's own name or a suitable business name. If a business name is used, it must be ensured that all business stationery and corporate communications display the trading name of the business along with the founder's name. Although it may be advantageous to register the business name for copyright purposes, this process is not compulsory. The business name may not be offensive and must not include the words Plc, Ltd, LLP or equivalent. Furthermore, words such as "Prince" or "Windsor" may not be used. A complete list of these words can be found on the website of Company House.

12.2.1.8 Transfer of Shares/Regulations in the Case of Shareholder Death

The law does not recognize the sole trader as being separate from the owner and as such, the business will cease upon the death of the owner.

12.2.1.9 Liability of Shareholders and Directors

The owner is personally liable for all debts and obligations incurred by his or her business. All business debts can be enforced against the individual's personal property.

12.2.1.10 Applicable Accounting Standards

The owner is obliged to keep appropriate records of the business. The accounting can be conducted as a simple profit and loss calculation on a monthly basis to meet tax requirements. One should be careful not to fall foul of the IR35 regulation. This rule shall prevent contractors from working for a single client for long periods of time, effectively acting as employees, but invoicing as a sole traders. A sole trader has to register for VAT from a taxable turnover of GBP 64,000.

12.2.1.11 Disclosure Requirements

A sole trader has no disclosure requirements other than related to tax payments.

12.2.1.12 Employee Participation

No legal workers' participation is required.

12.2.2 Ordinary Partnership

12.2.2.1 Legal Capacity and Power of Disposition

A partnership is created when two or more people come together to conduct business. Similar to the sole trader, the partnership does not have a separate legal personality (In Scotland however, the partnership is an independent legal entity). By default, all partners are entitled to share the profits and losses equally, no matter how much capital, effort or skill they bring into the business. All partners have an equal say in the business and in business decisions. The partnership can be ended by any partner by giving notice to all other partners. All partners are agents of the business and act on behalf of the other partners.

12.2.2.2 Process and Requirements for Incorporation

Persons can form a partnership by written or oral agreement, and a partnership agreement often governs the partners' relations to each other and to the partnership. A person can either be an individual, a corporation or other partnerships and business associations. In addition, a proof of existence of the partnership is needed when dealing with outside counterparties such as banks. As an ordinary partnership is not incorporated, it does not have to be registered with the Companies House. Thus, the formation is comparatively quick and a partnership can start operations immediately.

12.2.2.3 Requirements for Associates/Shareholders and Regulations Concerning Shareholders' Meeting

For ordinary partnerships, there are no requirements concerning associates and shareholder meetings.

12.2.2.4 Articles of Association

The internal work of a partnership is usually regulated by a partnership agreement. This agreement is equivalent to the memorandum and articles of association belonging to companies. The partnership agreement will set out procedures and rules related to capital requirements, profit sharing of partners, the admission of new partners, and the resignation of existing ones. The agreement is useful to overcome the above-mentioned regulations by law in which partners, for example, share profits and losses equally, regardless of the capital they brought into the corporation.

12.2.2.5 Minimum Contribution/Initial Capital

There is no minimum capital contribution for ordinary partnerships.

12.2.2.6 Commercial Register

An ordinary partnership is not listed with the Companies House.

12.2.2.7 Regulations Concerning Corporate Name

Similar to the sole trader, a partnership can conduct business under the founders' names or choose a business name. With regard to the business name, the same restrictions that were mentioned for the sole trader are valid.

12.2.2.8 Transfer of Shares/Regulations in the Case of Shareholder Death

By law, a partnership is dissolved if one partner dies. In practice however, partnership agreements can state a possibility for the other partners to purchase the stake of the departed partner and to continue the business.

12.2.2.9 Liability of Shareholders and Directors

All partners are jointly and severally liable for the liabilities of the company. This means that if a debt cannot be paid, then the creditor can pursue all the partners individually, and each partner may be forced into the position of paying the whole debt alone. Every partner is liable with his/her personal wealth.

12.2.2.10 Applicable Accounting Standards

A partnership maintains separate books of account, which typically include records of the partnership's financial transaction, each partner's capital contributions, and a withdrawal account that keeps track of the amount each partner has taken from the business for private use. Each partner must have access to the books and be allowed to inspect and copy them upon demand.

Although a partnership is required to file annual tax returns, it is not taxed as a separate entity. Rather, each of the partners is taxed on her or his proportional share of partnership profits. Except for the above-mentioned accounts, accounting for partnerships follows the same rules as for sole traders.

12.2.2.11 Disclosure Requirements

A partnership has no disclosure requirements other than related to tax payments.

12.2.2.12 Employee Participation

No legal workers' participation is required.

12.2.3 Limited Liability Partnership

12.2.3.1 Legal Capacity and Power of Disposition

A limited liability partnership (LLP) is a mixture between the above-mentioned ordinary partnership and the private limited company (Ltd.) that originated in 2000. A limited liability partnership is a corporate body with its own legal personality different from that of its members and thus, has unlimited capacity. Every member (the persons who subscribed their names to the incorporation document) of the limited liability partnership is agent to the corporation. Former members can also still act as agents juristically binding as long as the third partner may think that he still is a member of the partnership. If the drop out has been registered with the Companies House, this is no longer possible.

12.2.3.2 Process and Requirements for Incorporation

In order to form an LLP, at least two members need to subscribe their names to the incorporation document to form an entity for the sake of making profit. These members can be persons or corporations.

The incorporation of an LLP can be carried out quickly and is not very complicated. It can be done within a couple of days (GBP 20) and even in 1 day for an extra fee (GBP 50). The necessary registration forms can be found on the Website: www.companieshouse.gov.uk .

12.2.3.3 Requirements for Associates/Shareholders and Regulations Concerning Shareholders' Meeting

An LLP needs a minimum of two members, of which at least two have to be designated members. These designated members are comparable to directors of a Ltd. and have to take care of administrative requirements, such as filing the company's annual report. A person may cease to be a member of a limited liability partnership in accordance with an agreement with the other members or, in the absence of agreement with the other members as to end of membership, by giving reasonable notice to the other members. For limited liability partnerships, no regulations concerning shareholder meetings exist.

12.2.3.4 Articles of Association

The assignment of tasks and obligations shall be ruled in an LLP agreement. This agreement, similar to the case of the ordinary partnership, can also include special regulations concerning the sharing of profits, capital requirements and management of the LLP. This agreement does not have to be handed in to the Companies House. If no agreement is closed, legal regulations hold for LLPs. These can be found in "The Limited Liability Partnership Regulations 2001".

12.2.3.5 Minimum Contribution/Initial Capital

To incorporate an LLP, there are no regulations towards a minimum capital contribution. All members may, but are not obliged to bring capital into the company.

12.2.3.6 Commercial Register

A limited liability partnership has to be registered with the Companies House. As mentioned above, this process can be conducted online.

12.2.3.7 Regulations Concerning Corporate Name

The company can choose a business name. For this, the same regulations as for partnerships hold. In addition to that, the name of an LLP must end with the words "Limited Liability Partnership" or "LLP".

12.2.3.8 Transfer of Shares/Regulations in the Case of Shareholder Death

If a member dies, the respective share will be transferred in accordance with the LLP agreement. Generally, the LLP as a legal entity continues its existence regardless of the death of a member.

12.2.3.9 Liability of Shareholders and Directors

All members are only liable with their capital contribution to the LLP. The limited liability partnership itself is liable with its assets.

12.2.3.10 Applicable Accounting Standards

The same provisions that apply to limited companies with regard to auditing equally apply to LLPs. Thus, an LLP will be required to submit audited accounts, which give a true and fair view of LLP affairs. However, the exemptions open to small- and medium-sized companies also apply to LLPs.

With regard to taxation for an LLP, although being a company body, profit is taxed with the individual income tax rate of each member similar to an ordinary partnership.

12.2.3.11 Disclosure Requirements

Similar to limited companies, members of LLPs get the benefit of limited liability. This limited liability requires increased regulations concerning publicity and disclosure. In addition to indicating "limited" in their names, LLPs are required to submit their accounts and some of their affairs to public analysis by filing them with the commercial register. These requirements include the following:

- Accounts
- Annual returns
- General changes in membership
- Changes in designated membership
- A change to the registered office.

12.2.3.12 Employee Participation

No legal workers' participation is required.

12.2.4 Limited Partnership

12.2.4.1 Legal Capacity and Power of Disposition

A limited partnership is not a legal entity. It cannot contract, sue or be sued, or hold property. It operates within precisely the same legal framework as an ordinary partnership. Differences to the ordinary partnership arise from the fact that a limited partnership needs to be registered with the Companies House and from the limited liability of some partners, as will be explained below. Every general partner is an agent of the limited partnership.

12.2.4.2 Process and Requirements for Incorporation

A limited partnership must be registered under the Limited Partnership Act, 1907. To register, a statement (Form LP5), signed by all the partners, must be delivered to the Companies House. Until the partnership is registered, it will be regarded as an ordinary partnership with both the general and limited partners equally responsible for any debts and obligations incurred. The registration process is very quick and costs GBP 2.

12.2.4.3 Requirements for Associates/Shareholders and Regulations Concerning Shareholders' Meeting

For limited partnerships, there are no requirements concerning associates and shareholder meetings.

12.2.4.4 Articles of Association

The same regulations as for LLPs and ordinary partnerships apply.

12.2.4.5 Minimum Contribution/Initial Capital

For limited partnerships, no minimum capital contribution is required.

12.2.4.6 Commercial Register

A limited partnership has to be registered with the Companies House.

12.2.4.7 Regulations Concerning Corporate Name

Because a limited partnership is a registered entity, the name must be accepted by the registrar. In addition, the same regulations as for ordinary partnerships apply.

12.2.4.8 Transfer of Shares/Regulations in the Case of Shareholder Death

With regard to the case of partner death, the limited partnership is different from the ordinary partnership. If there is at least one general partner, the death or withdrawal of another general partner in a limited partnership will not result in a termination of the partnership. Moreover, a limited partner, as a passive investor, is like a shareholder of a corporation and his withdrawal or death will not affect the continuity of the partnership.

12.2.4.9 Liability of Shareholders and Directors

A limited partnership consists of one or more persons called general partners, who are liable for all debts and obligations of the firm. Furthermore, there are one or more persons called limited partners, who contribute money as capital, or property to the partnership. Limited partners are not liable for the debts and obligations of the firm beyond the amount contributed.

12.2.4.10 Applicable Accounting Standards

The same regulations as for the ordinary partnership apply.

12.2.4.11 Disclosure Requirements

The same regulations as for the ordinary partnership apply.

12.2.4.12 Employee Participation

No legal workers' participation is required.

12.2.4.13 General Remarks on the Formation of a Limited Company

All limited companies in England, Wales and Scotland are registered at Companies House, an Executive Agency of the Department for Business, Enterprise and Regulatory Reform (BERR). If you form such a company by yourself, you will need to send the following documents together with the registration fee to Companies House.

A Memorandum of Association

The memorandum is a written document, which sets out

- The company's name
- Whether the registered office of the company is to be situated in England and Wales (i.e. it may be situated in either), in Wales (i.e. it may be situated only in Wales) or in Scotland.
- What the company will do. The objective of a company may simply be to carry on business as a general commercial company (where applicable).
- That the liability of its members is limited (where applicable).
- The amount of share capital with which the company proposes to be registered and details of the division of those shares into fixed amounts.
- In the case of a public limited company, the fact that it is to be a public company.

Articles of Association

This document sets out the rules for the running and regulation of the company's internal affairs. The company's articles of association that are delivered to Companies House must be signed by each subscriber in front of a witness who must also sign. Regulations provide a complete set of articles of association.

A Completed Form 10

Form 10 gives details of the first director(s), secretary and the intended address of the registered office. As well as their names and addresses, the company's directors must give their date of birth, nationality, occupation and details of other director-ships they hold or have held within the last 5 years. Each officer appointed and each subscriber (or their agent) must sign and date the form.

A Completed Form 12

Form 12 is a statutory declaration of compliance with all the legal requirements relating to the formation of a company. A solicitor forming the company or one of the people named as a director or secretary of the company on Form 10 must sign the form. It must be signed in the presence of a suitably qualified person, for example, a commissioner for oaths, a notary public, a justice of the peace, or a solicitor. Form 12 must be signed and dated after all the other documents are signed and dated. This is because Form 12 confirms that all other registration requirements have been complied with.

12.2.5 Private Company Limited by Shares (Ltd., Limited)

12.2.5.1 Legal Capacity and Power of Disposition

Once registered, a company limited by shares has corporate personality. It is a legal entity (or a legal person) with its own legal rights and obligations, separate and distinct from those of its members. The company's property is its own and is not treated as belonging to the company's shareholders and directors. In favour of a person dealing with a company in good faith, the power of the directors to bind the company or authorize others to do so, is deemed to be free of any limitation under the company's constitution.

12.2.5.2 Process and Requirements for Incorporation

In the United Kingdom, the Companies Act allows one or more persons to form a company for any lawful purpose. In the Republic of Ireland, a private limited company may have a maximum of 50 shareholders. To incorporate a company in the United Kingdom (other than Northern Ireland), the following documents, together with the registration fee, must be sent to the commercial register:

- The memorandum of association
- The articles of association
- Form 10
- Form 12.

Each subscriber must sign the company's memorandum in front of a witness, who also must sign the memorandum before it is sent to Companies House. Each subscriber must take at least one share in the company and the number of shares that each subscriber takes must be written against the relevant subscriber's name. A private company must have at least one director. However, the company's articles of association may require more than one. A private company does not have to have a company secretary unless the company's articles of association expressly require the company to have one. The standard registration fee is GBP 20 and the documents are processed within 5 days after being received. If the requested documents are sent in electronically, the fee for the regular service is GBP 15. The company can be formed sooner if a premium service (GBP 30, electronically and in paper format) is requested, which provides formation on the same day as the formation documents are received. Furthermore, the company must have a registered office inside the United Kingdom.

12.2.5.3 Requirements for Associates/Shareholders and Regulations Concerning Shareholders' Meeting

The Companies Act, 2006 abolishes the current obligation for private companies to hold annual general meetings. The directors of a company may call a general meeting of the company. Members of the company also may require the directors to call a general meeting if they represent at least the required percentage of such of the paid-up capital of the company or if they represent at least the required percentage of the total voting rights of all the members having a right to vote at general meetings. How often the members should meet can also be formulated in the articles of association. A private company must have at least one director and must have at least one director who is a natural person. This requirement is met if the office of director is held by a natural person as a corporation sole or otherwise by virtue of an office.

12.2.5.4 Articles of Association

Regulations provide a complete set of articles of association. The articles for companies limited by shares are referred to as "Table A". A company limited by shares can adopt Table A in whole or in part as its own articles of association; but there is no requirement for it to do so, and it can, if it wishes, adopt Table A with modifications or even totally different articles. A company limited by shares that decides to adopt Table A without any modifications need not provide the Companies House with a copy of its articles of association. If Table A is adopted with modifications, the articles need to be provided for registration.

12.2.5.5 Minimum Contribution/Initial Capital

A share capital of only GBP 1 is needed to start up a private limited company. Limited companies are formed with both an authorized share capital and an issued share capital. The authorized share capital is the total number of shares existing in the company multiplied by the nominal value of each share. Not all such shares may have been issued. The issued share capital is the same calculation in respect of all the issued shares. A company incorporated in England and Wales can be created with any number of shares of any value, in any currency. Unissued shares can be issued by the directors at any time using a Form 123, subject to prior authorization by the shareholders and the directors having the power to allot fresh shares in accordance with the articles of association.

12.2.5.6 Commercial Register

When a new company is incorporated in either England and Wales or Scotland, it must be registered with Companies House, which is an executive agency of the Department of Trade and Industry. In the Republic of Ireland, the equivalent body is the Companies Registration Office, Ireland. Northern Ireland also has a Registrar of Companies.

12.2.5.7 Regulations Concerning Corporate Name

Generally, a company must not be registered under the Companies Act by a name if, in the opinion of the Secretary of State, its use by the company would constitute an offence, or if the name is offensive. The name of a limited company that is a private company must end with "Limited" or "Ltd." In the case of a Welsh company, the Welsh equivalents have to be used.

12.2.5.8 Transfer of Shares/Regulations in the Case of Shareholder Death

Generally, upon death, shares held in the sole name of the deceased vest in the personal representative or executor of the deceased. This person should inform the company and provide the necessary evidence so that it can register the fact and the personal representative can receive all notices and dividends relating to the shares. Companies' articles of association often provide that a personal representative cannot exercise the votes attached to the deceased's shares until he or she is registered as the holder of the shares. Shareholders in private limited companies address issues such as restrictions on the transferability of their shares and the absence of a market for sale of those shares, especially if the shareholder is not in a controlling position, in the shareholder's agreement. The document outlines the structure of the company, how it will be financed, who is on the board, what you can and cannot do with shares, what happens to the profits, protection of minority shareholders, what happens to the company if there is stalemate, how the venture can be terminated and what the business and shareholders are allowed to do. A well-thought-out agreement provides an orderly way to transfer shares in the business and helps keep the business running smoothly in the face of future events such as death, disability or retirement of a shareholder.

12.2.5.9 Liability of Shareholders and Directors

"Limited by shares" means that the company has shareholders and that the liability of the shareholders to creditors of the company is limited to the capital originally invested, i.e. the nominal value of the shares and any premium paid in return for the issue of the shares by the company. A shareholder's personal assets are thereby protected in the event of the company's insolvency, but money invested in the company will be lost. The directors, however, can be made liable for a company's losses or debts in a number of ways if they have been prosecuted by the following breaches:

- Dishonest dealings with the company's property or money
- Cheating the company's creditors or clients (both examples are known as fraudulent trading)
- Negligent actions or decisions (or negligent failures to act or take decisions), which result in the loss of the company's money or assets.

12.2.5.10 Applicable Accounting Standards

All limited and public limited companies must send their accounts to the registrar.

Certain information may be omitted from the accounts of small (including dormant companies) companies prepared under the special provisions of part VII of the Companies Act. These companies may further abbreviate the accounts they file at Companies House. Small companies and dormant companies may also be exempt from audit.

Generally, accounts must include the following:

- A profit and loss statement
- A balance sheet signed by a director
- An auditors' report signed by the auditor (if appropriate)
- A directors' report signed by a director or the secretary of the company
- Notes to the accounts
- Group accounts (if appropriate).

For accounting periods beginning on or after October 1, 2007, directors' reports must contain a business review. This does not apply to companies that qualify as "small". For financial years beginning on or after January 1, 2005, the accounts may be prepared in accordance with international accounting standards.

12.2.5.11 Disclosure Requirements

Constitutional Documents

1. The company's memorandum and articles
2. Any amendment to the company's articles (including every resolution or agreement required to be embodied in or annexed to copies of the company's articles issued by the company)

3. After any amendment of the company's articles, the text of the articles as amended
4. Any notice of a change of the company's name.

Directors

1. The statement of proposed officers required on formation of the company
2. Notification of any change among the company's directors
3. Notification of any change in the particulars of directors required to be delivered to the registrar.

Accounts, Reports and Returns

1. All documents required to be delivered to the registrar under Section 441 (annual accounts and reports) of the Companies Act.
2. The company's annual returns.

Registered Office

The company has to disclose the notification of any change in the company's registered office.

Winding Up

1. Copy of any winding-up order in respect of the company.
2. Notice of the appointment of liquidators.
3. Order for the dissolution of a company on a winding up.
4. Return by a liquidator of the final meeting of a company on a winding up.

Public Notice of Receipt of Certain Documents

1. The registrar must cause to be published:

   – in the gazette, or
   – in accordance with Section 1116 (alternative means of giving public notice) of the Companies Act.

1. The notice must state the name and registered number of the company, the description of document and the date of receipt.
2. The registrar is not required to cause notice of the receipt of a document to be published before the date of incorporation of the company to which the document relates.

12.2.5.12 Employee Participation

No co-determination is required.

12.2.6 Private Company Limited by Guarantee

12.2.6.1 Legal Capacity and Power of Disposition

The company with limited guarantee is a legal personality in its own right. It is separate from those who own or run it, and has limited liability. In favour of a person dealing with a company in good faith, the power of the directors to bind the company or authorize others to do so, is deemed to be free of any limitation under the company's constitution.

12.2.6.2 Process and Requirements for Incorporation

Please refer to process and requirements section of a private company limited by shares.

12.2.6.3 Requirements for Associates/Shareholders and Regulations Concerning Shareholders' Meeting

Please refer to the same section of a private company limited by shares.

12.2.6.4 Articles of Association

A company limited by guarantee must adopt the Table C articles of association in those forms, or as close to those forms as possible. It does not have the choice of adopting totally different articles.

12.2.6.5 Minimum Contribution/Initial Capital

A guarantee company does not have share capital, but has members who are guarantors instead of shareholders. The guarantors give an undertaking to contribute a nominal amount towards the winding up of the company in the event of a shortfall upon cessation of business. It cannot distribute its profits to its members, and is therefore eligible to apply for charitable status if necessary.

Its members cannot receive any dividend, profit or other income from the guarantee company, nor can they receive a share of its assets if it comes to liquidation.

12.2.6.6 Commercial Register

Please refer to the same section of the private company limited by shares.

12.2.6.7 Regulations Concerning Corporate Name

Like a private limited company, a company limited by guarantee must include the suffix "Limited" in its name, except in circumstances specifically excluded by law. One condition of this exclusion is that the company does not distribute profits.

Generally, a company must not be registered under the Companies Act by a name if, in the opinion of the Secretary of State, that its use by the company would constitute an offence, or if the name is offensive.

12.2.6.8 Transfer of Shares/Regulations in the Case of Shareholder Death

Please refer to the same section of the private company limited by shares.

12.2.6.9 Liability of Shareholders and Directors

The ordinary members of a company – that is, those who have signed guarantees, will only be liable for the maximum amount they have guaranteed if the company goes into insolvent liquidation. The members (in most cases) elect the board of directors (usually called trustees or governors to avoid connotations of salaries and bonuses), which is responsible for setting up and overseeing the policy of the guarantee company.

The directors, however, can be made liable for a company's losses or debts in a number of ways:

- Dishonestly dealing with the company's property or money
- Cheating the company's creditors or clients (one and two are known as fraudulent trading).
- Negligent actions or decisions (or negligent failures to act or take decisions), which lead to a loss in the company's money or assets.

12.2.6.10 Applicable Accounting Standards

Please refer to the applicable accounting standards of the private company limited by shares.

12.2.6.11 Disclosure Requirements

See the private company limited by shares disclosure requirements.

12.2.6.12 Employee Participation

No co-determination is required.

12.2.7 Private Unlimited Company

12.2.7.1 Legal Capacity and Power of Disposition

An unlimited company has all the other features of a private company limited by shares. It is registered at Companies House, has members, directors, memorandum and articles, etc.

12.2.7.2 Process and Requirements for Incorporation

Please refer to the process and requirements section of the private company limited by shares.

12.2.7.3 Requirements for Associates/Shareholders and Regulations Concerning Shareholders' Meeting

A private company must have at least one director. The Companies Act, 2006 abolishes the current obligation for private companies to hold annual general meetings.

12.2.7.4 Articles of Association

An unlimited company must adopt the Table E articles of association in those forms, or as close to those forms as possible. It does not have the choice of adopting totally different articles.

12.2.7.5 Minimum Contribution/Initial Capital

No initial capital is needed.

12.2.7.6 Commercial Register

Please refer to the same section of the private company limited by shares.

12.2.7.7 Regulations Concerning Corporate Name

The company name must end with the words "Unlimited" or its abbreviations or Welsh equivalents.

12.2.7.8 Transfer of Shares/Regulations in the Case of Shareholder Death

Please refer to the same section of the private company limited by shares.

12.2.7.9 Liability of Shareholders and Directors

The liability of the members is unlimited – that is, they are liable to contribute whatever sums are required to pay the debts of the company, should it go into compulsory liquidation.

12.2.7.10 Applicable Accounting Standards

An unlimited company usually does not have to deliver accounts.

12.2.7.11 Disclosure Requirements

Because there is no limitation on members' liability, far less of the company's affairs have to be disclosed publicly than is the case with the other types of companies. One major advantage is that the unlimited is not required to register annual accounts at Companies House.

Unlimited companies need only to deliver accounts to the registrar if, during the period covered by the accounts, the company was

- a subsidiary or a parent of a limited undertaking
- a banking or insurance company (or the parent of a banking or insurance company)
- a "qualifying company" within the meaning of the Unlimited Companies (Accounts) Regulations, 1993
- operating a trading stamp scheme.

12.2.7.12 Employee Participation

No co-determination is required.

12.2.8 Public Limited Company (Plc.)

12.2.8.1 Legal Capacity and Power of Disposition

The company with public limited guarantee is a legal person in its own right. In favour of a person dealing with a company in good faith, the directors' power to bind the company or authorize others to do so is deemed to be free of any limitation under the company's constitution.

12.2.8.2 Process and Requirements for Incorporation

To incorporate a company in the United Kingdom (other than Northern Ireland), the following documents, together with the registration fee, must be sent to the commercial register:

- The memorandum of association
- The articles of association
- Form 10
- Form 12.

Furthermore, a company registered as a public company on its original incorporation cannot commence business or exercise its borrowing powers unless the registrar has issued it with a certificate of entitlement to do business and borrow – the trading certificate – which normally takes approximately 2 weeks to process. To apply for a trading certificate, the company must send Form 117 to the Companies House. Concerning filing fees and timing, please refer to the process of the private company limited by shares.

12.2.8.3 Requirements for Associates/Shareholders and Regulations Concerning Shareholders' Meeting

English and Scottish Plcs require two shareholders and two directors, one of who may also be the company secretary. Shareholders can be natural persons or companies. A Plc must have at least one director who is a natural person. This requirement is met if the office of director is held by a natural person as a corporation, solely or otherwise, by virtue of an office. Every public company must hold a general meeting as its annual general meeting in each 6-month period beginning with the day following its accounting reference date (in addition to any other meetings held during that period).

12.2.8.4 Articles of Association

The memorandum has to state that it is a public company and that it has an authorized share capital of at least GBP 50,000 or at least GBP 65,600.

A memorandum and articles of association suitable for the particular type of company can be bought from a law stationer or company formation agent. Alternatively, one may prepare the form according to the regulations detailed in Table F in the Companies Regulations.

12.2.8.5 Minimum Contribution/Initial Capital

The Companies House will issue a trading certificate to a public company if the value of the company's allotted share capital is not less than GBP 50,000 or GBP 65,600. This requirement must be wholly satisfied either in sterling or in Euros, as a mixture of both will not meet the legal requirements.

12.2.8.6 Commercial Register

When a new company is incorporated in either England and Wales or Scotland, it must be registered with the Companies House. In the Republic of Ireland, the equivalent body is the Companies Registration Office, Ireland.

Northern Ireland also has a Registrar of Companies.

12.2.8.7 Regulations Concerning Corporate Name

The Plc's name ends with "Public Limited Company" or "Plc" or, if it is a Welsh company, it may use the Welsh equivalents.

12.2.8.8 Transfer of Shares/Regulations in the Case of Shareholder Death

Please refer to the same section of the private company limited by shares.

12.2.8.9 Liability of Shareholders and Directors

Please refer to the same section of the private company limited by shares.

12.2.8.10 Applicable Accounting Standards

A Plc normally has only 7 months after the end of its accounting reference period to deliver its accounts to the registrar. A civil penalty will be incurred if it delivers accounts to the Companies House after the statutory time allowed for filing. A UK Plc cannot take advantage of many of the provisions and exceptions applying to private companies under the Act, such as audit exemptions for small private companies. A Plc cannot apply for voluntary strike-off under Section 652A, Companies Act, 1985.

Generally, accounts must include the following:

- A profit and loss account (or income and expenditure account if the company is not trading for profit)
- A balance sheet signed by a director
- An auditors' report signed by the auditor (if appropriate)
- A directors' report signed by a director or the secretary of the company
- Notes to the accounts
- Group accounts (if appropriate).

For accounting periods beginning on or after October 1, 2007, directors' reports must contain a business review. This does not apply to companies that qualify as "small". For financial years beginning on or after January 1, 2005, the accounts may be prepared in accordance with international accounting standards.

12.2.8.11 Disclosure Requirements

Please refer to the disclosure requirements described in the private company limited by shares section. Additionally, the company has to disclose the following information.

Share Capital

1. Any statement of capital and initial shareholdings
2. Any return of allotment and the statement of capital accompanying it
3. Copy of any resolution under Sections 570 or 571 (disapplication of preemption rights, disapplication of preemption rights by special resolution)

4. Copy of any report under Sections 593 or 599 as to the value of a non-cash asset.
5. Statement of capital accompanying notice given under Section 625 (notice by company of redenomination of shares)
6. Statement of capital accompanying notice given under Section 627 (notice by company of reduction of capital in connection with redenomination of shares)
7. Notice delivered under Sections 636 (notice of new name of class of shares) or 637 (notice of variation of rights attached to shares)
8. Statement of capital accompanying order delivered under Section 649 (order of court confirming reduction of capital)
9. Notification (under Section 689) of the redemption of shares and the statement of capital accompanying it
10. Statement of capital accompanying return delivered under Sections 708 (notice of cancellation of shares on purchase of own shares) or 730 (notice of cancellation of shares held as treasury shares)
11. Any statement of compliance delivered under Section 762 (statement that company meets conditions for issue of trading certificate).

Mergers and Divisions

1. Copy of any draft of the terms of a scheme required to be delivered to the registrar under Sections 906 or 921
2. Copy of any order under Sections 899 or 900 in respect of a compromise or arrangement to which Part 27 (mergers and divisions of public companies) applies.

12.2.8.12 Employee Participation

No co-determination is required.

12.3 Summary

12.3.1 Advantages and Disadvantages of Different Legal Forms

12.3.1.1 Sole Trader

Advantages: As a sole trader, the owner has total control over the business. Furthermore, this structure is advantageous for tax reasons, as only the owner is taxed. Another advantage is the quick and straightforward formation process. Moreover, the low disclosure and accounting requirements keep bureaucracy to a minimum.

Disadvantages: The biggest disadvantage of this structure is its unlimited liability. If the firm goes bankrupt, the owner would also be liable with all personal wealth. The owner is also the only person to manage the firm and thus, personally accountable for all decisions.

12.3.1.2 Ordinary Partnership

Advantages: The ordinary partnership can react very flexibly towards a change in partnership. Furthermore, a partnership can be formed relatively cheaply and quickly. As in the case of the sole trader, the disclosure requirements are low and the income is taxed at the personal tax rate.

Disadvantages: The unlimited liability is the biggest disadvantage of the partnership. Here, other than with the sole trader, every partner is also liable for the debts and decisions of every other partner. Moreover, a partnership does not offer a structure that can be sold or passed on.

12.3.1.3 Limited Liability Partnership

Advantages: The LLP combines the strength of a Ltd. with those of an ordinary partnership. The legal personality allows an easy selling or passing-on process. More important is that the partners enjoy limited liability. In addition, the flexibility towards a change in partnership and the tax advantage of the ordinary partnership also apply for the LLP.

Disadvantages: Due to the limited liability disclosure, requirements are higher than for ordinary partnerships. The formation process is also more complicated and time consuming.

12.3.1.4 Limited Partnership

For the limited partnership, the same advantages and disadvantages as for the ordinary partnership apply. In addition, there is one important advantage, which is the greater flexibility towards capital sourcing. This results from the limited liability characteristics of some partners. As a further disadvantage it must be mentioned that the LP needs to be registered, as it is otherwise perceived to be an ordinary partnership.

12.3.1.5 Private Company Limited by Shares

Advantages: A major advantage of the company limited by shares is the low start-up investment and the fast ramp-up possibility. Furthermore, the company structure offers high flexibility in designing the articles of association. Another positive aspect is the high convertibility of the limited by shares in other legal company structures.

Disadvantage: The main disadvantage is the considerable disclosure requirement.

12.3.1.6 Private Company Limited by Guarantee

Advantages: This company type is used primarily to found non-profit organizations. It is commonly believed that it cannot distribute its profits to its members, and is therefore, often eligible to apply for charitable status. If a private company limited by guarantee in a charity business has high-profile guarantors, the access to funding or donations might be easier.

Disadvantages: A disadvantage is that the guarantors do not usually benefit from any profits of the company and therefore, do not have an incentive to offer high guarantees. Moreover, the structure of the company consisting of voting rights and no shares makes it hard to change the company.

12.3.1.7 Private Unlimited

Advantages: The private unlimited company has the advantage that the owner does not have to disclose a lot of information to the public.

Disadvantages: The liability of the members is unlimited – that is, they are liable to contribute whatever sums are required to pay the debts of the company should it go into compulsory liquidation. This is a major drawback of the decision to choose such a company format and is also the reason why this legal capacity is not found very often.

12.3.1.8 Public Limited

Advantages: A major advantage of the public limited companies is the possibility to raise money through trading the shares, for example, on a stock exchange. The public limited can use this money to finance investments.

Disadvantages: A severe disadvantage is the high disclosure responsibility. Furthermore, going public raises the risk of losing control of the company through hostile takeovers. Another downside is the dependency on the shareholder and their expectations. The final disadvantage is the high amount of capital required to start a Plc.

12.3.2 Recommendations Depending on the Individual Case

The potential start-up company in our case is a London-based Web 2.0 venture. The founder has GBP 10,000 in cash to realize his idea of creating a social network for expatriates all over the world. Of special importance to him is that the company has a limited liability so that he can only lose the GBP 10,000 in the case of insolvency. Furthermore, he wants the company to be a legal entity. As he is planning to start up without a partner or team, it is important to him that he can found the business as a single person. Moreover, the founder wants to start business as soon as possible and is thus, looking for a quick incorporation process.

When analysing the best fitting legal structure for the founder, we initially neglected the sole trader, partnership and limited partnership, as these forms do not have a separate legal entity. Furthermore, we neglected the limited liability partnership as we are faced with a sole owner of the company and an LLP requires a minimum of two founders. The unlimited company is not applicable as the founder is looking for limited liability. From the remaining companies, the Plc. does not fit the requirements of the founder, as he only has GBP 10,000 and not the necessary GBP 50,000 for the Plc.

Also, the limited company by guarantee can be ignored, as the founder has no guarantor for his venture.

In summary, the limited company by shares (Ltd.) is the best possible legal structure for the needs of the founder. It offers a single entrepreneur limited liability, an own legal entity, a minimum cash requirement of GBP 1, and in addition, a very quick and straightforward incorporation process. Thus, we recommend the founder to carry out the business under the legal structure of a Ltd. to capitalize on the stated advantages that fit his requirements.